Random House

harvest Moon

crosswords

edited by Stanley Newman

**Random House
Puzzles & Games**

NEW YORK   TORONTO   LONDON   SYDNEY   AUCKLAND

Visit the Random House Puzzles & Games Web site:
www.puzzlesatrandom.com

First Edition

Printed in the United States of America

10 9 8 7 6 5 4 3 2

ISBN: 978-0-8129-3628-5

Introduction

Welcome to *Random House Harvest Moon Crosswords,* with 100 cool and comfortable puzzles from some of America's most talented puzzlemakers. Each crossword has a theme, or central idea, running through its longest answers. The title provided at the top of each page will give you a hint as to what the theme is. And the answers are all in the back, just in case.

Thanks to Oriana Leckert and John Chaneski for their help in the preparation of the manuscript.

Your comments on any aspect of this book are most welcome. You can reach me via regular mail or e-mail at the addresses below.

If you're Internet-active, you're invited to my Web site, www.StanXwords .com. It features puzzlemaker profiles, solving hints and other useful info for crossword fans. There's also a free daily crossword and weekly prize contest. Please stop by for a visit.

Best wishes for happy solving!

Stan Newman

Regular mail: P.O. Box 69, Massapequa Park, NY 11762 (Please enclose a self-addressed stamped envelope if you'd like a reply.)

E-mail: StanXwords@aol.com

Join Stan Newman on His Annual Crossword-Theme Cruise!

You'll enjoy a relaxing vacation on a luxurious ship, plus a full program of puzzles, games and instructional sessions. For complete info on Stan's next cruise, please phone Special Event Cruises at 1-800-326-0373, or visit its Web site, www.specialeventcruises.com/crossword.html.

1 WHATEVER

by Fred Piscop

ACROSS

1 Free ticket
5 Ways' partner
10 Toddler's glassful
14 Aroma
15 Chance for a hit
16 Privy to
17 Like Andorra or Monaco
18 *Goosebumps* author
19 [ignore this deletion]
20 Joke-themed game show of yore
23 A Bobbsey twin
24 Impresario Hurok
25 '50s auto
28 __ *longa, vita brevis*
31 Shrink back
35 Unruly mane
36 Air, to a jet engine
39 Unload, in a way
40 Dave Clark Five tune of '66
43 Actress Petty
44 Steering device on a boat
45 Hope/Crosby destination
46 Standing upright
48 Pt. of a V-8
49 Driver's one-eighty
51 Campers' org.
53 Masseur's milieu
54 Not both
61 Bowled over
62 *The Tempest* sprite
63 Golfer's selection
65 Prefix with god or john

66 Monster portrayer in *Young Frankenstein*
67 Use a stopwatch
68 Author unknown: Abbr.
69 Hostel visits
70 On the rocks

DOWN

1 Basic bed
2 Of Pindar's work
3 "__ Lisa"
4 *The Scarlet Letter* surname
5 Burr role
6 Ides of March rebuke
7 In __ (soon)
8 "One-billionth" word form

9 *The 39 __*
10 Letter to Santa, maybe
11 Opposition member
12 Misfortunes
13 Busy bug
21 New Haven collegian
22 Stranded motorist's need
25 *South Pacific* hero
26 Sorrow
27 Cathedral topper
28 Storage area
29 Long-distance auto race
30 Expertise
32 India's first prime minister
33 "__ de Lune"

34 Pop singer John
37 Hoops tourney, for short
38 __ out a living
41 Contributed
42 Blow one's top
47 As well
50 Gauguin's island home
52 Syrians and Iraqis
53 Cobbler's supply
54 Author Wister
55 *Nautilus* skipper
56 Easy pace
57 "Howdy!"
58 Hard to grasp
59 Idle or Ambler
60 Trevi Fountain locale
61 Oklahoma city
64 Beatty or Buntline

2 BOOKS AND AUTHORS

....

by Rich Norris

ACROSS

1 House in the woods
6 "Very funny!"
10 Not active
14 Have one's say
15 Shelley alma mater
16 Women
17 *War and Peace* author
19 Word of woe
20 Advantageous position
21 "__ Misbehavin'"
22 Jeweled crown
23 Take five
25 Too thin
27 Agra attraction
31 Danish physicist
32 Be patient for
33 Recorded
35 WV clock setting
38 Tailless cat
39 Tree with spreading branches
40 Word form for "within"
41 Storm center
42 Waiter's request
43 Desi's daughter
44 Subtle quality
46 Windshield cleaners
48 Tidal wave
51 Author Lofting
52 Yacht spot
53 Eighteen-wheeler
55 Stable staple
59 *Leave __ Beaver*

60 *Advise and Consent* author
62 Financial claim
63 Harness strap
64 Helpers
65 Frame insert
66 RBI, e.g.
67 Place for a sash

DOWN

1 Nat or Natalie
2 Imitated
3 Life story: Abbr.
4 Commingle
5 New beginning
6 Was unconfident
7 Envelope abbr.
8 Night noises
9 Whatever

10 Book before Jeremiah
11 *Sons and Lovers* author
12 Pay attention in class
13 Francis Bacon product
18 Mascara target
22 Trampled
24 Wolf down
26 "Good buddy"
27 Bring under control
28 On vacation, maybe
29 *Pride and Prejudice* author
30 Puts in a hold
34 Diploma paper
36 Be up and about

37 Shoe parts
39 Stuff (into)
40 Exaggerated happiness
42 Algerian port
43 Fall behind
45 Labor groups
47 Bane
48 Govt. obligation
49 French composer
50 Castaway's home
54 Lamb's pen name
56 Autobahn auto
57 "__ bien!"
58 Pt. of SSS
60 __ *Poetica* (Horace poem)
61 Margery of nursery rhymes

3 PRAISE PHRASE

by Patrick Jordan

ACROSS

1 Fast-food phrase
5 Author Oz
9 Social stratum
14 Abu Dhabi dignitary
15 Luncheonette list
16 Female voices
17 Main part of a church
18 With 34 Down, Monty Python member
19 Calf roper's rope
20 Start of some advice
23 Is in possession of
24 Keep a hinge quiet
25 Stimpy's sidekick
26 Part of TAE
28 Lippizaner's routine
33 Card dealer's device
34 Item in Woods' bag
35 Neither's partner
36 Middle of the advice
40 Bovine bellow
41 Baba and MacGraw
42 "A Little Bitty Tear" singer
43 Like snobs' noses
46 River navigated by Charon
47 Columnist Smith
48 Sigma successor
49 MD's org.
52 End of the advice
58 Actress Ekberg
59 Army members
60 Cotton deseeders
61 Rustic
62 Filleted fish
63 House of York symbol
64 Bergen dummy
65 Thunderstruck
66 "Johnny's Theme" composer

DOWN

1 Extra inning
2 Nebraska's largest city
3 Cares
4 Hydrox competitor
5 Aviator Earhart
6 She won an Oscar as Sophie
7 Step __ (hurry)
8 __ as (for example)
9 "Bette Davis Eyes" singer
10 Straightens the wheels
11 Stick around
12 Dorothy's dog
13 Biblical brother
21 Original
22 Actress Dunne
27 Comic Costello
28 C-3PO or R2D2
29 Pulls a heist
30 Attachment
31 Olympus residents
32 Timeline segment
33 Patronize the mall
34 See 18 Across
36 Mustangs' sch.
37 *Who's the Boss?* star
38 Approach for a loan
39 Creeping vine
44 Heavy overcoat
45 Scurrilous
46 Talked back to
48 Ownership evidence
50 Capital of Belarus
51 Perplexed
52 Giant Hall-of-Famer
53 Shakespearean "soon"
54 Adidas rival
55 Juárez house
56 Be acquainted with
57 Taj Mahal site

4 LOOKING UP

by Lee Weaver

ACROSS

1 Suspect's story
6 "Do __ others . . ."
10 Stack
14 Steel reinforcement rod
15 __-do-well
16 On the ocean
17 Caribbean dance
18 Enormous
19 Old Russian ruler
20 Anywhere on earth
23 St. Francis of __
25 Affirmative votes
26 Impractical
30 Party poppers
31 Military subdivision
32 Can material
35 Music halls
36 High-flying toys
38 Lion's pride
39 Not used
40 Assistant
41 Handbag
42 Ill-fated
45 Pet adoption grp.
48 Do better at the plate
49 One with a second job
53 Gangster's gal
54 Bread spread
55 V-shaped cut
59 Supplemented, with "out"
60 Computer owner
61 Raccoon cousin
62 Not as much
63 History
64 Kuwaiti kingpins

DOWN

1 Elbow's site
2 Grassy field
3 Apple competitor
4 Woman's head scarf
5 Literary incongruities
6 Reveal
7 In the neighborhood
8 Examination
9 Word form for "straight"
10 Country singer Cline
11 Debate subject
12 Inclines
13 Corn serving
21 Soldier's medal: Abbr.
22 Compass point
23 Battery terminal
24 Scatter about
26 Sacred picture
27 External
28 One, to Pierre
29 Belittle, slangily
32 Foot bones
33 Map close-up
34 Requirement
36 Hobbyist's purchase
37 Boise is its cap.
38 Pizza topping
40 Straight __ arrow
41 Authoritative power
43 Associate
44 Wagon-wheel path
45 Fire result
46 Gdansk natives
47 Winter ailments
50 Half-mask
51 Ingrid, in *Casablanca*
52 The Bee __
53 Actor Gibson
56 __ chi (martial art)
57 Midpoint: Abbr.
58 Towel inscription

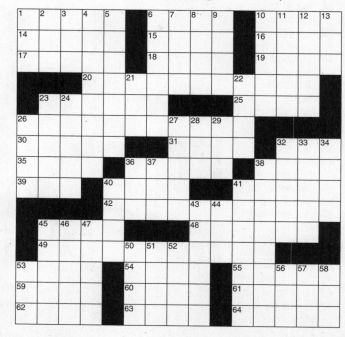

TREE DIMENSIONAL

by Bob Lubbers

ACROSS

1 Spouses
6 Formal dance in France
9 Sand bar
14 Hersey's bell town
15 Yoko __
16 __ firma
17 Layered pastries
19 Red-waxed cheeses
20 Rosy-complected
22 Communications co.
23 Couple
24 Very happy
28 Are: Sp.
30 Greek peak
33 "__ Got a Crush on You"
34 Spade the detective
37 Power measurements
40 Memorable Hughes plane
42 Unevenly matched
44 Dissenting votes
45 Actress Ruby
46 Consider
48 __ Championship Season
52 Fish's __ fin
55 Motorists' org.
58 Altar words
59 Lineman's boom
63 Birch craft
66 Most sincere
67 Boxing venue
68 Poetic night time

69 __ blanche
70 Cried like a kitten
71 Commercials
72 Firemen's needs

DOWN

1 Cope
2 Modifies
3 Part moved by a 63 Down
4 Organic compound
5 Thick-__ shoes
6 Blubbery sound
7 Author Tyler
8 Mislay
9 Refined iron
10 Hopper of gossip

11 "Are you a man __ mouse?"
12 Forelimb
13 __ Vegas, NV
18 Euro predecessor
21 Buster or Diane
25 Buster Brown's dog
26 First lady
27 __ Moines, IA
29 Small vipers
31 Stockholm citizen
32 Droop
35 Onassis' nickname
36 Confused state
38 Also
39 DA's aide

40 Fortune teller
41 Average grade
42 Unusual
43 Classic beginning
47 Central Americans
49 Backpackers
50 "__ Fideles"
51 Rich cakes
53 Scottish quickbread
54 Leading
56 Spring mo.
57 Eighth letter
60 Actress Perlman
61 Oboist's need
62 "So long, signor!"
63 Machine part
64 Exist
65 Freshly made

6 HEMMERS AND HAWERS

by Fred Piscop

ACROSS

1 ___-Man (video game)
4 Finger or toe
9 Baseball features
14 Stutz Bearcat contemporary
15 Texaco rival
16 Piano technician
17 Cube inventor
19 Madrid museum
20 High points
21 Suffix with rocket or racket
23 Well-worn
24 Getz of jazz
25 WWII correspondent
28 Serbian city
31 "Just a moment!"
32 Forty-niner's find
33 Radial pattern
36 1980 DeLuise film
37 *Happy Days* actress
39 '50s toothpaste
42 Grafting shoot
43 Lacto-___-vegetarian
46 BLT need
48 Reporter's tablet
50 *Fear of Fifty* author
53 Trevi fountain cash
54 Mach 1 breaker
55 ___-mo replay
56 Lucci of soaps
58 Middle of some plays
60 French composer
63 Leg part
64 See eye to eye
65 Paranormal skill
66 Marsh plant
67 Has to have
68 ___ Na Na

DOWN

1 ___-K (toddlers' school)
2 Aquarium device
3 Like some lenses
4 Have the courage
5 Morning-radio name
6 Dollop
7 More slippery, in winter
8 Keepsake
9 Oil-treatment letters
10 Old-world
11 Wall Street worker
12 Is a Nosy Parker
13 Sign of stage success
18 It means "all"
22 Cruise port
24 ___-cone
25 Shangri-las
26 ___ *terrible*
27 *The Name of the Rose* author
29 Levels of society
30 *Exodus* role
34 HBO competitor
35 "Nothing ___!"
37 Making into law
38 Aussie bounder
39 Meteor tail?
40 German auto engineer
41 Spielberg film of 1997
43 Sedatives
44 Furniture topping
45 Poem of homage
47 Breakfast quaffs, for short
49 Socialite Maxwell
51 New York city
52 Word on Oslo coins
56 Slate, for short
57 Puts to work
58 Stubborn beast
59 ETO nickname
61 Ill temper
62 Antipollution org.

by Rich Norris

ACROSS

1 Be up and about
5 Boiling byproduct
10 __ mater
14 Singer Braxton
15 Alabama city
16 Arctic barker
17 Informal conference
19 School monitor's domain
20 Doesn't do much
21 Vert.'s counterpart
22 Heated argument
23 Total failure
25 TV fare
27 Computer button
28 Capt.'s prediction
30 Zhou En-__
31 Language ending
32 Mets' home
34 Med. insurance plan
36 Brought up
38 '20s saloon
41 Watercraft
44 Ted's *Cheers* role
45 Being, to Brutus
49 Bank acct. entry
50 Swiss peak
52 Canyon edge
54 Bagel filling
55 Online meeting place
58 Abate
60 Gets a handle on
61 Rhythm keeper, sometimes
63 Caterpillar competitor
64 Part of a curriculum
65 Hard candy
67 Teen woe
68 Mr. T's TV outfit
69 Exam
70 Rural tracts
71 Day openers, poetically
72 Scraps for Fido

DOWN

1 Bitter conflicts
2 Froglike
3 Properly positioned
4 Goes up
5 Draft org.
6 Pianist John
7 *Silas Marner* novelist
8 Unprincipled
9 Fellow
10 Former embers
11 Boot material
12 Sort of sugar
13 Gave one's approval for
18 Verbal suffix
22 Upper regions
24 Shakespearean tragedy
26 University of Wyoming site
29 "I __ Rock" (1966 song)
33 Beast of burden
35 Signs off on
37 Aberdeen affirmative
39 Anjous and Boscs
40 Musical ability
41 Food
42 Improve
43 Staying power
46 More glossy
47 Most vinegary
48 Pundits
51 Side dish
53 Built
56 French heads
57 Lawn-care tool
59 Former defense org.
62 *My Country* author
65 Traffic trouble
66 Rental ad abbr.

8 CAR THEFT

by Bob Sefick

ACROSS

1 Jeansmaker Strauss
5 Charitable donation
9 Legendary lawman
13 Dr. Seuss' *If __ the Circus*
14 Hard work
15 McCarthy's trunkmate
17 Become tiresome
18 Charlie, for one
19 Opposite, globally
20 New York City college
23 Scratching, as a cat
25 Smithereens
26 "Diamond" lady
27 "Winner __ be present"
30 Legendary lifter
32 Summer Games mgmt. grp.
33 Starting
37 Two golf comedy films
41 Pain in the neck
42 Cariou of Broadway
43 Makes hermetic
44 Polygraph exam, informally
47 Asian occasion
48 Saloon chit
52 Swift sorts
54 Raymond Massey film of 1940
57 Bugs' voice
58 Tranquillity
59 Sounds of disapproval
62 Marsh plant
63 Bible book
64 Problematical
65 Flour sources
66 Impress, in a way
67 Worshiper's locale, often

DOWN

1 Backtalk
2 Important period
3 Shrines of a sort
4 Newlywed's acquisition
5 Blend in
6 Cocktail place
7 Short skirt
8 Bulgar, e.g.
9 __ de corps
10 Have __ for news
11 Dinosaur
12 Idle chatter
16 WCTUers
21 European capital
22 Important period
23 Hands do it
24 Supple
28 "If I __ Care"
29 Refusals
31 Legislation
33 Old pro
34 Leaves the rink
35 Valdez vessel
36 Dukes
38 Cover story?
39 Society-page word
40 Houston player
44 Joust needs
45 Stock-ticker mastermind
46 Most balanced
48 Heiress Hutton, in headlines
49 Comparatively fit
50 Prepared
51 Soupçon
53 Shinbone
55 Prime role
56 Flimsy, as excuses go
60 Ghost __ chance
61 Isr. neighbor

9 COVER STORY

by Norma Steinberg

ACROSS

1 Pacifies
6 Pal
10 Christmas poem opener
14 Ryan or Tatum
15 Carson's successor
16 Epitome of thinness
17 Heraldic design
19 Singer Guthrie
20 __ Arbor, MI
21 Martini component
22 Astronomical event
24 Store preserves
25 Milkmaid's seat
26 Bath for a roast
30 Teeter
34 Got down
35 Skulk
37 Practiced, as one's trade
38 Monkee Jones
39 Put in the bank
41 *Lad, __* (Terhune book)
42 Gather
44 Fishing cord
45 Precinct
46 Rang
48 Met
50 Furious
52 Roof waterproofing
53 Abominable
56 Wine-bottle word
57 Leprechaun
60 Cubbyhole
61 Agricultural flyer
64 Alternative word
65 Perry's creator
66 "Once __ time . . ."
67 Skyrocket
68 Recolored
69 Manilow tune

DOWN

1 Caesar's sidekick
2 Soon, in poems
3 Trimmed of fat
4 Small rug
5 Catchword
6 Family group
7 That woman
8 Like some expectations
9 Russian capital
10 Pioneer
11 Twist out of shape
12 Feels poorly
13 Kind of plum
18 Term-end tests
23 Chicago area
24 Suave urbanite
25 Start of play, in tennis
26 Displeased with
27 Bowie's last stand
28 Competitor
29 Twofold
31 Try to buy at auction
32 Sierra __
33 Bordered
36 Vegas game
40 Slightly marred
43 Dry
47 Did the twist
49 Household appliance
51 __ *and the Pirates*
53 Singles
54 String tie
55 Chicago home-run hero
56 Hurried
57 British prep school
58 Give temporarily
59 Make ragged
62 Bullring cheer
63 Hot tub

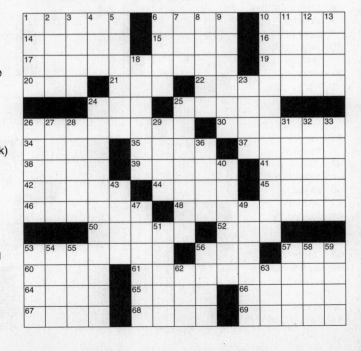

AT THE TRACK

by Rich Norris

ACROSS

1 Lively party
5 Offend the nose
10 Clever maneuver
14 Sandwich cookie
15 Kid around with
16 Author Jaffe
17 Paper measure
18 Like Santa Claus
19 High schooler's concern
20 Uninvited guests
23 Go bad
24 Most current
28 Rusty of baseball
31 Summer mo.
34 Book after Ezekiel
35 They blink in traffic
38 Greek letter
39 *Planet of the __*
40 Bulgaria's capital
41 Kazakhstan sea
42 Military leader: Abbr.
43 Ritzy car
45 Make happy
47 Magazine inserts
48 Take in, perhaps
49 Medicinal amount
51 Play about Capote
52 Noon follower
59 Witticism
62 Brownish gray
63 Inkling
64 In excess of
65 Actress Burstyn
66 Asta's owner

67 Arms of the sea
68 Sign a new lease
69 __ onto (take possession of)

DOWN

1 Five-time Wimbledon champ
2 Region
3 Couch or chair
4 Mark McGwire specialties
5 Athletic pursuit
6 Oompah instrument
7 Followers: Suff.
8 Have a snack
9 Prepare to propose, perhaps

10 Quite fast, in music
11 Brunch fish
12 Three __ match
13 November veggie
21 Corn holders
22 Stadium sounds
25 Lively intelligence
26 __ *Street*
27 Make fit
28 Presented, as a show
29 Elvis' birthplace
30 Places to play
31 Ancient marketplace
32 Starving
33 Trot and canter
36 Performer's suffix

37 Varnish ingredient
41 Referring (to)
43 Showy lily
44 Mata __
46 Becomes narrower
50 Vegetable oil, e.g.
51 Lott of the Senate
53 Story
54 Ponder
55 Sort of sword
56 Object of worship
57 Architect Saarinen
58 Polite address
59 Nine-to-five activity
60 Latin eggs
61 Door opener

11 FEATHER OR NOT

by Bob Lubbers

ACROSS

1 Reads quickly
6 British guns
11 Incite to attack, with "on"
14 Well-groomed
15 The Pentateuch
16 Syr. neighbor
17 Yankees manager
18 Loos or O'Day
19 Thailand native
20 Informer
22 Many oz.
23 Tiny bits
24 Danny and Stubby
26 Component
30 Glittery bit
32 Embellish
33 Preceding
35 Aria, e.g.
36 Pitcher Satchel
37 Vein glory
40 Spoils
42 Dinero
43 Distant fort
45 Put the collar on
46 Bridge type
47 Acoustic measure
49 Old salt
50 Easy target
57 Antiaircraft sound
58 Ford family member
59 Of hearing
60 Compete
61 Plunder
62 Billiard shot
63 __ Khan
64 More achy
65 Gladden

DOWN

1 Atl. crossers
2 Blood blockage
3 Prefix for nautical
4 Roman ruler
5 Funny Red
6 Sober-minded
7 Ice-cube grabbers
8 One of HOMES
9 Mil. alliance
10 Sitarist Ravi
11 Fool
12 Peron's third wife
13 La __, WI
21 Average
25 Deer horn
26 Scale notes
27 Fuss
28 Abruptly
29 Soldiers
30 Autograph
31 "The Raven" author
33 That was then
34 *Flying Down to* __
36 Footlike part
38 John __ Passos
39 *Id* __
41 Coin throwers
42 Warm-up time
43 __ rima (eight-line stanza)
44 RNA component
45 Columnist Landers
47 McQueen or Martin
48 Persian Gulf visitor
51 Logical starter
52 Despot
53 Two-handed
54 __ Major (Big Dipper)
55 Fling a fly
56 Swiss abstractionist

12 CARDINAL ANATOMY

by A.J. Santora

ACROSS

1 Monk's garment
6 Actress Verdugo
11 Aviate
14 Copland ballet
15 Where Mocha is
16 Wade opponent
17 Slots
20 County place
21 Mixture
22 Retrial seekers
26 Spread joy
30 Musical ability
31 Dregs
32 Genesis place
33 Stream overflows
36 To the end, in music
38 Critical agreement
40 Diner delivery
42 Diner order
45 Let out
46 Relish
47 Club for exercisers
48 Lincoln in-laws
50 The taxpayers
53 Jump
55 Marie Wilson role
56 Woodward film, with *The*
63 Water in Bordeaux
64 Bye-byes
65 Chest wood
66 Color
67 Praying figure
68 Bergen coin

DOWN

1 To's opposite
2 Actor Ely
3 Rhyming tribute
4 Shut down
5 China neighbor
6 Canines
7 Was ahead
8 Decorate, in a way
9 *Hud* star
10 Sandy's owner
11 Wk. day
12 Fate
13 Positive response
18 Xylophone need
19 Sad
22 WWI troops
23 __ for the couse
24 Feign
25 Job-seekers' needs
27 Fatty
28 Perfect score
29 Chemical suffix
34 Bandage
35 Coal scuttle
36 Soothers
37 WWII craft
39 Most untidy
40 Lunch order
41 Classic car
43 Barbary beast
44 Mi followers
46 *Viva __!* (Brando film)
49 Do
51 Painter's garb
52 More secure
54 Way out there
56 Cartoonist Key
57 Dry grass
58 Have regrets
59 Is able to
60 Conductor de Waart
61 It may move you
62 Clemens stat

ON THE BLINK

by Patrick Jordan

ACROSS

1 Interstate entrance
5 Feel sympathy (for)
9 Moral principle
14 Lab-culture medium
15 *Life* rival, once
16 Lariat loop
17 Start of a motorist's shout to a passerby
20 Racecar sound
21 Gladiatorial venues
22 Beaming brightly
25 On the ___ (secretly)
26 65 or so
27 Eddie, in *Beverly Hills Cop*
28 Account subtraction
30 Camera type, briefly
31 In heaps
33 Vigilant
36 End of shout
41 Dog-___ (bent at the corner)
42 Treat with milk
44 Former draft org.
47 Choreographer Tharp
50 Pennsylvania port
51 Peg for 59 Down
52 Bandleader Baxter
53 Bested
55 More pretentious
57 Spelling of *S.W.A.T*
58 The passerby's reply
63 *Norma Rae* group
64 Glance from Groucho
65 Tater
66 Lustrous velvet
67 Poet Teasdale
68 Glass' ancestry

DOWN

1 Cheer from the bleachers
2 Beauty's predecessor?
3 Armed Forces Day month
4 Special benefit
5 Chocolate-bar nut
6 Wile E. ___
7 *All About Eve* star
8 ___ out a living
9 Something to mail in
10 Carryall
11 Pursues doggedly?
12 Playwright Horovitz
13 Balsam burner
18 Mexican Mrs.
19 Show hesitation
22 It's taken by a fall guy
23 X or Y, to a mathematician
24 Food shop
25 Cylindrical storehouse
29 Coarse
32 Modern evidence source
34 *King Kong* studio
35 Fatigued feeling
37 Highway
38 Ayres and Wallace
39 Detective Wolfe
40 Cross the threshold
43 "Didn't I tell you so?"
44 Skip one's bedtime
45 *Porgy and Bess* role
46 Starts to take effect
48 Repair-shop substitute
49 Dawn goddess
52 Director Sergio
54 Stocking stuffer
56 Privy to
57 Cruising
59 Golfer from South Africa
60 Jacuzzi locale
61 Convent member
62 Bizarre

BOO HOO

by Rich Norris

ACROSS

1 PC key
4 Topples
9 Truman's birthplace
14 Health farm
15 Beginning
16 Papal vestment
17 Poor explanation
19 Room at the top
20 Be dependent (on)
21 Drove too fast
23 "__ little teapot . . ."
24 Cartoonist Peter
25 Malt brew
27 Son of Seth
28 Dickens pen name
29 Home buyer's outlay
31 African language
33 Listens to
34 Like 2, 4, and 6
35 Swing around
37 Confuse
40 Construction worker's protection
44 Quietly persuasive
48 Human ancestor
49 Improves, as wine
50 Evaluated
51 "__ Lang Syne"
52 Two-bagger: Abbr.
53 Fortune's partner
54 Car part

55 __ Lama
57 Casual pants
61 Lacking skill
62 Appliance manufacturer
63 Communications corp.
64 "Phooey!"
65 More achy
66 Storm center

DOWN

1 Curved letter
2 Small bird
3 Concerto solo
4 Cunning
5 Very old: Abbr.
6 Baton Rouge sch.
7 Class unit
8 Increase by degrees
9 Put ammo into

10 Museum content
11 Afternoon show
12 Ex claim?
13 Hires different actors
18 "Evil Woman" band
22 Greek vowel
24 Sit-up targets
25 Filleted fish
26 Exact duplicate
27 Fix firmly
29 Pearl seeker
30 "__ one to talk!"
32 Gives a hand
35 Actress Elisabeth
36 Frying medium
37 Magic-lamp owner

38 Plant with a bitter root
39 Resident
41 Transportation charge
42 Galore
43 Baseball great Williams
45 Important time
46 Rhythmic dances
47 Sailors' patron
51 Lumberjack's tool
53 Looks well on
54 Hardly open
56 Likely
58 Former Mideast alliance: Abbr.
59 U-turn from WSW
60 Use one's peepers

15 CHOICE WORDS

by Fred Piscop

ACROSS

1 "Howdy!"
5 Diameter halves
10 Gibraltar landmark
14 Bug-eyed
15 Gives off
16 Arthur of tennis
17 Get clobbered
20 Festive night, often
21 Not masc. or fem.
22 Most trifling
23 Marking on a MiG
25 Indigestion cause
27 Tree-dwelling primates
29 Singer Damone
32 Command to Fido
35 __ *pro nobis*
36 Pocket bread
37 1957-63 sitcom
41 Suffix with kitchen
42 Actress Thompson
43 Vicuña kin
44 __ Plaines, IL
45 Old-fashioned cooker
48 Hook's henchman
49 Popping up
53 Ruhr Valley city
56 Agitate
57 Shad eggs
58 Final offer of a sort
62 Bone-dry
63 Like Cheerios
64 Not __ many words
65 Godiva's title
66 "It's a work __!"
67 Noticed

DOWN

1 Bigoted one
2 "__ at the office!"
3 Joined, as oxen
4 Ripen
5 Rip again
6 Loves: Fr.
7 By __ of (owing to)
8 Addams Family cousin
9 "Sort of" suffix
10 Competed at Indy
11 Workers' protection org.
12 Greek Xs
13 Superman alias
18 Pipe opening
19 Yalies
24 Barrel strip
25 Aviation word form
26 Zodiac animal
28 Tiny bits
29 __ *Zapata!*
30 List member
31 "__ Mia" (1965 song)
32 Musher's vehicle
33 Folk singer Seeger
34 Vittles
36 Loses color
38 "Would __ to you?"
39 Starter with gram or graph
40 __ *Madigan*
45 Bygone science mag
46 *The* __ (Addison/Steele publication)
47 Point in the right direction
48 Like a fleabag
50 Castle of the ballroom
51 Library no-no
52 Board, as a bus
53 List-ending abbr.
54 Lee of cakedom
55 Lose traction
56 Sp. miss
59 Overly
60 Clod
61 Word on either side of "-à-"

by Bob Lubbers

ACROSS

1 Chore
5 God of love
9 Urge forward
14 Fit
15 Tibetan monk
16 Valiant
17 Gray or Moran
18 Maturing agent
19 Mideast belief
20 Small sponge cakes
23 Daub
24 Kiln
25 Female sheep
29 Actress Patricia
31 Stretchy
33 "__ du lieber!"
36 Oklahoma city
38 Cay
39 Brief outline
43 Eastern Egypt
44 Mil. alliance
45 Ave. crossers
46 Plead
49 Canasta holding
51 Office aide: Abbr.
52 Grouchy one
54 Theater pathway
58 Fast on the uptake
60 Army glitch
64 *Charles in Charge* star
65 Get the __ of (learn)
66 Lecterns
67 Rubik of cube fame
68 Pennsylvania port
69 "The Sheik of __"
70 Cong. meeting
71 Split in two

DOWN

1 Chinese weights
2 Biblical patriarch
3 Trombone adjunct
4 Nairobi native
5 Jai __
6 Southern tree
7 Greek letter
8 Most uncommon
9 Nile wader
10 __ *Miniver*
11 Buddy
12 Ms. Perón
13 Moon lander
21 It's on the house
22 66, for one: Abbr.
25 Being, in Latin
26 Sags
27 Put into office
28 Clock maker Thomas et al.
30 Massachusetts cape
32 Writer Gogol
33 Sailing
34 Does pull-ups
35 Forages
37 Racket
40 Trade center
41 Sweetie-pie
42 Canonized fem.
47 Puncture or pressure preceder
48 Indian groups
50 Excited state
53 Without __ in the world
55 Ogle, with "at"
56 Vladimir Ilyich __
57 Like swords
58 Wharf
59 Courts
60 Aerobics center
61 Neither mate
62 Orthodontists' org.
63 Little lie

LOOK OUT

by Brendan Quigley

ACROSS

1 Hanging scenery in *Hamlet*
6 Dentist's directive
11 Jay-Z's genre
14 Parasite
15 *"Vive ___!"*
16 Pride
17 Start of a quip
19 Playing-card spot
20 Fancy cakes
21 Chris of the courts
23 Sgt., e.g.
24 Part 2 of quip
28 Drives
31 Squeal
32 Spanish pronoun
33 Hugs, symbolically
35 Part of NAACP
38 ___ Lingus
39 Part 3 of quip
43 Where St. Pete is
44 Branch of sci.
45 Simile center
46 Godparent, sometimes
48 Literary monogram
50 Bridge guarder of folklore
54 Part 4 of quip
58 ___ Speedwagon
59 Shortstop Derek
60 Turin tongue
63 French dance
64 End of quip
67 It's N of Colo.
68 Bring out
69 To go: Fr.
70 Adherent: Suff.
71 Certain yeller
72 They're on tap

DOWN

1 Makes adjustments
2 Restore, as walls
3 Gymnastics star of '84
4 Yearning
5 Mets' home
6 Bending muscle
7 Author Wallace
8 Mesabi product
9 Philosopher Kierkegaard
10 Baker's tool
11 Retaliation
12 Hot under the collar
13 Cold drink
18 Tenure, on Broadway
22 Somme summer
25 Milli ___
26 French state
27 Common correlative
29 "Absolutely!"
30 Number
34 Poetic form
36 38 Across competitor
37 Absorbed (in)
39 '93 World Series winners
40 *Camelot* character
41 Marsh bird
42 Former two-nation grp.
43 All rival
47 Expression of disbelief
49 Whine
51 Baltimore bird
52 Horseshoes shot
53 Hermits
55 Pass on
56 Treasure stash
57 Jeanne d'Arc, e.g.
61 Part of 42 Down
62 Julia's ex
63 Caribbean island grp.
65 *My Three Sons* son
66 Get with difficulty

18 URBAN SPRAWL

by Eric J. LeVasseur

ACROSS

1 Golfer Ballesteros
5 Open courts
10 Misses the birdie
14 Arabian Nights Festival site
17 Alamodome locale
18 __-squared (circle formula)
19 High degree
20 Electra's brother
24 Toledo cabbage
28 Anecdotal wisdom
29 Play for time
31 Orbital sections
32 Brit. medals
33 Starch medium
34 *Familia* members
35 Ring surface
36 "To the max" indicator
37 Canine cleaner: Abbr.
38 Lively, in mus.
40 Didn't budge
42 What some cards provide
43 Andean Indian
44 Import
45 Is at a loss for words?
46 Letter opener
48 A Square was named for it
50 Kind of camera: Abbr.
51 Fem. forces
52 Iditarod start
61 "Soybean Capital of the World"
62 Ken or GI Joe
63 Of punishment
64 Erupter of 1852

DOWN

1 Call for help
2 Air-pollution org.
3 Moving vehicle
4 Passes by
5 Caster's choice
6 Boxing decision
7 Managed
8 "__ Ruled the World"
9 *The Heart Is __ Hunter*
10 Get the oven ready
11 __-en-Provence
12 Nutritional datum: Abbr.
13 Flyer to Stockholm
15 Sleep __ (decide tomorrow)
16 Mel's family
20 Match game
21 Gilda's *SNL* reporter
22 Some art
23 Biblical fisherman
24 Oscar-winner of 1986
25 Three-day religious observance
26 College life
27 Snaky 1974 horror film
30 Fiery felony
39 Dillon's job
40 Foothold
41 Sheetrock material
42 Trickery
47 Schedule section
49 Ankles
52 Put in
53 Opposite of paleo-
54 M divided by IV
55 Auxiliary verb
56 Sloe product
57 High note of old
58 Brooks persona
59 Relatives
60 Mad __ hatter

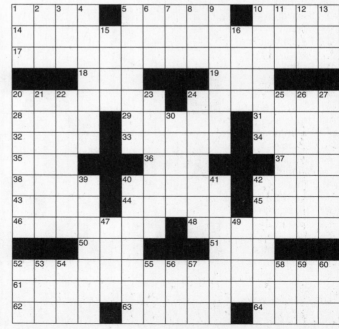

JEWELRY BOX

by Lee Weaver

ACROSS

1 Former UN member
5 Falls short
10 Cloth unit
14 Ration (out)
15 Japanese immigrant
16 Kuwaiti ruler
17 Brace
18 Franchise emporium
20 Large ferns
22 Frog sound
23 Pepper grinders
24 Calf call
25 Plains Indian
27 Australian beast
32 Poetic Muse
33 Alumnus, for short
34 River sediment
35 Vietnamese festival
36 Vocally
37 Pilot's heading: Abbr.
38 Engrave with acid
40 Road curve
41 Music-licensing grp.
43 Putting back on the payroll
45 Fast skiing maneuver
46 "That's incredible!"
47 Chops into cubes
48 Salt Lake City inhabitant
51 Wild cats
54 Engine-cylinder part
56 Wedding-cake feature
58 Steinbeck character
59 Rationality
60 "__ on the Range"
61 Ship of 1492
62 Festive celebrations
63 State of agitation

DOWN

1 Ref's counterpart
2 Belgrade resident
3 Weather alert
4 Apply a new coat
5 Not at all loyal
6 Fireplace residue
7 "This __ outrage!"
8 Keepsakes from Oahu
9 Sermon topic
10 Sells out
11 Melville novel
12 Capri cash, once
13 Difficult expedition
19 "Go away!"
21 1963 role for Liz
24 Anti-DWI org.
25 Leader of the disciples
26 Mountain ridge
27 Fork feature
28 Praise
29 Sewing-box item
30 Forearm bones
31 Stair parts
33 Secluded valley
36 Irish Rose lover
39 Light supper, to a Brit
41 Part of CPA: Abbr.
42 Close-fitting dresses
44 Betting setting
45 Prolonged attacks
47 Tightly packed
48 "__ my word!"
49 Polynesian carving
50 T __ "Tom"
51 Hudson Bay tribe
52 Indirect suggestion
53 Type of truck
55 Stamp on a bad check
57 Finished with the USAF

20 IT'S A GUY THING

by Norma Steinberg

ACROSS

1 Meander
5 Iron fishhook
9 Cookies quantity
14 Exclusively
15 Singer Guthrie
16 Worship
17 Elevator inventor
18 Approach
19 Marc Antony, e.g.
20 Look
23 ABC rival
24 Incantations
25 Navigate
27 Destinies
30 Refer (to)
33 Command in a library
36 Mime Marceau
38 Money in Malta
39 Baby grand, e.g.
41 Meander
42 Lawyers' work
43 __ Stanley Gardner
44 Courteney, on *Friends*
46 Female sheep
47 Mar
49 Beatle drummer
51 Make reparations
53 Entertain, as kids at bedtime
57 Embassy figure: Abbr.
59 Spontaneous discussion
62 *The Today Show* host
64 Distribute

65 Detroit products
66 Synthetic fabric
67 Level
68 Poker fee
69 "Land __ alive!"
70 Tears
71 For fear that

DOWN

1 Alex Haley opus
2 Ready to pour
3 Identically
4 Yours truly
5 Rap-music variety
6 Vicinity
7 Spanish custard
8 Crosses, as a stream

9 Wooden container
10 Uproar
11 *Top Gun* star
12 Lobster kin
13 Egg producers
21 Bowie's last stand
22 And the rest: Abbr.
26 Singer Fitzgerald
28 Therefore
29 Reads quickly
31 Comic Carey
32 Comfort
33 Exceeded the limit
34 Employ
35 Fifty cents
37 Check copy
40 Spiffy

42 "Who __?" (Gershwin song)
44 Bill of fare
45 Lurches
48 Venomous snakes
50 Scoundrel
52 Rabbit hunter Fudd
54 TV journalist Sawyer
55 Civil offenses
56 Beginning
57 "__ fair in love . . ."
58 Poet Angelou
60 Pants maker Strauss
61 Part of a process
63 Before, in verse

21 *VAGUE VISTAS*

by Rich Norris

ACROSS

1 Strike back, e.g.
6 Translator's obstacle
11 Rhine whine?
14 Kate's TV pal
15 Look closely (into)
16 Murmur romantically
17 Field-goal specialist
19 Word on a towel
20 "Boy, am __ trouble!"
21 Absconded with
22 Word in a sermon
24 Downward path
26 Beer buy
27 Co.
28 Weight watchers watch it
32 Actor Baldwin et al.
35 Went down
36 Future atty.'s exam
37 Defraud
38 Chicago cagers
39 Auto make, familiarly
40 Fish fooler
41 Mixture
42 Nut tree
43 Customer-file entry
45 Singer Shannon
46 __ la Douce
47 Artificial tan source
51 Scold
54 Graduation month

55 Postal Creed word
56 Woodsman's tool
57 Football strategy
60 Barrie hero
61 Still-life subjects
62 Not available
63 Tiny, in Troon
64 Twisting
65 Eagle claw

DOWN

1 Moving quickly
2 Southfork matriarch
3 King and Ladd
4 Presidential title: Abbr.
5 Looks unstable
6 Dostoyevsky title character
7 Ship surface
8 Kind
9 Farmer's garb
10 Least
11 Muscular distress
12 Quarter, for one
13 Party planner
18 *King* __
23 With reckless abandon
25 Manhattan, for one
26 Yo-Yo Ma's instrument
28 Prove false
29 "That's clear now!"
30 *The French Connection* cop

31 Design using acid
32 "SOS" pop group
33 Make-up artist?
34 Nobelist Wiesel
35 German river
38 Rapidly growing burg
42 Fund raiser
44 Drives bananas
45 Sand formation
47 Like dishwater
48 Make void
49 Rapid: Mus.
50 Dress smartly
51 Puppy patter
52 Student's concern
53 Singer Horne
54 Quick pull
58 Teachers' grp.
59 Bambi's aunt

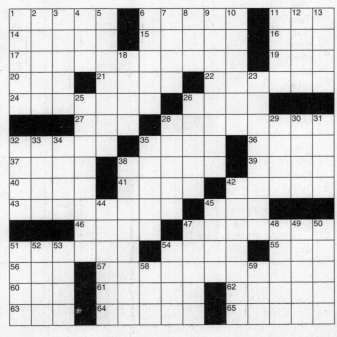

22 EXECUTIVE SEARCH

by Bob Lubbers

ACROSS

1 Houston team
7 Jazz singer Laine
11 Patrolman
14 Dash
15 Dog complaint
16 NBC's former owner
17 Snap
19 Whitney or Wallach
20 Pirate's knife
21 Steal
22 Dress up
23 Puts in the kiln
24 Swiftly
26 Turn back
30 Traders' wares
31 Piano-key material, once
32 *The __ Falcon*
35 Twosome
36 "We're in the __"
37 Labor strenuously
40 Lounging robes
42 Wild card, often
43 Vistas
45 Analyzed grammatically
46 Wear away
47 Central Asian
50 Tyler or Ullmann
51 Big Band brother
53 Washed-out feeling
57 Poor grade
58 Type of TV commercial
60 Bobby of hockey
61 Bread spread
62 "More volume!"
63 Submissions to an ed.
64 Boss Tweed basher
65 Quiver contents

DOWN

1 Small cobras
2 __ *City* (Fox sitcom)
3 Kilmer subject
4 Paddy product
5 Single
6 "Enough!"
7 Themed group of poems
8 Thumbs (through)
9 Actress Sommer
10 Run
11 Dinosaur-extinction period
12 "One __ Jump" (Basie theme)
13 Satchel's kin
18 Evergreen tree
23 Cook, in a way
25 Placard
26 "Let 'er __!"
27 Model Herzigova
28 Offscreen announcements
29 Short trip
30 Pig digs
32 New Zealand bird, once
33 Adviser Landers
34 Bandleader Brown
36 Rainier and Everest: Abbr.
38 Crook's diamonds
39 Directed
41 Uses for nourishment
42 __ es Salaam
43 Infrequently
44 18th-century newsmen
45 '50s scandal subject
47 Attempts
48 Broad tie
49 Golf peg
52 Earthen pot
53 Foggy image
54 Venice beach area
55 __ *Good Men*
56 Towel term
59 Supporting

23 SWING TIME

by Patrick Jordan

ACROSS

1 Supersonic speed unit
5 Measurement for Noah
10 Radar image
14 A woodwind
15 Quickly
16 All the __ (wildly popular)
17 See 56 Across
19 Eden's earldom
20 Hog haven
21 Without a warranty
22 Iguana, for one
24 Go for a dip
25 Ripped
26 See 56 Across
32 Selective
33 Klutzy types
34 Equi- kin
35 Talk wildly
36 Honey holder
37 Aware of
38 Stat for Seaver
39 Grad
41 Villain's expletive
43 See 56 Across
46 Attention-getting cries
47 *Gilligan's Island* dwellings
48 Holdings
51 Bethlehem trio
52 Actress Gardner
55 Go off course
56 What the theme answers have in common
59 Cram-session cause
60 Snuffy Smith's kid
61 Leisure
62 Vega's constellation
63 Wide-mouthed pitchers
64 Turned blue, perhaps

DOWN

1 Janitorial implements
2 Lie next to
3 Facsimile
4 With it
5 Keith Partridge portrayer
6 When computers are working
7 Ram's remarks
8 Roll-call response, in Rouen
9 Rebuke
10 Shameless
11 Igneous-rock source
12 Inventor Sikorsky
13 Remain undecided
18 Two-masted vessels
23 Pupil controller
24 Flue residue
25 Pre-1917 despot
26 Puppeteer Lewis
27 Late-night TV name
28 Gads about
29 Knife name
30 Cosmetician Lauder
31 Outback critters
32 Liner laborers
36 Bleach bottles
37 Assns.
39 Disarm the alarm, perhaps
40 Newborn's outfit
41 Rocky Mountain predators
42 *Wait __ Dark*
44 Jenna Elfman role
45 "Casey at the Bat" poet
48 Daredevil Knievel
49 Alluring
50 Eye drop
51 Parcel (out)
52 Off somewhere
53 Ming thing
54 Had more birthdays
57 Hem's partner
58 Did a tour guide's job

24 *SHH!*

by Lee Weaver

ACROSS

1 Humdrum
5 Spinning toys
9 Hugely popular
12 Dull people
14 Cool in manner
16 Luau strummer
17 Nonetheless
19 Bro's sibling
20 Joke
21 Living-room pieces
23 Functional
26 All excited
27 __ Lanka
28 Briny septet
30 Repairs, as software
33 Close associates
35 __ spumante
37 Word form for "paired"
38 From the top
39 Intends (to)
41 Rotisserie part
42 Stereo component
44 In the money
45 Oven glove
46 Regard highly
48 Membership fees
50 Author Umberto
51 Vaulted recesses
53 Jaunty
55 Least honest
57 Burgundy, in Burgundy
58 River inlet
59 British matriarch, familiarly
65 Hockey great Bobby

66 Ushers in
67 Harvests
68 Trainer's place
69 Kind of terrier
70 Take five

DOWN

1 Air-gun pellets
2 Home builder's need
3 Onassis' nickname
4 Hagar the Horrible's wife
5 Sunbather's goal
6 Ancient
7 Prepare an egg
8 Went it alone
9 Southern side dish

10 Steinbeck character
11 Mrs. Dick Tracy
13 Thick slices
15 Grooved, as a column
18 Radiant
22 Geometric art style
23 Seventh planet from the sun
24 Burglar deterrent
25 Alleviator
27 Sudden outpouring
29 Conservative
31 Minor malfunction
32 __ voce (softly)

34 Tidies the terrace
36 Acquire
40 Gather wheat, e.g.
43 Updates (the clock)
47 Matches up
49 Slalom contestant
52 Porterhouse or T-bone
54 Word before tube or sanctum
55 Toad relative
56 Well-ventilated
60 Amount: Abbr.
61 Put into service
62 Ginnie __
63 FedEx rival
64 Denver hrs.

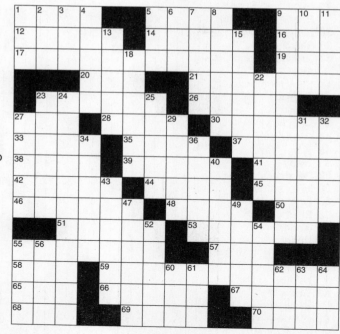

by Bob Lubbers

ACROSS

1 Bona __ (authentic)
5 Saudi, e.g.
9 Hoaxes
14 Fruity drinks
15 Singer McEntire
16 *Objet d'art*
17 Op-Ed piece
20 Pronounce
21 Russian river
22 Speechifies
23 Ashen
24 Top cards
25 Most scarce
28 Self-images
29 Hoover, for one
32 Like Santa Claus
33 __ Alto, CA
34 Positive
35 Sugar and Rose Bowls, e.g.
38 Singer Adams
39 Sketched
40 Greenspan and Arkin
41 Cozy room
42 Slapstick missiles
43 "And how!"
44 Scarfs down
45 *You __ Live Twice*
46 Desdemona's love, in opera
49 One against
50 Bit of cream
53 Upright citizen
56 Visored helmet
57 Waste allowance
58 "Thanks __!"

59 Director Sergio
60 Hernando de __
61 Back of the neck

DOWN

1 Aficionados
2 Brainstorm
3 Moist, as a lawn
4 Slalom curve
5 Ark berth
6 Clear, as a debt
7 Cain's brother
8 Watering hole
9 Beats the goalie
10 Hippy dances

11 In __ (stuck)
12 Marceau's art
13 Male heirs
18 Racetrack prizes
19 Tight-fitting wrap
23 *Beau __*
24 Radiant
25 Competed in a rodeo
26 Domicile
27 Varnish ingredient
28 Soothes
29 Aramis' creator
30 Coliseum
31 Not at all neat
33 Peels

34 Actress Struthers
36 Magazine supervisor
37 French
42 Taste center
43 Completely
44 Barkin or Burstyn
45 Beginning
46 Milky gemstone
47 Lose energy
48 Ticklish doll
49 Hair style
50 Oscar __ Renta
51 On
52 Computer unit
54 Tiebreakers in hockey: Abbr.
55 Author Fleming

26 CORNY

by Fred Piscop

ACROSS

1 Lighter igniter
6 Relay-race hand-off
11 Dustcloth
14 Ancient Greek colony
15 Wine's bouquet
16 In the past
17 Squander slowly
19 Long-jawed fish
20 Contest hopeful
21 Physically fit
23 Passionate
25 Closing word
26 Last mustachioed president
29 Small bill
30 Incas' land
32 Ticked off
34 Distributed
36 To's partner
39 Puzzle smudge
41 Tiny marine animal
43 "A mouse!"
44 Corday victim
46 Ouzo flavoring
47 Catch sight of
49 Cue-stick end
51 Division word
52 *Elephant Boy* boy
54 Betterment
56 Barbecue fuel
59 Discriminatory sorts
63 Call __ day
64 Bit of electronics
66 Popular Christmas tree
67 Barely sufficient
68 Word form for "bull"
69 Nourished
70 Republic founded in 1836
71 Icy forecast

DOWN

1 Piccolo relative
2 Bereft
3 "What's __ for me?"
4 Fertilizer chemicals
5 Mongol invader
6 Tom Cruise, in *Cocktail*
7 Palindromic constellation
8 Namely
9 Muscat's land
10 Contrary votes
11 Oliver Twist, e.g.
12 Slack-jawed
13 Bridge expert Charles
18 Opposite of exo-
22 Hardy follower
24 Society-page word
26 Locust or linden
27 Suffix for million
28 Compressed wood shavings
30 Arafat's grp.
31 Singer James
33 Trash place
35 Dig discoveries
37 Sit a spell
38 Creme-filled cookie
40 Actor Walston
42 Harmful
45 Chowed down
48 Have an evening meal
50 Okefenokee possum
52 Adorn, with "up"
53 Shaw of swing
54 Take a load off
55 Monopoly payments
57 Mgr.'s helper
58 "Good work!"
60 Andrew of *Melrose Place*
61 Wear out
62 Dick and Jane's pooch
65 "__ pig's eye!"

SPOONFUL OF SUGAR

by Patrick Jordan

ACROSS

1 Tinseltown turkey
5 Roach and Linden
9 Locomotive sounds
14 Mimic
15 Saudi Arabia neighbor
16 Comics maid
17 Robert De __
18 City near Lake Tahoe
19 Politeness pundit Post
20 Speaker of quote
23 Brunch selection
24 Work unit
25 Tarzan's kid
28 Vail vacationer
31 Second-smallest continent
33 Watch type, for short
36 Start of a quote
38 Came down to earth
40 ". . . __ wood-chuck could chuck wood?"
41 Off-white
42 Middle of quote
47 Chess pieces
48 Chaperone
49 Extreme hardship
51 Classic car
52 H, to Homer
54 Camden Yards ballplayer
58 End of quote
61 *Cheers* actor
64 *Persistence of Memory* painter
65 Eve's youngest
66 Philip Nolan, e.g.
67 Big birds
68 Raison d'__
69 Went a few rounds
70 Give the appearance
71 No layabout

DOWN

1 Bluegrass instrument
2 YSL fragrance
3 Country crooner Haggard
4 Grills in the oven
5 Hubert __ Humphrey
6 1980s Hemsley sitcom
7 Crow's-nest cry
8 Night noise
9 Annoy the teacher, maybe
10 Smokehouse offerings
11 Israeli gun
12 Hairstyling goop
13 Guileful
21 Frightened cries
22 ". . . __ saw Elba"
25 __ buddy
26 Editorialize
27 Saudi Arabia neighbor
29 Exude
30 Send elsewhere
32 CSA soldier
33 Modern medical tool
34 End the business day
35 Donna Summer's genre
37 "Rikki-Tikki-__"
39 Candlelight-dinner quorum
43 Built
44 Katharine's *Butch Cassidy* role
45 Conceit
46 Director Ephron
50 Ran under the tap
53 Lake Titicaca's range
55 "__ a Nightingale"
56 Petrol unit
57 Outmoded anesthetic
58 Unfounded, as rumors
59 Work with circus lions
60 Swing around
61 Part of WWW
62 Prefix for sphere
63 Veto

28 FOWL FARE

....

by A.J. Santora

ACROSS

1 Half a South Pacific island's name
5 Singer Tormé
8 Belt
13 South Carolina athletes
15 Make a call
16 Submissive, in a way
17 Ignited again
18 Camera part
19 Abe's youngest
20 Dress trimming
21 Writer Josephine
22 Vittorio De __
23 Acclaim
26 Type of joint
30 Playwright Fugard
31 Solzhenitzyn subject
32 Genetic letters
33 Some officers, so to speak
36 Raggedy doll
37 Big blows
38 *Man Crazy* novelist
39 Cocky ones
41 To date
42 Knitting stitch
43 French wheat
44 Compensation
47 Live and breathe
48 Hammett hound
52 Solve
53 Arguments
55 Be as one
56 It's water repellent, so they say
57 Yes-man
58 *Norma __*
59 Hand-raising activity

DOWN

1 '30s heavy-weight champ
2 It means "everything"
3 Agents, for short
4 High card
5 *My Wide World* author
6 __ out a living
7 British money of old: Abbr.
8 Hughes aircraft
9 Something to chew
10 Deep-massage developer
11 Blue dye
12 Oil company, in stock-market slang
13 Alphabetic trio
14 Chamber group
20 Foe
21 Gets down to business
22 Goes alone
23 Word form for "race"
24 Pants fabric
25 __ cit.
26 Tubes
27 Mountain ridge
28 Cove
29 Young girl
30 Rent-__
31 Distort
34 Pitchers' place
35 Voice vote
40 Set apart
41 Dripping, to Donne
43 Robert the __
44 "Be off!"
45 Jason's ship
46 Zhivago's love
47 Water color
48 Eban of Israel
49 Blinds part
50 Cal __
51 Seek to know
53 Transmitter: Abbr.
54 Beantown music grp.

ACROSS

1 Senegalese capital
6 "Surely, you __!"
10 Big party
14 Bert's Muppet roommate
15 __-friendly
16 Choir voice
17 Flour or milk
19 Show appreciation
20 Blasting need
21 2,000 pounds
22 Apparatus
24 Blushing
25 Enjoy the hot tub
26 Sit astride
30 Oman bigwig
34 Low-fat, as meat
35 Yearn (for)
37 Telegraph inventor
38 Composer Satie
39 Someone to respect
41 Comedienne Martha
42 School assignment
44 Actress Olin
45 The __ Piper
46 Fond of
48 Scraps
50 Rubbish
52 Peas holder
53 Talkathon
56 Astronaut Grissom
57 Neighbor of Mont.
60 Role for Leslie Caron
61 "To" and "too," for two
64 Role model
65 Microwave
66 British nobles
67 Slugger Ruth
68 Used to be
69 Beer mug

DOWN

1 Skillful
2 Presley's middle name
3 Entwine
4 Lend a hand
5 Took five
6 San __, PR
7 Intuition: Abbr.
8 Alabama city
9 Picks up the check
10 Single guy's home
11 "You're __ Need to Get By"
12 Comic Laurel
13 A cardinal virtue
18 Walk like a child
23 Pal
24 Union members
25 Binges
26 Aerodynamically designed
27 Concise
28 Salary increase
29 Hang around
31 Part of a bridal dress
32 To date
33 Prerequisites
36 Actor Wilder
40 Increase, as effort
43 Yesteryear
47 Appointment breaker
49 Eats between meals
51 Kitchen range
53 Talkative
54 Verdi heroine
55 Shapeless mass
56 Out of sight
57 About
58 Sandwich shop
59 Special-interest grp.
62 French sea
63 Cereal grain

THE DATING GAME

by Rich Norris

ACROSS

1 Lincoln's namesakes
5 Abbey residents
10 Current choice, for short
14 Play group
15 Eero Saarinen's dad
16 Karmann __ (sports car)
17 Johnson of *Laugh-In*
18 San __, CA
19 Breather
20 Site of some legal challenges
23 More silly
24 Driver's license datum
25 Do some tailoring
27 __ Lingus
28 Feels unwell
31 Oration
33 Eye annoyance
34 Passion
36 Poetry Muse
37 React to a punch, perhaps
40 Tavern seat
43 Singer Paul
44 Enzyme suffix
47 TV collie
49 Meeny preceder
51 Zero
52 Coat part
53 Owns
55 Soot spot
57 Exit grandly
61 "__ Rebel" (1962 song)
62 Composer Erik
63 Draft rating
64 Elevator inventor
65 PR firm's concern
66 Abbr. on an envelope
67 Verbal nudge
68 *Frasier* character
69 Examination

DOWN

1 Small shrubs
2 British noble
3 Where river meets sea
4 Harsh
5 Learn, as lines
6 Name of five Norwegian kings
7 Actress Talbot
8 Holds on to
9 Skiing locales
10 Taj Mahal site
11 First daughter
12 Do a bio-lab assignment
13 Popular pet
21 Hot drink
22 Throw out
26 Reporter's question
29 Mother of Castor and Pollux
30 French river
32 Before, poetically
35 Gospel writer
37 Sea plea
38 1912 Nobelist Root
39 Wailing spirits
40 Hearst's kidnappers: Abbr.
41 Clay pigeons, e.g.
42 Gradual absorption
44 Slow tempo
45 Official seals
46 Classy
48 Orders takeout
50 Singer Sumac
54 Hindu teacher
56 *Lusitania* sinker
58 Malt-drying kiln
59 Sloping type: Abbr.
60 Buster Brown's dog
61 Short flight

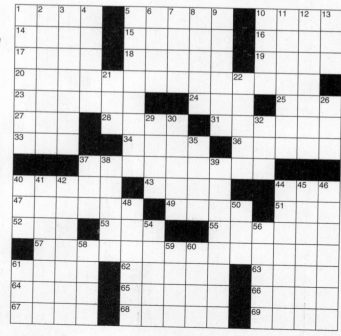

31 METALLIC MENAGERIE

by Greg Staples

ACROSS

1 Uses a swizzle stick
6 "I've __!" ("Enough!")
11 Sign, as a contract
14 Golfer with an army
15 Barely winning
16 Stimpy's pal
17 Fairy-tale fowl
19 Be in the red
20 Glacier Bay locale
21 Make-believe
23 Foxy
24 UFO passengers
26 Part of MIT
27 Trash
30 Valerie Harper role
33 El __, TX
36 Spacious
38 Kind of exam
39 The Auld Sod
40 Island near Venezuela
41 Analogy words
42 Untamed
43 French cubist painter
44 Without ice
45 Relish
47 Football blitz
49 Airline to Tel Aviv
51 Posed for a portrait
52 Clock setting at LAX
55 Trajectory shape
59 More cheerful
61 Canine cry
62 Vodka drink
64 Corp. bigshot
65 *A Passage to* __
66 Ride at anchor
67 Bill add-on
68 Driver's ed students
69 Computer-printer pioneer

DOWN

1 Long stories
2 Folklore being
3 Type of filling
4 Disencumbers
5 Diogenes, for one
6 Embrace
7 Per item
8 Way out
9 Cartographic closeup
10 Be on the brink
11 Steam locomotive
12 Part of CNN
13 Proposer's prop
18 7 or 11, in Vegas
22 Imitating
25 Nighttime annoyance
27 Venetian taxi
28 Woodworking tool
29 Fixes firmly
31 Figures to be crunched
32 Oodles
33 Sunday seats
34 Verdi song
35 Charlie Rich's nickname
37 Place for a sail
46 Bugs, for one
48 *My Favorite Year* star
50 Ben on *Bonanza*
52 __ Peak, CO
53 Take care of
54 Check for fit
55 Covenant
56 Real-estate calculation
57 Fill a hold
58 D __ "day"
60 Use scissors
63 Carrier to Stockholm

32 DINNER CIRCLES

by Patrick Jordan

ACROSS

1 Not quite shut
5 Poet Teasdale
9 Does a hatchet job on
13 CBS eye, e.g.
14 Element #5
15 Leave the stage
16 Two examples of 56 Across
18 New Haven school
19 United
20 Green Hornet's driver
21 Amateurs
23 Bunker, to his buddics
24 Meat in a pita
25 Two examples of 56 Across
31 Les __-Unis
32 Pub pints
33 George Bush's '70s grp.
35 Love god
36 Telemarketing tasks
38 Barry's *Going My Way* costar
39 Kipling character
40 They're divided into periods
41 Breadth
42 Two examples of 56 Across
46 Spherical bodies
47 Sow sound
48 Prepare a floppy disk
51 Casino game
52 Soup veggie
55 Mecca man
56 Theme of this puzzle
59 Bethlehem visitors
60 Makes less burdensome
61 Criticism, so to speak
62 Threat-ending word
63 Added to, with "out"
64 Brokaw and Berenger

DOWN

1 Purina competitor
2 Enlist in
3 1958 Pulitzer author
4 Hold up
5 Offer comfort to
6 Jason's ship
7 Nancy's youngest
8 Critiques
9 Attention-getter
10 See 49 Down
11 Artifice
12 British gun
14 Chess choice
17 Gumbo veggies
22 Pinball paths
23 Book after John
24 Flounder's filter
25 Cheat at hide-and-seek
26 Just clear of the seabed
27 One of the Judds
28 Model-plane material
29 Hockey infraction
30 Slight coloration
34 Stress or worry, e.g.
36 *Little Rascals* teacher
37 Oohs' partners
38 Cottonwood covering
40 Poet Pound
41 __-the-mill
43 Horror-film menace
44 Lamented
45 Aviary population
48 Debbie Allen TV series
49 With 10 Down, grad student's hurdle
50 Teases, with "on"
51 Car part
52 13th-century explorer
53 Wax-coated cheese
54 Begins a Q&A session
57 __ Ridge, TN
58 Poetic adverb

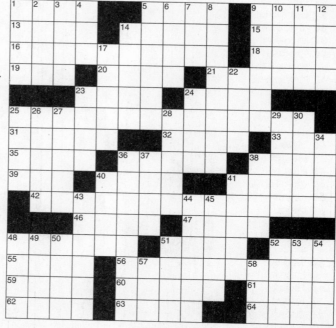

ACROSS

1 Kisses partner
5 Comes down with
9 Comic pianist
14 LAX postings
15 Party to
16 Worrier's risk
17 Start of a John Wooden quote
20 Like Gen. Powell
21 Singer DiFranco
22 Cold capital
23 Foul up
24 Leap of faith
26 Apr. 15 advisor
29 Upside-down sleeper
31 USNA grad
32 Fairy-tale tyrants
34 "Auld Lang __"
35 Gentle handling
36 Slings partner
37 Middle of quote
40 Express distress over
42 Gene material
43 Having only length
46 Wide awake
47 Deposit
48 More than enough
49 Platoon members
50 Keystone Kops, often
53 Scale notes
54 Horse's stride
55 Go bad
56 Here on the Riviera
57 End of quote

62 What like poles do
63 *Star Wars* series creature
64 Highlander
65 Fills up
66 Moist in the morn
67 Sun. talks

DOWN

1 Gloria Vanderbilt, for one
2 Plumb
3 Food fanciers
4 Compass reading
5 Ferber novel
6 100%
7 Slinky, for example
8 Schnozzolas
9 Protestor's prop
10 Ersatz butter
11 Elvis' record label
12 Hamburg's home: Abbr.
13 East ender?
18 Slice and dice
19 Trojans' sch.
25 Bands' bonuses
26 Future king
27 Church perch
28 Stubborn sort
30 Pavarotti, e.g.
33 Horse handler
35 Hamilton's bill
36 Wanted-poster letters

38 Jeers
39 Riptide pull
40 Baseball base
41 Inventor Whitney
44 College member?
45 Stops
47 Took to the tub
48 Regarding
51 Sellout
52 Not at all smooth
54 High spirits
57 Taxing org.
58 Mad hatter's drink
59 Fitting
60 Flabbergast
61 Battleship initials

34 POTABLES

by Lee Weaver

ACROSS
1 Pay attention to
7 TV alien
10 "Don't look __!"
14 A ham on stage
15 Souvenir from Kauai
16 Chair or sofa
17 Picnic dessert
19 Narrative
20 Legalese adverb
21 Acknowledges an officer
23 Down in the dumps
24 "No ifs, __, or buts!"
26 Defense grp.
27 Certain Alaskan
28 Taffy consumer
31 Doorway sides
34 Less cooked
36 Greek vowel
37 Newsman Sevareid
38 Butterfly relatives
39 Counterfeit coin
40 House addition
41 Musical Count
42 "If You Knew __"
43 Hoosegows
45 Bean or Welles
47 Mardi __
48 __-do-well
49 Two-bagger: Abbr.
52 Time off
55 Canadian province
57 Word of regret

58 Breakfast sweet
60 Stand up
61 Feel bad about
62 Thin pancakes
63 Rolling stone's lack
64 Before, in odes
65 Evaluate

DOWN
1 Small salamanders
2 Nebraska city
3 Carried piggyback
4 Roman road
5 Breakfast foods
6 Royal fur
7 The whole enchilada
8 Most August babies
9 Money matters
10 Very bright
11 Dish-drying cloths
12 Buck or bull
13 Summers, on the Riviera
18 Grueling auto races
22 *The Wizard of Oz* actor
25 Train stop
27 Easy as __
29 Decorative case
30 Fury
31 All-terrain vehicle
32 Singer Guthrie
33 Vase material
35 "I know __ I speak!"

38 Defeat decisively, in sports
39 Energy source
41 Necklace component
42 Post-office machines
44 Showy flowers
46 Iroquois tribe
49 Window covering
50 Two-wheelers
51 Windblown soil
52 Do damage to
53 Hodgepodge
54 *You Bet __ Life*
56 Experts
59 Lawyer's payment

ACROSS

1 Not first-quality: Abbr.
4 Molten rock
8 Leads into wrongdoing
14 Average grade
15 Makes angry
16 Algonquian language
17 *Hallelujah, __ Bum*
18 Expensively finished
19 Smith's gun partner
20 High-school subject
23 Summer pest, informally
24 Type of tire
28 Tenure of office
29 __-Locka, FL
31 Ivy League school
32 Young seal
35 Flying "A" competitor
38 VCR button
39 October sports event
42 Cellular letters
44 Russian refusal
45 The whole shebang
46 Offender, in cop lingo
48 TV's "Science Guy"
50 Othello's betrayer
54 French painter
57 Rubbed with one's nose
60 Shakespeare play site
62 Autobiography
65 Dry, as champagne
66 Retains
67 Actor Rains
68 __ avis
69 Golfer Ernie
70 Junior watcher
71 Major work
72 Nabokov novel

DOWN

1 Most unfriendly
2 1976's *King Kong*, e.g.
3 Parent
4 Ignite
5 Respond to reveille
6 Zipper alternative
7 Wine city
8 Urban area, old-style
9 Cockpit bailout button
10 Stephen King novel
11 *Nova* network
12 Eagle on a par four
13 __ Remo, Italy
21 Metronome speed
22 Clear the board
25 Dumbo's wings
26 Pub brew
27 Morning condensation
30 Annoying
33 Java holder
34 Tissue layer
36 Madrid Mrs.
37 Tin Man's need
39 Toad feature
40 Star in Cygnus
41 *My Fair Lady* lady
42 Tachometer abbr.
43 Teachers' org.
47 Engorge oneself
49 Lure into crime
51 Tennis great Gibson
52 President Ford
53 Black Sea port
55 Playground item
56 More achy
58 Robert Ruark novel
59 Greek letters
61 River of Aragón
62 Roast hosts, for short
63 Actor Wallach
64 Shoe-wiping place

by Bob Lubbers

ACROSS

1 Abominable Snowman
5 Flambé maker
11 British sports cars
14 __ *for All Seasons*
15 Tell
16 High-school course
17 Visiting many bars
19 Needlefish
20 Writer Rand
21 Actress Portman
23 Ghana's capital
26 T-shirt size: Abbr.
28 French movie
29 Chinese drink
31 Most current
33 Rocky peak
34 Shine brightly
36 Yo-yo trick
41 Most flexible
42 Dyer's container
44 Chronicles
47 Exhaust tube
50 Exude joy
51 JFK arrival, once
52 Of yore
53 Rogers' partner
56 Yoko __
57 Apt name for a cook?
58 Out of control
64 Musket suffix
65 Sharp-witted
66 Pennsylvania port
67 He followed HST
68 Divisions of Australia
69 Proofreader's mark

DOWN

1 Puppy complaint
2 Ostrich cousin
3 Bar bill
4 __ of (postal phrase)
5 Kukla's friend
6 Actor Ayres
7 100%
8 Bangor's home
9 Sicilian spouter
10 Troop group: Abbr.
11 '50s pitcher Sal
12 Cereals
13 Avenue crosser
18 Tatum's dad
22 Played a role
23 G-man: Abbr.
24 Boast
25 Wax: Lat.
26 Inclines
27 Gizmos
30 Jazz combos
31 Christine of *Chicago Hope*
32 Partook of
35 Where __ (center of activity)
37 Andes animal
38 __ Nidre (Hebrew prayer)
39 Roman poet
40 Gawk
43 Perfect gymnastics score
44 Reduced in rank
45 Like some tables
46 Basic quality
48 Extended
49 __ under (overwhelmed)
51 Actress Berger
54 Retirees' accts.
55 Corrosion
56 Change for a five
59 Bolt fastener
60 Chemical ending
61 Wrath
62 __ *Abner*
63 About a 62 average

LITERARY SANDWICH

by Rich Norris

ACROSS

1 Finish third
5 Auditing employees: Abbr.
9 Coll. at Amherst
14 Spelunker's bailiwick
15 In addition
16 Festive occasion
17 Like some testimony
18 San __ Obispo, CA
19 Took a shot
20 *The Human COMEDY* author
23 It may precede a fall
24 Bodkins lead-in
25 Small boats
28 "__ boy!"
30 Engine housing
33 Breezed through, as an exam
34 *Silas Marner* novelist
35 Lawyers' grp.
36 *An American TRAGEDY* author
40 Food fish
41 Succulent
42 Bird house
43 Today: Sp.
44 Residents: Suff.
45 Tea types
47 Honest __
48 Balkan War participant
49 *The Human COMEDY* author

56 Concealed
57 Make or break
58 Trompe l'__
59 Advance warning
60 Villainous
61 Mock fanfare
62 Japanese-American
63 Bank chamber
64 Klondike carrier

DOWN

1 Dilapidated vessel
2 Spydom name
3 Model-train layout
4 Rolling in dough
5 French port
6 Expand, as hot dogs
7 Without warranties
8 Cubs slugger
9 Modern
10 Shelley and Stuart
11 *Rigoletto* solo
12 British weapon
13 One of the Chaplins
21 Steam up
22 Turning part
25 Nab
26 It may precede a blessing
27 Worthy of help
28 Guinness' namesakes
29 In apple-pie order
30 Leisurely stroll

31 Too big
32 Pub contest
34 Buffalo's lake
37 African nation
38 External
39 Rorschach test images
45 Bit of gravel
46 Epoch
47 Pianist Watts
48 Sans __ type
49 Port opening
50 Tram loads
51 Preceding periods
52 Hindu god
53 Eager desire
54 Helper
55 Bedecked
56 Rotate, as a camera

38 YOU BET

by A.J. Santora

ACROSS

1 Naughty kids
6 Sch. subject
9 WWII craft
12 Scribe
13 Son of Venus
14 Social finish
15 '70s game show
17 Sympathy partner
18 Doddering
19 __ podrida
20 Agenda listing
21 Ancient Persians
22 Money holders
24 Mai __
26 Together
27 Innocent one
30 Forest creatures
33 White's partner
36 Texas tea
37 Train components
39 Sean Lennon's mom
40 African cattle pen
42 Shopper's bag
43 Native ability
44 Coagulation
46 Average
48 Expressionless one
52 Minimum
56 Javanese ruler
57 Coll. sports group
58 Offspring
59 __ glance
60 Salty snacks
62 Last mo.
63 Solar disk
64 Oscar and Cornel
65 Orson's planet
66 Hitched
67 Stratum

DOWN

1 Pickling need
2 Unyielding
3 Center or skier
4 Singer Brewer
5 Full-house sign
6 Be suspicious
7 Reef formers
8 Treasury Dept. agency
9 *Bonanza* role
10 Horse
11 Groups of horses
12 Explosive sound
13 "For __ know . . ."
16 Tennis shot
20 New York school
23 Conductor Lukas
25 Altar words
27 Derek of Harvard
28 Breeze, essentially
29 Pershing sobriquet
31 Drew out
32 Coll. course
34 Purchase from 33 Across
35 __ Nidre
37 Something indistinct
38 Tie fabric
41 Zone
43 Anew
45 Memorable
47 Actress Witt
48 Spanish museum
49 Hollywood staple
50 *The Godfather* actor
51 Nosh
53 Stage remark
54 Excellent
55 Hardy girl
60 Ben, to 9 Down
61 Temple player

IN THE DOUGH

by Norma Steinberg

ACROSS

1 Accomplishment
5 Alan Alda sitcom
9 Spigot
12 Made eyes at
14 Soak in water
15 Boater's tool
16 Racecar safety feature
18 Exist
19 Tire type
20 Poisonous snakes
21 Blotch
24 "No more!"
26 Auto frame
28 5/15 or so
31 Places of refuge
32 Frog kin
35 Norman Vincent __
36 Neckwear
37 One-eyed monster
39 Hot tub
40 __ nous (confidentially)
42 Soprano __ Te Kanawa
43 Singer Redding
44 Talk out again
46 Thwart
48 Real-__ broker
51 Conscious
52 One of the Three B's
54 Distant
56 Time period
57 Excellent
62 Deer family member
63 Ascends
64 Ms. Hawkins of Dogpatch
65 Enemy
66 Words of understanding
67 Physique

DOWN

1 In favor of
2 Self
3 A hundred percent
4 __ Aviv
5 Slugger Roger
6 Slugger's opportunity
7 Israeli greeting
8 Girl's pronoun
9 Banquet figure
10 Org. for seniors
11 Chief executive: Abbr.
13 Day of *Pillow Talk*
14 Garden plot
17 Narcissism
20 Assistant
21 Holy place
22 Be extraordinary
23 Beast of burden
25 Gladys Knight backup
26 Supply the food
27 Argyle, e.g.
29 Of Swiss mountains
30 Baking ingredient
33 Actress MacGraw
34 Village
37 "__ la vie!"
38 Captain Kidd, for one
41 Ill-considered
43 Eggs
45 __ Tweed (fabric)
47 Washstand pitchers
49 Annoy
50 Show's introducer
52 Complaint
53 Folk singer Guthrie
55 Gives the go-ahead
57 Dernier __
58 Boxing punch
59 Fuss
60 El __ (Spanish hero)
61 Vital

by Fred Piscop

ACROSS

1 Atlas pages
5 Stadium souvenirs
9 Soup-eater's sound
14 Balm ingredient
15 Fictional Uriah
16 Schlepper
17 Delivery to a printer
20 Battery terminal
21 Writer Roth
22 Type of apple
25 Originally named
26 "__ De-Lovely"
29 Bummed out
30 Negative prefix
32 Artist Gauguin
33 Jeans, for example
35 *My Cousin __*
36 Solicitious phrase
40 Mountain group
41 Orderly formation
42 __-European languages
43 "Indeed!"
44 Peat source
47 Dispenser candy
48 "Just __ thought!"
51 Natural gases
54 "There __ be a law!"
57 Boxing site
58 Sporty wheels
62 Hoopster Shaquille
63 Symbol of holiness
64 Brainstorm
65 Dayan of Israel
66 Every twelve mos.
67 Toward sunrise

DOWN

1 Colorful parrot
2 Pop star Morissette
3 Southern California city
4 Sowed
5 Half a dance's name
6 __ Lingus
7 Chick sound
8 Pitching great Warren
9 Do hair
10 Central spots
11 Idealists
12 Iron-pumper's unit
13 Be a Nosy Parker
18 Scale notes
19 Tool's partner
23 Economist Smith
24 One of a 1492 trio
27 __ out (ignore)
28 Foxy
31 Fairy tale, e.g.
32 Singer Zadora
33 Dessert choice
34 Wild time
35 *"Oy __!"*
36 Ebb
37 Gridiron areas
38 In the past
39 Endure
40 Tear up
44 Bestselling doll
45 Iroquois tribe
46 Rock and rap, for two
48 Light on one's feet
49 __ Na Na
50 Needing to scratch
52 Possess, to Scots
53 Anwar of Egypt
55 Four Corners state
56 In the distance
58 Lap dog, for short
59 Yoko __
60 Out of sorts
61 Judge Bean

41 FOOD FOR THOUGHT

by Bob Lubbers

ACROSS

1 Boom supports
6 Banquet platform
10 Arizona city
14 *Heidi* author
15 Brown shade
16 Prayer end
17 Green veggie
19 Sawbucks
20 Deep red
21 Sunny lobbies
22 Tend a tot
25 "__ No Strings" (*Pinocchio* song)
26 Baby powder
27 African fly
30 Before
31 Russian range
33 Food from heaven
35 Salad ingredient
39 Fallen rocks
40 Outfit
43 __ *Abner*
46 San Simeon builder
49 Coffee servers
50 Let up
52 Kind of pudding
54 Special Forces cap
55 Actress Danes
57 Iroquoian Indian
58 Campbell can
62 Actor Neeson
63 Mine: Fr.
64 Tussle
65 HS exams

66 Greek letter
67 Crystal-ball gazers

DOWN

1 Submissions to an ed.
2 Quick to learn
3 Neighbor of Leb.
4 Kids' vehicles
5 Trig functions
6 Bookkeeping entries
7 Top cards
8 *"Dies __"*
9 Cal. column
10 Dull finish
11 Come into view
12 Of greater tenure
13 Having a handle
18 Pluck
21 Thoroughfare
22 A/C unit
23 Swiss river
24 Boring
25 "__ that special?"
28 Abu Dhabi leader
29 Make lace
32 Scented sack
34 Agree
36 __ Scott Decision
37 Meadow
38 Continental currency

41 Ltd. cousin
42 Bible book: Abbr.
43 Tags
44 Spain + Portugal
45 Wrangler's rope
47 Sports arenas
48 Follow
51 Abounds
53 Basketball tactic
55 "__ and get it!"
56 Booty
58 Run in
59 Comstock load
60 Former Mideast org.
61 Ltr.'s second add-on

42 THAT'S ENTERTAINMENT

by Rich Norris

ACROSS

1 Ready for trimming, as a sail
6 Masseuse employer
9 Keep under wraps
14 Madrid museum
15 Capote nickname
16 Game fish
17 Robust specimen
20 Ace, perhaps
21 "Great!"
22 Diminutive ending
23 Kind of inspection
26 Like a 17 Across
28 Fall behind
29 Run __ of (conflict with)
30 Fixes socks
32 Type of stock option
33 Actress Farrow
35 Look for
36 Lighter alternative
40 Fraternal group
41 Arafat's org.
42 Loft contents
43 Monarch
45 Break up, informally
47 "Time __ Bottle" (Croce song)
50 Actor Stephen
51 Pencil topper
53 Binary digits
54 Rub the wrong way
56 Biting flies
58 Appreciative gesture
61 Track official
62 Kimono sash
63 Deli dozen
64 Spurt of energy
65 Clamor
66 Senator Kefauver

DOWN

1 Consternate
2 Factoids
3 Part of NASCAR
4 Collar attachment
5 Show displeasure
6 Camping need
7 Expert
8 "__ Wiedersehen!"
9 Cooked, in a way
10 "Dies __"
11 Like some calls
12 Summaries
13 High degree
18 Tanning site, maybe
19 FDR's successor
24 Legal citation
25 Pelvic bones
27 "For shame!"
29 Diving bird
31 Pale
32 Prepare for pictures
34 Eager (for)
36 Kind of stock
37 Ponca City's home
38 Dog bane
39 Cool dude
40 Go wrong
44 Betterment
46 Keep from leaving
47 Rude remark
48 Tease
49 Size up
52 Rink arbiter
53 Preminger and Graham
55 Fills with wonder
57 Ireland, to the Irish
58 City-map lines: Abbr.
59 Agnes of __
60 Stat for Sosa

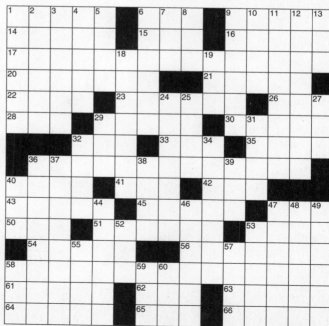

by A.J. Santora

ACROSS

1 French feline
5 It might be pale
8 Gum __ (ink ingredient)
14 Actress Skye
15 . follower
16 Part of FDR
17 Dependency adage, with "It"
20 Blot out
21 Preppy school
22 In order
23 Actress Hagen
25 Dubliners
27 Perry Como song
33 "Nothin' doin'!"
34 Barbary beast
35 Epic poem
36 Rabbit kin
39 Fierce
41 Devil Rays home
42 Veteran
43 "__ only me!"
44 Gradually
49 Less wild
50 Monopolize
51 "Take __ Train"
54 Med. course
56 Start
60 Australian ditty
63 Following closely
64 Bran source
65 Slave away
66 English counties
67 Sailing dir.
68 Saber relative

DOWN

1 Refer to
2 Frosty covering
3 "Diana" singer
4 Readies to drive
5 Play part
6 Kitty Litter inventor
7 Showing passion
8 Handsome guy
9 Emeritus: Abbr.
10 Denver's sitcom boss
11 Bugaboo
12 Actress Swenson
13 Diving bird
18 Bristle
19 Went fast
24 Jai __
26 Hit, old-style
27 Heathen
28 "Oh, give me __ . . ."
29 Mission control, for short
30 Half note
31 Sew, in a way
32 Praiseful poems
33 Global alliance
37 Plattsburgher, to a Bronxite
38 "Bye!"
39 NYC transit line
40 Wyle of *ER*
42 Ideal
45 Sends, in a way
46 *Bonnie and Clyde* director
47 Spree
48 Start burning
51 Xmas poem start
52 "Hell __ no fury . . ."
53 Pre-coll.
55 Federal agent
57 Splash
58 Singer Adams
59 Story
61 Sleep unit?
62 Had a bite

EASY AS PIE

by Bob Lubbers

ACROSS

1 Historical periods
5 Meal
11 Actress Lupino
14 Eyelid projection
15 "We'll turn Manhattan into __ of joy"
16 Veto
17 __ Major (Big Dipper)
18 Lowest part
19 Golf-ball holder
20 Type of pie
23 Lauder of cosmetics
24 No longer working
27 Ave. crossers
28 Endure
32 "__ bleu!"
33 Greek
36 Composer Coward
37 Type of pie
39 Impartial
41 Soaks up
42 Tapestry
44 Exxon, once
45 Map abbr.
48 Baggage carriers
51 Wary
53 Type of pie
57 Orange pekoe, e.g.
59 Baltimore player
60 Like a Nash lama
61 Blyth or Jillian
62 Swear (to)
63 Tardy
64 Clampett patriarch
65 Like some boxes
66 Considerably

DOWN

1 Gives the slip to
2 Most uncommon
3 Good traits
4 Physique
5 1944 Nobel physicist Isidor
6 Son of Seth
7 Essential part
8 "When You Wish Upon __"
9 Inclination
10 Entices
11 Office communication device
12 Backgammon cube
13 Bunyan's tool
21 Excises, editorially
22 Jungle vines
25 Before, to a poet
26 Tierra __ Fuego
29 Canadian province: Abbr.
30 Litterbug, e.g.
31 Uptight
33 Mr. Greeley
34 Sgts., e.g.
35 Strays
37 Jazz club named for Charlie Parker
38 Christ Stopped at __
39 Remote
40 "How __ you?"
43 Pacific islander
45 Of a sovereign
46 __ form (as expected)
47 Shoelace opening
49 Door: Fr.
50 Tizzies
52 __ Gay (WWII plane)
54 Champagne name
55 "What __ is new?"
56 Sent back: Abbr.
57 __ Mahal
58 Compass pt.

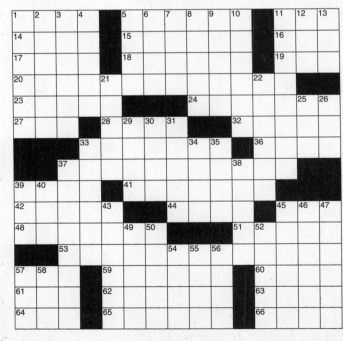

45 IT HAD TO BE HUE

by Richard Silvestri

ACROSS

1 Seaweed substance
5 Exile isle
9 Walked through water
14 Where Timbuktu is
15 Boulevard
16 Swell smell
17 Caan's *Funny Lady* role
19 Bolshevism founder
20 Rome residents
21 Ancient prophet
22 Gloss
23 Surge
25 Inc., in England
27 __ *gratia artis*
28 Work unit
31 Biting
35 "Do __ fa . . ."
37 Squeeze (in)
38 Leg part
39 Short putt
40 Killer whale
41 Pushpin
42 Alaska's first governor
43 Senior member
44 Flood floater
45 GI's address
46 Govt. purchasing org.
48 Have in mind
51 Prop for Groucho
55 Widen
57 Caught on to
60 Get around
61 "Three Little Words" songwriter
62 "Land __ alive!"
63 Church section
64 Willow or walnut
65 Like krypton
66 Do some gardening
67 Stood firm

DOWN

1 Prefix for "both"
2 Ways of walking
3 God of Islam
4 Moon valley
5 Wandering
6 Diving bird
7 Low man at La Scala
8 Lemon finish
9 Tusked mammal
10 Regions
11 Jazz trumpeter
12 Actor Jannings
13 Jutlander
18 Street sign
21 Senator Hatch
24 Identifying
26 Mythical reptile
29 Compete at Indy
30 FBI guy
31 Nick and Nora's dog
32 Turn to cinders
33 TV talk-show host
34 Ready the press
36 MPG raters
37 Bill's partner
39 Home of the brave
43 Every 24 hours
45 Bear witness (to)
47 Threw fear into
49 Consumer champion
50 Hang decoratively
52 Circumference
53 Sky color
54 Mutineer
55 He loved Lucy
56 __ the Terrible
58 Language of Eire
59 Prepared Easter eggs
61 Half a bray

ACROSS

1 Sticky, as in summer
6 Small plateau
10 OT book
14 Make up (for)
15 Golden __ (senior)
16 Was dressed in
17 Bushwhacker
19 Slang expert Partridge
20 Bangkok resident
21 Has a bite of
23 Govt. hush-hush group
24 South American capital
26 *Hee Haw* persona
28 Swiss canton
30 *Nixon* director
32 Rose Bowl site
34 Actor Erwin
35 Sticking point
36 Road curve
38 Little more than
42 Listening device
45 Having gear
48 Emulate a couch potato
52 __ *Pinafore*
53 Bureaucratic ritual
54 Bridal path
56 "__ you serious?"
57 Spill the beans
59 Iowa city
62 Shout
64 Butcher buy
66 Tony relative
67 Container weight
68 Livy's land
69 Russian refusal
70 Moved with ease
71 Promote

DOWN

1 Biblical verb
2 Zion National Park state
3 Da Vinci masterpiece
4 Columbus' 1492 goal
5 Society newcomer
6 *YM* or *GQ*
7 Farm products
8 Fume
9 Old debts
10 Have debts
11 Indonesian island
12 Gotten out of bed
13 The '90s, for one
18 Dickens title opener
22 Part of CBS
25 Peas' home
27 Baffle
28 Some market moves
29 Sought office
31 Still-life subjects
33 Sports figure
37 Blew up a storm
39 Paper collectibles, e.g.
40 Sleep state
41 MS. preparers
43 Biological sci.
44 Feasts
46 One of the archangels
47 Preconditions
48 Tot's writing tool
49 Contract term
50 Antarctic penguin
51 __ *Weapon*
55 Rubber source
58 Garr of *Mr. Mom*
60 Viscount's superior
61 Three-player card game
63 Court call
65 Sault __ Marie

47 SNOOZE BREAK

by Patrick Jordan

ACROSS

1 Editor's note
5 Peddles
10 Sing like Ella
14 Long stride
15 Goody
16 Roof overhang
17 Definition of "alarm clock," part 1
20 Scam target
21 Chronic complainers
22 "Why?"
24 Talkative
25 Funnyman DeLuise
28 Pool distance
29 Highest USMC rank
30 Do one's bidding
32 In great supply
34 Pursuit
39 Part 2 of definition
42 Alabama city
43 British noble
44 Pack down
45 Coal carrier
47 Director Van Sant
49 Country singer Clark
50 ". . . and __ a good night"
53 Betting setting
55 Cheerful
57 Erle colleague
61 End of definition
63 New Rochelle college
64 Radiate, as charm
65 Faucet flaw
66 Golf gadgets
67 War horse
68 Blunders

DOWN

1 Balkan native
2 Singer Braxton
3 Monumental
4 First extra inning
5 Goblets, e.g.
6 Directional suffix
7 Turn loose
8 Hibernation location
9 Larry or Shemp
10 Grinch's creator
11 Get down to __
12 Murphy's infant
13 Danson and Knight
18 Cello kin
19 Subtle distinction
23 Was malicious
25 Tiny circles
26 Woodwind
27 Whimper
29 Comic Gobel
31 Sweet potato
33 Mortgage agcy.
35 Very popular
36 Way over yonder
37 Japanese sport
38 Catch a glimpse of
40 Coffee-flavored liqueur
41 Late sleeper
46 Pizza topping
48 Adventurous tale
50 Western lake
51 Standing __ foot
52 Turkish nobles
53 Trial setting
54 Luxuriant fur
55 Houlihan portrayer
56 Teller's call
58 Wedding-cake level
59 Take in aurally
60 Poses a riddle
62 Rhymed tribute

48 *SEE YOU LATER*

by A.J. Santora

ACROSS

1 Raggedy doll
5 French cop
9 Jersey's chew
12 Words of a song
14 Spore sac
16 Important numero
17 Medical practice
19 Hwy.
20 *Rhoda* production co.
21 Runner Sebastian's kin
22 Eagle, e.g.
24 Tea cake
26 Ornamental plant
27 Actress Thurman
28 Tap drink
29 French film
32 European tree
34 Weevil
36 Lawn bowling
37 Peppermint product
38 TV doc Art
39 Gourd-like plant
41 Take a cab
42 Run-down area
43 Before
44 Like
45 Pontifical
47 Plate armor
51 Sketcher's need
53 Now, to Caesar
54 Scrooge word
55 Heavy weight
56 Socialize
59 Piece of the action
60 Shoe material
61 Lessened
62 "__ So Fine"
63 Sugar source
64 Predicament

DOWN

1 Meek as __
2 "Night" word form
3 Oil barrels
4 Lyricist Harburg
5 Aspect
6 WWII craft
7 Hosp. area
8 Ives partner
9 Cut short
10 Golden Rule word
11 Active one
13 Pickle, once
15 Navy commando
18 "Thought" word ender
23 Odd
25 Ginger plants
26 Horner find
28 Keen
30 Evening hour
31 Want-ad abbr.
32 Music genre
33 Residents
35 Ornamental stroke
36 Chemist's deg.
37 "Material __"
40 Zoo attraction
44 Fritzi, to Nancy
46 Soup veggies
47 Gem face
48 Belittle
49 Fills fully
50 Molts
51 Draw with acid
52 Rascal
53 Nylon shade
57 So-so mark
58 Zodiac animal

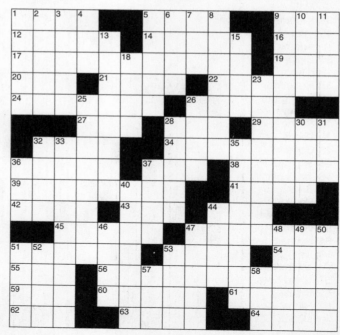

49 CAN WE TALK?

by Norma Steinberg

ACROSS

1 Choir voice
5 Cry loudly
9 Tonic's partner
12 Expressed displeasure
14 Condor's nest
15 Fuss
16 "Ten items or less" place
18 Classic car
19 __ out (parachuted)
20 It's north of Nebr.
21 Borg of tennis
24 Water channel
26 City of Spain
28 Cavort
31 Singer McEntire
32 Ill-mannered
35 Photographer Adams
36 Diplomatic official: Abbr.
37 Pretender
39 Smidgen
40 Annoyance
42 So long, in Leeds
43 Comfort
44 Sign up
46 Track official
48 Broadens
51 Forest components
52 Wearing loafers
54 Pointed beard
56 Ad-__ committee
57 Is the boss
62 Irritate
63 Highly sloped
64 Marinara, e.g.
65 Salary
66 Light throw
67 Casino transactions

DOWN

1 Mary Todd's spouse
2 Smoked salmon
3 Go one better
4 Above, to a poet
5 Ringing instruments
6 The Little Mermaid
7 Pitcher's procedure
8 Confederate general
9 New Jersey nickname
10 Brainstorm
11 Cubbyhole
13 Actress Winger
14 "__ live and breathe!"
17 Justice __ Day O'Connor
20 Read a bar code
21 German city
22 Carroll poem
23 Stop __ dime
25 "Dies __"
26 Wine fruit
27 Mom's sister
29 Desists
30 Church official
33 Genetic initials
34 Has a snack
37 Join metal
38 "__ down the hatches!"
41 Null's partner
43 Before
45 Musically smooth
47 Vicinities
49 Pokes (around)
50 Strongboxes
52 Destroyer, e.g.
53 Israeli dance
55 Piece of advice
57 DDE's predecessor
58 Science class
59 Take to court
60 Pretense
61 "Okay!"

BOOKMAKING

by Rich Norris

ACROSS

1 Living-room piece
6 Glacial formation
11 Air-rifle ammo
14 Greek letter
15 Fight site
16 Bullring shout
17 Unrealized gain
19 Uncooked
20 Adam's mate
21 Pleads
22 Flabbergast
24 French river
26 At ease
28 Vacation memento
30 Color again
31 __ Bator
32 Desert wet spots
33 European airline
36 Signed agreement
40 Throw in
41 Baseball Hall of Famer Rod
42 One of the Brontës
43 Honored, as with a party
44 Poker player, at times
46 Pertinent
49 Connects emotionally
50 Island west of Curaçao
51 Golf stroke
52 Very long time
55 "Let 'er __!"
56 Nightclub fee
60 Shelley work
61 Special talent
62 Banish
63 Abigail Adams, __ Smith
64 Have a feeling
65 Direct elsewhere

DOWN

1 __ Cod
2 Norwegian royal name
3 Advantage
4 Friend of Fidel
5 Docking area
6 Bilko, casually
7 Love god
8 Hockey official
9 Black cuckoo
10 Chemist's facilitator
11 Cleansing powder
12 Conflagration
13 Repaired a shirt
18 Confined, with "up"
23 Actress West
25 *Golden* __ (Drake's ship)
26 Plant anew
27 Genesis site
28 Oompah instrument
29 Lost traction
30 Went fast
32 Fairy-tale baddies
33 Typeface description
34 Teen trouble
35 Poll or trick follower
37 Sprain treatments
38 Kosovo peacekeeping grp.
39 Surprise attack
43 Watch pocket
44 Campus recruiting org.
45 Flower part
46 Brother of Moses
47 __ and joy
48 Calcutta coin
49 Delta of *Designing Women*
51 Chest muscles, briefly
53 Stare at
54 __-do-well
57 Latish lunch hour
58 Furniture carrier
59 Woodsman's tool

ON THE GRIDIRON

by Bob Lubbers

ACROSS

1 Oodles
6 Watering hole
9 Scatter
14 Copier need
15 Bar bill
16 Verily
17 Inside covers
19 Washer cycle
20 Mexican money
21 Circle segment
22 Evades
23 "Yes __, Bob!"
25 "__ Got You Under My Skin"
26 Big Apple arts mecca
31 Popeye's nemesis
33 Guzzler
34 Went in a hurry
35 Mountain ending
36 Yuletide drink
39 Funny Charlotte
41 Estuary
42 Thresholds
44 Used to be
46 Anon
48 Hook, line and sinker
52 Orange cooler
53 Insurgent
54 Playful talk
57 "We __ not alone"
58 Sailor's saint
62 Madonna role
63 Highway barrier
65 Ninesome
66 PA clock setting
67 Nimble
68 Saw wood
69 Mao __-tung
70 Pita sandwiches

DOWN

1 "__ lively!"
2 Ice-cream holder
3 "No ifs, __ or buts!"
4 Down payment
5 Lady of Sp.
6 Sound system
7 Packages
8 Pecs neighbors
9 Tried mightily
10 Neptune's spear
11 Ladder bar
12 Alternatively
13 Divining-rod shapes
18 Green space in Paris
22 Pronouncements
24 Party to
26 Entices
27 Postal Creed word
28 Nutty cake
29 One of HOMES
30 Bring up
31 Cattlemen's concern
32 With 45 Down, jeans giant
37 Proprietor
38 One-liner
40 Actress Sommer
43 Break apart
45 See 32 Down
47 Sneeze inducer
49 Conceive
50 Add fizz to
51 Trucker, often
54 Affleck et al.
55 English county
56 Bolivian boy
59 Den
60 *Venus de* __
61 Corrida cries
63 "__ the lead out!"
64 Statesman Hammarskjöld

52 FREEZE FRAME
. . . .

by Ray Hamel

ACROSS
1 Bamboo eater
6 It's from hunger
10 Feds
14 Unfamiliar
15 Solicitous response
16 Function
17 Sound of wet impact
18 Spatting
19 __ Major
20 1968 Hepburn film
23 Lennon mate
24 Meal starter
25 1997 Kline film
31 Pat
34 Soil
35 McGwire stat.
36 Winter Olympics event
37 Days in a novena
38 Shopping binge
40 Newspaper notice
41 Scant
42 Cote sound
43 Cause to jump
44 Ship heading: Abbr.
45 1983 Berenger film
48 Objective
49 Sidelines yell
50 1995 Schlesinger movie
59 Neighborhood
60 Seaport of Algeria
61 Ancient Greek region

62 Ripoff
63 Mr. Mostel
64 Cohort
65 Brinker of fiction
66 Garden spot
67 Pooh pal

DOWN
1 Days of old
2 Coleridge's sacred river
3 Green shade
4 Business proposition
5 Ohio college
6 Steinway output
7 Wine region
8 No from Kohl
9 Go downhill
10 Sty sound
11 Cartoonist Walker
12 Otherwise
13 Close by
21 A person
22 *Just As* __ (Billy Graham book)
25 Strained
26 Waves at
27 Bert's roommate
28 Inventory unit
29 Pulsate
30 Assay subject
31 Mideast emirate
32 "I want __ just like . . ."
33 Asian palm
36 __ Ness

38 Chitchat
39 Author of "The Gold Bug"
43 Comic bit
45 Quirk
46 Kind of patch
47 Long-jawed fish
48 Smart portrayer
50 ATM output
51 Dolphin relative
52 Incline
53 TV palomino
54 Meter reading
55 __ song (cheaply)
56 Presently
57 Betrothal token
58 Poet Angelou

by Fred Piscop

ACROSS

1 Keep __ (persist)
5 Capacitance unit
10 Morning radio talker
14 Klinger portrayer
15 Battleground of 1836
16 It means "billionth"
17 Corny baseball great?
20 Send to Congress
21 British novelist
22 Ad follower
23 Walkie-talkie word
24 Where many vets fought
25 Tankard filler
26 Most AARP members
27 Leave out
31 More moth-eaten
33 Inventor Otis
35 Plus
36 Corny baseball great?
39 Hole goal
40 *Tristram Shandy* author
41 Garfield's girlfriend
44 Aardvark's meal
45 *Pygmalion* monogram
48 Propel, as a shot
49 New Haven student
51 Dostoyevsky character
53 Wood tool
54 Puts up, in a way
57 "Tiny Bubbles" singer
58 Corny nickname for Pee Wee Reese?
61 Circle dance
62 Standing upright
63 Critic Sheraton
64 Respectful reply
65 Taboos
66 Burpee bagful

DOWN

1 Dessert, to a Brit
2 Polk's successor
3 Factory seconds: Abbr.
4 White flag's message
5 Partner of away
6 Winged
7 Zany Martha
8 Mideast capital
9 "De Camptown Races" word
10 Neither Rep. nor Dem.
11 Bening's sister-in-law
12 Squeaky, maybe
13 Blubbering sort
18 Amble along
19 Verne's submariner
28 .001 inch
29 Nature goddess
30 Greek letter
32 Hang in the hammock
33 De Valera's land
34 "You said it!"
36 Ballroom dancers
37 Oils and the like
38 Like some jobs
39 Alaskan bay
41 "I don't care" attitude
42 Radar's quaff
43 On cloud nine
45 __ Mae
46 Puccini's *La __*
47 Showing no emotion
50 Emcee's spiel
52 Colgate quarters
55 Campbell of country
56 Splinter group
59 Beat it
60 Some chessmen: Abbr.

ACROSS

1 Joe of *My Cousin Vinny*
6 PDQ relative
10 Tube commercial
14 Pandora's box contents
15 *Sesame Street* regular
16 Residence
17 Greek letters
18 Spill the beans
19 Conceits
20 Gambler's nightmare
23 Most greasy
26 Ladies' men
27 The Bard of __
28 Home of CNN
31 Used a stopwatch
33 Fluish feeling
34 Airline to Stockholm
37 Pressure-laden time
41 123-45-6789, for one: Abbr.
42 Debatable
43 Silly goose
44 Mechanical-man science
47 Farmland
48 Paying customer
51 Acorn creator
53 Recipe item
56 Govern
57 Choir voice
58 Assistants
62 Smeltery stuff
63 Stead
64 Make impure
65 Ship pole
66 "__ we forget"
67 Snow boards

DOWN

1 Candy in a dispenser
2 Abel's mother
3 Take a load off
4 Goodman's instrument
5 Magazine copy
6 Costello's partner
7 Part of SASE
8 Bedouin
9 Circus man
10 Actress Ritter
11 *Glamour* rival
12 Mobil rival
13 Office furniture
21 Govt. code breakers
22 Be overfond of
23 Affirmations
24 Some poison plants
25 Miller's salesman
29 Christine of *Chicago Hope*
30 Ripen
32 Game tile
34 Mexican mister
35 "Tomorrow" singer
36 In thing, in fashion
38 Step sound
39 Bricks measure
40 Hung-jury result
44 Urgent prompting
45 Lame excuse
46 Schlemiel
48 Kind of computer drive
49 Designer Ashley
50 Ocean oases
52 *Endymion* poet
54 Ballet bend
55 Summers in France
59 Gaming cube
60 Swan song
61 Peter and Paul: Abbr.

55 DESCRIPTIVE LETTERS

by Bob Lubbers

ACROSS

1 Greek porticos
6 Damage
10 Alumnus
14 Eagle nest
15 Draft classification
16 Meander
17 Dairy product
19 Prayer ender
20 Sea eagle
21 Music for two
22 Diner
24 In tatters
26 Ere
28 Clapton or Sevareid
30 Poseidon's spear
34 Slay
37 Lasting impression
39 TV host
40 Actor Milo
42 Corp. takeover
43 Center of power
44 Quay
45 On the summit
47 Air out
48 Arp's art form
50 Fairy
52 __ Family Singers
54 Get lower
58 Bible book
61 Alda of *M*A*S*H*
63 __ Speedwagon
64 Butter substitute
65 First assembly-line car
68 Arabian sultanate
69 Probabilities
70 Golfer Palmer
71 Chico or Karl
72 Thumbs-down votes
73 Theater sections

DOWN

1 Wiser
2 __ firma
3 Asian ape
4 Lend a hand
5 Lawn tool
6 Native land
7 Singer Baker
8 Fam. member
9 __-break (crucial)
10 Family fare
11 The Eternal City
12 State confidently
13 Disavow
18 German autos
23 Shakespearean sprite
25 Baby Boomer's kids
27 Western comedy series
29 Carpenter's compressor
31 __ *homo*
32 Nine, in Nuremberg
33 Trial period
34 Mamie Eisenhower, née __
35 Workers' safety org.
36 "If __ a Hammer"
38 Approximately: Abbr.
41 In flames
46 Go biking
49 Up-river swimmer
51 Wedding tux, often
53 Rice field
55 Antler tip
56 Spooky
57 Protuberances
58 Adverse fate
59 __ mater
60 In the neighborhood
62 Minus
66 Harem room
67 To and __

56 BIRD CALLS

by Norma Steinberg

ACROSS

1 Run in neutral
5 Shower alternative
9 Naughty
12 Lunchtime, often
13 Mistake
15 Mosaic piece
16 Pigeon blow?
18 Undulation
19 Bandstand box
20 Harvest
21 Kind of salad
23 Metropolis
24 __ noire
25 Obis
28 Off-tour jaunt
32 Woodwinds
33 Fabricated
34 Put out of sight
35 Diminish
36 Gave in
37 Eve's address
38 Quickly: Abbr.
39 Sign seen by seers
40 Astronomer Carl
41 Put back
43 100%
44 Oxidation
45 Endure
46 South Seas island
49 Ambience
50 Court
53 Julia Roberts' brother
54 Crows' cooperation?
57 Part of a chain
58 Sharon of Israel
59 Medicinal tablet
60 Youngster
61 Actor Wilder
62 As well

DOWN

1 Ancient Peruvian
2 Dire destiny
3 Plane stunt
4 Finale
5 Engenders, in the Bible
6 Military force
7 Golf hazard
8 Ad __
9 Prejudice
10 Menlo Park middle name
11 Bambi and others
14 Flowed back
15 Songbird's love?
17 Iroquoian Indians
22 Eroded
23 Chicken chicanery?
24 Delaware senator
25 To date
26 Defame
27 Soft drinks
28 In the bank
29 Mountain crest
30 Perfect
31 Director Marshall
33 *Glengarry Glen Ross* playwright
36 Napoleon's birthplace
40 Brooke Shields role
42 Ump's call
43 Early release
45 Light-bulb unit
46 Have an effect
47 Song from *Rigoletto*
48 Prefix for sight
49 Pierre's pal
50 Emulate banshees
51 Nocturnal birds
52 Norwegian capital
55 Web site suffix
56 Apr. number cruncher

by Rich Norris

ACROSS

1 Wild guess
5 Comes to an end
11 *Beverly Hillbillies* paw
14 Jason's craft
15 Intensely devoted
16 Chemical word form
17 Summer cooler
19 Coq au __
20 Escalating trend
21 Create high-level advertising?
23 9 Down suffix
24 Signed, in a way
26 *Peter Pan* pirate
27 Assured, as victory
29 Mingo on *Daniel Boone*
33 Literary collection
36 Identifies
38 Caesar's partner
39 Personnel task
43 Well: Fr.
44 Make a point
45 Golf gadget
46 Where the Nile flows
49 See 33 Down
50 Plants grass, in a way
52 Mil. rank
53 Valise
56 Portuguese ladies
60 Safe from harm
62 PGA player
63 Small-scale vehicles
65 Pub selection
66 Actress Burke
67 Blinds part
68 Singer Tillis
69 Hair-setting appliance
70 Wood-shaping tool

DOWN

1 Nachos partner
2 Stumbles
3 Texas A&M player
4 Danish physicist
5 San Francisco treat
6 Goof up
7 Citrus drinks
8 Looks for
9 Food processor
10 Prepared, as prunes
11 Rock singer Jon Bon __
12 Way out
13 Unit of force
18 Arduous
22 Get to
25 Floor models
28 Poker card
30 Champagne choice
31 Behold: Lat.
32 Rice wine
33 With 49 Across, Israeli statesman
34 Greenhorn
35 Maple genus
37 Nose-in-air types
40 Potato concoction
41 Auto racer
42 Point of focus
47 Valleys, in Britain
48 Nimble
51 "I'm sorry to say . . ."
53 Put up
54 Desilu name
55 *Beau* __
56 Unwanted E-mail
57 __ Stanley Gardner
58 Seasonal song
59 Deal in
61 Pablo's pad
64 Tell it like it isn't

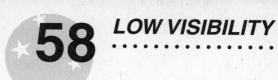

58 LOW VISIBILITY

by A.J. Santora

ACROSS

1 Pointer
6 Liquid asset
10 Tranquility, for one
13 "__ evil, . . ."
14 Sills songs
16 Snooze break
17 Moving
18 Bugle signal
20 Billy Rose tune
22 Swiss river
23 Graph lines
24 Box
27 Clothesless culture
30 *Bonfire of the Vanities* author
31 Junior, to Senior
36 Mesabi resource
37 Doesn't like
41 *Exodus* hero
42 Is over-sentimental
43 *SCTV* star
45 African menace
49 Today, in Roma
50 Record
53 Goddess of plenty
54 Withhold info from
59 Looked like rain
61 CBS anchor
62 Solo in space
63 Public square
64 Oman man
65 Custard base
66 Printing direction
67 Visionaries

DOWN

1 *End __* (Willingham book)
2 Network
3 Make slow
4 Getting __ years
5 Promise
6 Flower part
7 Come up
8 Weary sounds
9 Laughs
10 Highway clearer
11 __ *de vie* (brandy)
12 Relevant
15 Part of EST
19 Fair
21 Man, for one
25 Huge hairstyle
26 Shoal
28 Adjective suffix
29 Impudent
30 Milldams
32 Tokyo, once
33 Close relative, for short
34 Emissary: Abbr.
35 Gripe
37 Sonora sandwich
38 ". . . __ ' a bone . . ."
39 Fay Wray film
40 Language suffix
44 *"Mon __!"*
46 Exactly
47 More agile
48 Glacial formations
50 18th-century French printer
51 Harden (to)
52 March honoree
55 Writer LeShan
56 Tent holders
57 __ out a living
58 Everage title
59 1996 role for Antonio
60 Trail behind

ACROSS

1 Depend
5 Slightly open
9 Gratuity
12 Wading bird
13 The life of __ (ease)
15 Muscle condition
16 Become smitten
18 Vases
19 Murphy Brown's program
20 Head: Fr.
21 Just about
23 Actress Harper
24 Boring, colorwise
25 Groups of bees
28 Boxer's crew
32 "__ hell": Sherman
33 Seeing red
34 Director Kazan
35 On
36 Raised, as an ante
37 Building extension
38 Netlike material
39 Prerequisite
40 Quit
41 Pontificated
43 Dissertations
44 State of mind
45 Framework
46 Minor quake
49 *Misery* star
50 Actress Farrow
53 Doughnut feature
54 Upholsterer's project
57 Former UN member
58 Lauder of cosmetics
59 Printer's purchases
60 Recolor
61 Danson and Turner
62 Has to

DOWN

1 Repeated musical phrase
2 Web-auction site
3 Role for Leslie Caron
4 High-fashion monogram
5 He played Marshal Dillon
6 Leaves at the altar
7 Skin-cream ingredient
8 Gun, as a motor
9 Matador's opponent
10 Roadside rests
11 Pain in the neck
14 Pined (for)
15 Desert-region plant
17 Entries in a list
22 Youngster
23 Machine part
24 Acted riskily
25 Boggy area
26 Tend the houseplants
27 Ascended
28 Aspired
29 Inventor Howe
30 Washer cycle
31 Wise men
33 Velocity
36 Topple, as a jouster
40 Trousers material
42 Pigeon sound
43 Tiny amounts
45 Stared with dropped jaw
46 Dull sound
47 Optimistic
48 Otherwise
49 Refer to
50 List of choices
51 Annoys
52 Aide: Abbr.
55 WWII craft
56 Pep

60 FEET FIRST

by Lee Weaver

ACROSS

1 Make embarrassed
6 Confidence game
10 Ram's remark
13 Flycatching bird
14 Thomas __ Edison
15 Bell sound
16 Aromatic evergreen
18 Topnotch
19 Marked down
20 Movie-set boss
22 Noggin, in Nantes
24 In a vague manner
25 Frolicking about
29 Shoe bottom
30 Montevideo is its cap.
31 Asta's owner
33 Established belief
36 Poker raises
39 Varnish ingredient
40 Urged, with "on"
41 More than sufficient
42 Tarzan's neighbors
44 Summer, in Lyon
45 Some batteries
47 Deletions
50 Grass-cutting tool
52 Muffin ingredient
53 Single-sail vessels
55 On fire
59 Hodgepodge
60 Very stubborn
62 Become tiresome
63 Dutch cheese
64 Tongue-lash
65 Writer Rand
66 Society newcomers
67 On the peevish side

DOWN

1 Lhasa __
2 Pinto or lima
3 Barley beards
4 Serene
5 Physician
6 Carpenter's tool
7 Blockhead
8 Keep away from
9 Indian seaport
10 Rumrunner
11 Pester
12 Ripening agent
15 Accumulation of work
17 Open the door to
21 Destroy slowly
23 __ Gay
25 Castro's island
26 Calla-lily family
27 Shotgun-loading maneuver
28 Raisin, originally
32 Very tart
34 Dole (out)
35 Fruity drinks
37 Certain pleasure-seeker
38 Former defense org.
43 Actress __ Jessica Parker
46 Disgraced
48 Least risky
49 Prepare to remove oxfords
50 Astronaut Ride
51 Piano piece
53 Comedienne Imogene
54 Thick slice
56 Hullabaloos
57 Lose solidity
58 Whirlpool
61 Els' followers

UNSTEADY

by Bob Lubbers

ACROSS
1. *Les États-__*
5. Deli meat
8. Adolescent
13. WXY, on a phone
14. Writer LeShan et al.
16. Take in, perhaps
17. Adherents: Suff.
18. Mom's sister
19. Enjoys a book
20. Acrobat's lifter
23. Mum
24. *Flying Down to __*
25. Mach-speed jets: Abbr.
29. Pre-weekend shout
31. 1776 soldier
33. IRS specialist
36. Eternity
38. Ancient Greek region
39. Recess ride
43. "Yes __ Bob!"
44. DEA agent
45. Consumed
46. Boxer Holyfield
49. Allen's *Tonight* successor
51. Solidifies
52. Scale notes
54. *The __ of Wrath*
58. Chuck Berry's genre
60. Pitcher Satchel
64. Ireland, to the Irish
65. Gen. Robert __
66. From Formosa, e.g.
67. E-mailed
68. Clearheaded
69. Chef Julia
70. "Mayday!"
71. Ensnare

DOWN
1. Inventory count
2. Second-generation Japanese
3. Computer-chip maker
4. Sonnet part
5. More exuberant
6. Rub follower
7. Big house
8. Play area
9. Arena cheer
10. Actress Hagen
11. "Excellent adventure" dude
12. Stat. for Sosa
15. Step series
21. Betrothed
22. Caviar
25. Tug tow
26. Braga of films
27. Pollute
28. The boards
30. Egg __ yung
32. Toss out
33. Church sections
34. Critic Barnes
35. Jeweler's weight
37. Holy sister
40. Achings
41. 40 winks
42. Police searches
47. WWII battle zone
48. Prepares potatoes
50. Most infrequent
53. "Blue __" (Berlin tune)
55. Of the Arctic
56. Actress Verdugo
57. 40 winks
58. Tear apart
59. Cartoonist Peter
60. Lobbying org.
61. Bat wood
62. Jr.'s son, perhaps
63. "My __ Sal"

62 LEADING MEN

by Rich Norris

ACROSS

1 Stick around
5 *ER* network
8 Start to grow
14 Stopped at sea, with "to"
15 Mars or Venus
16 Satisfy
17 Dentist's request
18 Compete
19 Wickerwork material
20 Zephyr
23 Luau instrument
24 Simple shacks
28 Scot's refusal
29 __ wave
31 Range
32 Pick up the plates
33 Diner's protection
35 Eurasian wild goat
36 Bankruptcy option
40 Idle of comedy
41 Hearst's kidnappers: Abbr.
42 Steam up
43 Offends the nose
45 Honor __ thieves
47 Toothpaste-endorsing org.
50 Washington player
52 Took as one's own
54 Embroidery technique
56 Mackerel relative
59 Cold-day feature
60 Part of TLC
61 Bjorn Borg's homeland
62 Yoko __
63 Maple genus
64 Brooks of *Mother*
65 Mil. rank
66 __-Ball (arcade game)

DOWN

1 Japanese leader of yore
2 Midwest capital
3 Map line
4 1983 Streisand film
5 Buck and Crane
6 Paid off
7 "Smokey" spotter
8 Shopper's indulgence
9 Public squares
10 Having a good memory
11 Morsel for Mister Ed
12 "Born in the __"
13 Countdown component
21 Subside to a drizzle
22 Jock Ewing's spouse
25 Shakespearean soliloquy starter
26 Pizza place?
27 Driver's license datum
30 Garfield's middle name
32 Relapse into bad habits
34 Rearview-mirror concern
36 Algonquian speaker
37 Hurried off
38 African antelope
39 Cereal fungus
40 Answer incorrectly
44 Olympics competitor
46 Working in a crew, maybe
47 Go after
48 Judicial order
49 Be attached (to)
51 "__ Need You" (Kenny Rogers song)
53 Type sizes
55 Grandson of Adam
56 Character-building org.
57 Pea-green boat passenger
58 S. Dak. neighbor

63 ALCHEMY

by Eugene W. Sard

ACROSS

1 Side dish
5 Arrests
9 Grapefruit holder
14 Like a bagatelle?
15 French 101 verb
16 Edmonton skater
17 Bad
18 Bad
19 Hearings outlet
20 START OF A WORD CHAIN
23 ___ *Miz*
24 Be a know-it-all
25 Sailing vessel
29 French cheese
30 Israel follower
32 Greek letter
33 Egyptian god
36 PART 2 OF CHAIN
38 Hit location, often
39 College aides: Abbr.
40 Singer Page
41 PART 3 OF CHAIN
43 Not more than
44 Nav. rank
45 '70s radical grp.
46 Err
47 Feel one's ___
49 George's partner
51 Literary monogram
54 END OF CHAIN
57 Henri's headgear
60 Internet addresses: Abbr.
61 Not calm
62 New Zealand native
63 Give up
64 Sprinter's goal
65 Small songbirds
66 Durbeyfield girl
67 Cassandra was one

DOWN

1 Odor
2 River embankment
3 1987 peace Nobelist
4 Metal link
5 Source of harm
6 Standing order?
7 Slow down
8 Password askers
9 Caesar's foil
10 Hazardous
11 High mountain
12 Beverage
13 Direction ending
21 Cowboys' gear
22 Kett of the comics
26 Vinegary word form
27 Sharpens
28 Cap
29 Raised
31 All used up
33 Path proceder
34 Tuscany town
35 That is
36 Smidgen
37 Press down
39 Eye neighbor
42 Gymnast Korbut
43 Wanted-poster info
46 Reprimands
48 Violinist Isaac
50 Be of one mind
51 Caesar's robes
52 It may be slippery
53 Garden tool
55 Revolutionary pamphleteer
56 Rods
57 Audi competitor
58 Musical discrimination
59 Shad eggs

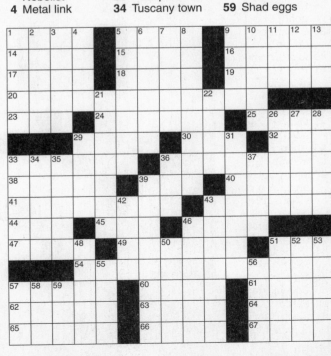

64 GROUP THINK

by Norma Steinberg

ACROSS

1 Unruly pile
5 Lunch or dinner
9 Eleventh-graders: Abbr.
12 Singer Guthrie
13 Playwright Edward
15 Boyfriend
16 Trash tossers
18 Thor's father
19 Zodiacal lion
20 Origin
21 Difficult
23 Forehead
24 Start of Caesar's boast
25 Actress Stone
28 Tire-tread loss
32 Indonesian island
33 Peddle
34 Metric weight
35 Dagwood's young neighbor
36 Lark
37 Actress Russo
38 "When I was __ . . ."
39 Sword handle
40 Pronouncements
41 Nobel's invention
43 Cold season
44 Mercedes-__
45 Crooner Crosby
46 Straight man
49 Ocean movement
50 __ Tse-tung
53 Ballerina's skirt
54 Bankroll holder, perhaps
57 Fixed quantity
58 Wee
59 "Do __ others . . ."
60 __-relief
61 Hunter's quarry
62 Fortune teller

DOWN

1 Corridor
2 Pennsylvania city
3 Voice range
4 Food cooker
5 Dark red
6 Macaroni shape
7 Lie adjacent to
8 Journey part
9 *Star Wars* knight
10 Precipitation
11 Performed an aria
14 Golden Girl Getty
15 Site for a fight
17 Typo, e.g.
22 In addition
23 Fret over
24 Gentleman's gentleman
25 Place
26 Like Rome or San Francisco
27 Jordan's capital
28 Uncle Miltie
29 Upright
30 Pierre's health
31 Daub
33 '72 Olympics swimming star
36 Black eyes
40 Eatery
42 Actress Ryan
43 To a great extent
45 The Good Book
46 Check end
47 Salad fish
48 Singer Redding
49 Ski lift
50 Horse hair
51 Card-game stake
52 Bloodhound's clue
55 Diamond arbiter
56 Urban vehicle

65 TITLE SEARCH

by Randolph Ross

ACROSS

1 Per-diem staff
6 Board game
11 3-D med. exam
14 The Little Mermaid
15 Nobel category
16 Excellent, slangily
17 *The Graduate* character
19 Puppeteer Baird
20 Sharp
21 Distinct
23 Lasting impression
25 Abhors
26 Lowered in dignity
30 Round roof
31 "Choice" words
32 Sublease
34 Former Treasury secretary
37 Pocketbook item
39 Small change
41 Columbus Day event
42 Tailless marsupial
44 Spiral shell
46 Golf position
47 Enclose
49 Enjoyed the boardwalk
51 Fly chaser
54 Roll-call response
55 Informal restaurant
57 Not straight
61 __ Baba
62 Pageant winner
64 Reading room

65 That is: Lat.
66 Mortise partner
67 CBS logo
68 Simmons rival
69 Closes, as an envelope

DOWN

1 Author Janowitz
2 Makes a mistake
3 Atomizer output
4 Examine
5 Miniature racer
6 Raises may depend on it: Abbr.
7 Coop group
8 __ off (slackened)
9 Looked over, with "out"
10 Gore or Bradley, once
11 Tom Selleck film of 1992
12 Country singer Bonnie
13 Runs in neutral
18 Struck in the head
22 Fictional uncle
24 Clue to the past
26 Landing pier
27 Suffix for switch
28 Publication founded in 1972
29 Audition CDs
33 Agent's take
35 Contemporary of Jimmy and Bjorn
36 Scholarship criterion
38 Intense campaign
40 Horror-film sound
43 Goddess of the hunt
45 Stinging insects
48 Mock
50 Stowe ogre
51 Sleuth Sam
52 Aviator Post
53 Chorus platform
56 Helper: Abbr.
58 Director Wertmuller
59 Earth sci.
60 Rather and others
63 One __ time (singly)

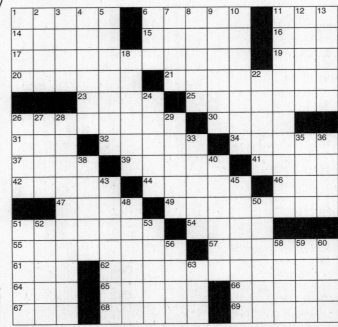

66 CANE KIN

by Bob Lubbers

ACROSS

1 Single girl
5 Insect sensors
10 Keystone figure
13 Academy student
14 "Farewell, Françoise!"
15 Roth plan: Abbr.
16 Expiate
17 Lake landers
19 Crook of a sort
21 SSW opposite
22 Cribbage piece
23 ___ in the Crowd
27 Watch winder
29 Also-ran
33 Tennis champ Lendl
34 Rink surface
36 State of need
38 Coffee flavorer
41 Certified to drive
42 Gel
43 German coal region
44 Perfume resin
46 Wobbles in orbit
50 Having a key
52 Cuckoo
54 "Vive le ___ !"
55 Barn topper
60 Limit
63 "... and ___ a good night!"
64 Coming
65 Poet Doolittle
66 Indian princess
67 Jeanne d'Arc, e.g.: Abbr.
68 ___ Park, CO
69 Env. notation

DOWN

1 Dormant
2 Actress Renee
3 Transmit
4 Sharply inclined
5 "Do not ___" (Monopoly phrase)
6 Summer drinks
7 South Pacific maiden
8 Salt-n-___ (rap pair)
9 Burn treatment
10 Family
11 Lode load
12 ___ de deux
13 Songwriter Sammy et al.
18 Natural liking
20 Liberation
24 With: Fr.
25 Rum barrel
26 Nav. rank
28 Apatite and melanite, e.g.
30 English china
31 One billion years
32 The Barber of Seville composer
35 Turner TV network
37 Map abbr.
38 Genoa greeting
39 Optimistic words
40 Singer Tormé
41 WWII vessel
45 Heavenly foods
47 Out-and-out
48 Made of fleece
49 Slink along
51 Supple
53 Prefix for coastal
56 Spanish cubist
57 "Stop!"
58 Bay of Fundy phenomenon
59 Barnyard beast
60 Music purchases
61 Ump's call
62 Society-page word

IN THE BAG

by Rich Norris

ACROSS

1 Chew (on)
5 Hair holder
9 Larger than large
14 Fa followers
15 Meet event
16 Workers' group
17 Like Nash's lama
18 About the same
19 Works in the yard
20 Annoying passenger
23 Symbol of might
24 Metric opening
25 Leg bones
28 *American Gothic* painter
34 "Do __ Diddy Diddy" (1964 song)
35 Bother persistently
37 Cube man Rubik
38 Opposite of *sans*
40 Al __ (pasta order)
41 Food plan
42 Biblical builder
43 Comeback
45 Gobble down
46 Recyclable metal
48 Lauren of *Dumb & Dumber*
50 Striped-shirt wearer
51 Gold unit
52 Deli order
60 Cake-pan type
61 Lipinski leap
62 Festive affair
63 Eero's father
64 Composer Bartók
65 Telltale sign
66 Like a rain forest
67 Subordinate title: Abbr.
68 Eleven o'clock fare

DOWN

1 Shapeless hunk
2 *Peter Pan* dog
3 Actor Baldwin
4 Small part
5 Alabama Indian
6 Volcanic output
7 *Ricochet* actor/rapper
8 Be undecided
9 Legal scholar
10 Like promises never made
11 Recording tool
12 Transvaal native
13 Switch positions
21 Window part
22 Dishwasher, at times
25 Graceful birds
26 Great destruction
27 "Do __ a Waltz?"
28 Actress Garson
29 Totaled
30 __ Martin (007 auto)
31 Cantilevered window
32 Actor Ryan
33 Eccentric
36 In need of wind, perhaps
39 Game using body language
44 Melt
47 Mortar partner
49 Crater Lake locale
51 It's a bit higher than A
52 Be in charge
53 Getting __ years
54 __ Wawa (Radner character)
55 Former pairs
56 Snakelike fish
57 Florida's Miami-__ county
58 Radiance
59 Listening devices
60 Rose home

68 MUSKETEERS' MOTTO

by R.J. Hartman

ACROSS

1 King or Shepard
5 It can be a gift
8 Withdraw
14 Actor Rob
15 Heredity inits.
16 Floor worker
17 Musketeer's favorite sport?
19 American Leaguer
20 Publicity, slangily
21 Radioer's word
22 Michaelmas daisies
23 "__ of the Tiger"
24 Pasture
25 Schubert's *Mass __-Flat*
26 Musketeer's favorite magazine?
32 Gives up
35 Sault __ Marie
36 Mishmash
37 Salty sea of Asia
38 Bravery
40 Camp shelter
41 Caron film
42 Author Levin
43 Sends off, in a way
44 Musketeer's favorite dessert?
48 Massachusetts cape
49 __ carte
50 Cunning
53 Measure of profit
57 Open a crack
58 Overly
59 Army command
60 Musketeer's favorite greeting cards?

62 Bakery items
63 Boola-boola boy
64 *The African Queen* screenwriter
65 Get in the way of
66 Belonging to *moi*
67 Places of refuge

DOWN

1 1966 Michael Caine role
2 Foolish
3 Shut off the alarm
4 New Jersey cager
5 Crawl
6 Toughen up
7 '30s heavyweight champ
8 Camus title character
9 Wipes out
10 Insincere talk
11 *The __ of Night*
12 Bambi and kin
13 Blows it
18 Wyoming neckties
25 A fan of
26 Trace of the past
27 Mohammed's faith
28 Absolute
29 *Family Ties* role
30 Confused actor's request
31 Subdivision subdivisions
32 City in Colombia
33 Guitarist Clapton

34 Roy's wife
38 __ table (dessert buffet)
39 Ireland's __ Islands
43 Road signal
45 Built
46 Sweet-talk
47 Singer Morissette
50 Put on
51 1961 Best Actress winner
52 Crossbars
53 African country
54 Onetime AEC symbol
55 Harvest
56 Collapsed
57 "Pardon me!"
61 Satire magazine

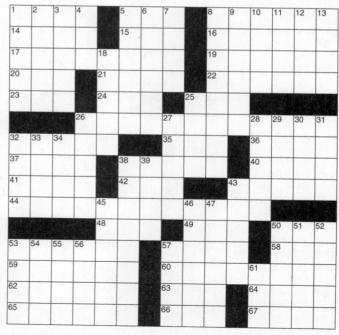

69 GO WITH THE FLOW

by Fred Piscop

ACROSS

1 Timber wolves
6 Hammer-wielding god
10 Completed
14 __ fours (crawling)
15 Bar mitzvah dance
16 "Not on your __!"
17 Skylit courts
18 Prayer ender
19 Burrowing mammal
20 Free-for-all
22 "Ah me!"
23 Spigot
24 Present from birth
26 Apply quickly, as brakes
30 Ore seeker
32 Chinese cuisine
33 Tag-sale shopper, often
37 Word form for "all"
38 Berra and Bear
39 Low-lying area
40 Giving one's name to something
42 __ stone (unchangeable)
43 Wal-Mart competitor
44 Encroachment
45 Triangular Greek letters
48 __ Lanka
49 Poet Khayyám
50 In a tough spot
57 Calamitous
58 Additional
59 Islamic text
60 Gymnast Korbut
61 On the briny
62 Beethoven dedicatee
63 Appear to be
64 Kitchen pro
65 Taylor of *The Nanny*

DOWN

1 Dryer batch
2 Not tricked by
3 Square-dance site
4 Ken or Lena
5 Astronaut Deke
6 Choreographer Twyla
7 __ sapiens
8 Creme-filled cookie
9 Results of a coaches' poll
10 *Show Boat* song
11 Cello's cousin
12 D's upper neighbor
13 Pee Wee of baseball
21 Make illegal
25 Arts-supporting grp.
26 Brogan or loafer
27 Gravy imperfection
28 Part of AD
29 Widely accepted
30 Yuletide trio member
31 Pupil surrounder
33 Rude dude
34 Defense grp. since 1949
35 Lamb's nom de plume
36 Tear apart
38 Peruvian-born singer
41 Thumbs-up vote
42 Half-suppressed laugh
44 Ill temper
45 Long-gone birds
46 Author Zola
47 Humongous
48 Wheat bundle
51 Ritzy
52 Sloth's home
53 Part to play
54 The Emerald Isle
55 Comfort
56 __-slapper (riot)

BREAD BOXES

by Rich Norris

ACROSS

1 Overconfident
5 Mets' home
9 Terrify
14 Texas city
15 Ping-__
16 Citified
17 Golfer's choice
18 Garage occupant
19 Nouveau __
20 Frequent Astaire partner
23 Detection device
24 Champion
28 This minute
30 Actor Erwin
31 Water: Fr.
32 Annoying type
36 Masking sound
39 Community spirit
41 Chemical suffix
42 Cuts into small pieces
43 Job for a diner cook
46 For fear that
47 To a __ (exactly)
48 Belly muscles
49 Corker
51 Seasoned veteran
53 Start a winning streak
58 '60s Neil Simon musical
62 Coffee variety
65 Open to discussion
66 Farm crawlers
67 Primitive weapon
68 Office note
69 Logical beginning?
70 Frets (over)
71 Yemen's gulf
72 Rotate

DOWN

1 Gulps of a drink
2 Donny's sister
3 The Huskies of the NCAA
4 Chinese percussion instruments
5 Small songbird
6 Datebook division
7 "Within" word form
8 Very excited
9 Enclose entirely
10 Invigorating, as air
11 2 on a telephone
12 Stadium sound
13 WSW opposite
21 Very long time
22 Diminutive ending
25 Melt the frost from
26 Fertile areas
27 Register signer
29 Revolving hums
30 Expensive
32 Basil-based sauce
33 Singer Merman
34 Did a blacksmith's job
35 High peak
37 Neither Dem. nor Rep.
38 Vinegar partner
40 1977 sci-fi classic
44 One of the reeds
45 To the point, in slang
50 Tiny legume
52 "Nonsense!"
54 Characteristic
55 Like Gandhi
56 Aquatic frolicker
57 Boxer Mike
59 Madame Bovary
60 __ the line (obeyed)
61 Tag along
62 Ed.'s concerns
63 Withdraw, with "out"
64 Average grade

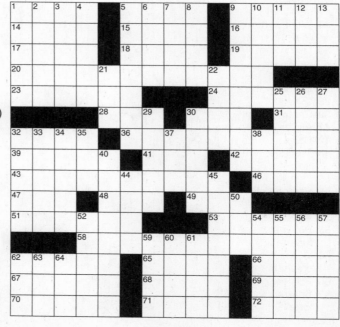

71 CLOTHES CALLS

by Bob Lubbers

ACROSS

1 Coll. course
5 __ Hari
9 WWI battle site
14 Corporate image
15 Noodles, on a Chinese menu
16 Goes off-stage
17 "__ right with the world!"
18 Drill sergeant's call
20 Worked diligently at
22 New York port
23 Third-generation Japanese-American
25 Combatants
29 Work unit
30 *Casablanca* star
33 Work without __ (dare)
34 Like some cereals
35 Subway entrance
36 "Shut up!"
39 Spout rhetoric
41 Picker-upper
42 Raise
43 Precede, with "to"
45 Fast jet: Abbr.
48 Scraped off
50 Boil over
52 Aborigine
55 Brownstone feature
56 '60s catchphrase
60 Folklore giant
61 Sharon of Israel

62 Fiery saint
63 Evening, on marquees
64 Jazz pianist Wilson
65 Faculty head
66 Cong. meeting

DOWN

1 Slip by
2 Cleric's wear
3 Eyeing
4 Something to count
5 CCL x X
6 Space starter
7 Ascots
8 Talk back
9 Join lanes
10 Self-evident
11 Semi

12 High degree
13 Superlative suffix
19 E-mailed
21 Candidates' one-on-one
24 Smidgen
26 Monogram unit: Abbr.
27 Conger, e.g.
28 Sault __ Marie
31 Toothpaste type
32 Pointer or O'Day
34 Was senior to
35 Takes potshots
36 Carson's predecessor
37 Cabinet dept.
38 Burden

39 Mouths, in Latin
40 Civil War soldier
43 Latvian
44 Prepared for publication
45 Cheap cigar
46 Two-reelers
47 Conical abodes
49 Like some newspapers
51 Collar types
53 Garden tunneler
54 Poet Lazarus
56 Calendar col.
57 Aluminum source
58 El __ (Spanish hero)
59 Eternity

WHEN IN ROME . . .

by Norma Steinberg

ACROSS

1 Porcelain flaw
5 Catches sight of
10 Reminds too often
14 ". . . __ wonder what you are"
15 Waste maker?
16 Swear
17 Bates or Arkin
18 Author Jong
19 Paul Sorvino's daughter
20 Cryptologist's code
21 Utter bliss
23 Storms
25 Feedbag kernel
26 Horse mackerel
27 Army activity
32 Mrs. Phil Donahue
34 Swamp
35 Marker
36 Became more mature
37 Menu
38 Flexibility
39 Exist
40 Helps with the dishes
41 Rhymes
42 Support with springs
44 Part of the leg
45 Get hitched
46 Artist's paint holder
49 CBS News show
54 Giant's word
55 April forecast
56 VIP of '50s TV
57 Nevada city
58 "__, a bone . . ."
59 Renter's paper
60 Ball-game quaff
61 New Haven campus
62 Actress Burstyn
63 Very small

DOWN

1 Singer Khan
2 Golfer's goals
3 Urban thoroughfare
4 Brooch
5 Australian girl
6 Helen's abductor
7 "__ soup yet?"
8 Draw with acid
9 Aquarium creature
10 Broadway Joe
11 Tel __
12 Author Vidal
13 Ugly Duckling, eventually
21 *In __ veritas*
22 Per capita
24 "__ Lang Syne"
27 Stable mothers
28 Part of A&E
29 What a klutz may have
30 Linguist Chomsky
31 Men
32 Word of respect
33 Taj Mahal site
34 "__ oui!"
37 Trustworthy
38 Gdansk resident
40 A trio for Hans
41 Coterie components
43 Small pain
44 Stagger
46 Vital sign
47 Melodies
48 Atlanta university
49 Medical picture
50 Pasternak heroine
51 Lab container
52 Scoundrel
53 Spoken
57 Hitter's stat.

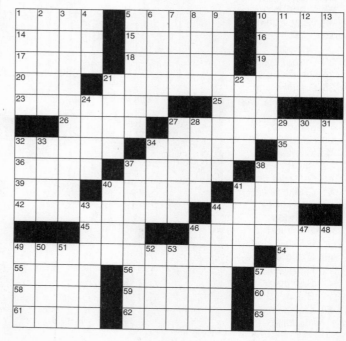

73 THE OLD SWITCHEROO

by Manny Nosowsky

ACROSS

1 Overfills
6 Wild revelry
10 Aerosol output
14 Very lean
15 Queen of heaven
16 "Well, Did You __?" (Porter tune)
17 *Mother Night* star
18 Roundish
19 Actor Waggoner
20 Bother a time-waster?
23 Smirnoff rival, familiarly
24 One-time Korean leader
25 That, in Tijuana
26 Okays
28 Prepare for battle again
30 __ *Man Answers*
33 Burger bread
34 Pie slices
35 Result if you don't quite leap over the mudhole?
38 Fence or baby follower
39 Short
40 Guitarist Paul
41 Chekhov or Bruckner
42 Joyrides
44 Transport for E.T.
45 Explorer Hernando de __
47 Composer Blake
51 Ovens on fuel haulers?
54 Art Deco designer
55 Tough spot
56 Wholeness
58 *Nada*, in Nancy
59 Theme
60 Watch again
61 [leave as is]
62 Sentence length
63 Knockout drops

DOWN

1 Wolf Blitzer's employer
2 Tops
3 Black key
4 Seder fare
5 Like some glances
6 "Oops!"
7 Whom to blame for 20, 35 and 51 Across
8 Flip-chart art
9 One from the 11 Down
10 Card combination
11 College group
12 Order takers
13 St. Louis team
21 Four-in-hand clasp
22 Yankee Jeter
27 Early riser?
29 Henry James biographer
30 Malfeasant's lament
31 Be perfect
32 In the matter of
34 __ *World*
36 Good thinking
37 X as in Xenophon
38 44 Across et al.?
42 In __ (calmly)
43 Thread for doctors
46 Way around
48 "John Brown's Body" poet
49 Linen or coffee preceder
50 Ronald Lauder's mom
52 Spring time
53 First mate
57 "__ out!" (ump's call)

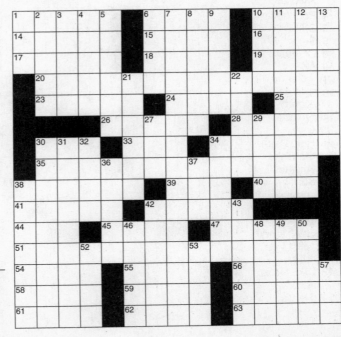

74 READING MATERIAL

by Rich Norris

ACROSS

1 Belly pain
5 Steffi of tennis
9 Latin ballroom dance
14 Impressionist David
15 Singer McEntire
16 Flu type
17 Seer's reading material
19 Is resentful about
20 Grain cutters
21 Excited sensation
22 Here, in Le Havre
23 Train component
24 Pool stick
25 Started a fire
26 Sell
28 Olympics prize
30 Average grades
31 __ nous
33 Susan Lucci role
35 Contract reading material
40 Civil War side
41 Black-and-white snacks
43 Tears
46 Be in charge
49 Big-eyed birds
50 Literary collection
51 Hawaiian instrument
52 Go bad
54 State with keys: Abbr.
55 Wolf in __ clothing
57 Feature of some cars
59 Tropical trees
60 Seer's reading material
62 *Dallas* matriarch
63 *Damn Yankees* role
64 Draft status
65 Passed out cards
66 Charged amount
67 Broadway diva Linda

DOWN

1 Back, on a ship
2 Moon phase
3 Garden plant
4 Hard to hold
5 Alexander __ Bell
6 Admire
7 Lincoln and Fortas
8 Musical notes
9 Wife of Ike
10 X __ "xylophone"
11 Join the crowd
12 Golfer's predicament
13 Beginnings
18 List ender: Abbr.
21 Bell-shaped flower
22 __ *Got a Secret*
24 Poet Sandburg
27 Attire
29 New __ India
30 Egypt's capital
32 That, in Toledo
34 __-Magnon
36 Glooms
37 Suit to __
38 Recently discovered
39 Like an 800 number
42 Fed. entitlement org.
43 Spoke hoarsely
44 Get some air
45 Spanish dish
47 Thin cereals
48 Like skim milk
51 Overturn
53 Capote, to friends
56 Actor Jannings
57 "Go away!"
58 Oklahoma native
60 RN's specialty
61 Corn portion

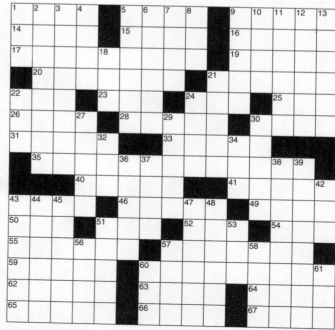

by Bob Lubbers

ACROSS

1 DiMaggio and DeLuise
5 Classic autos
9 Heineken competitor
14 Part of BTU
15 Forearm bone
16 Greek market
17 "Push my buttons!"
19 Columnist Barrett et al.
20 Vaulted
21 Column style
23 Equipment
26 Step supports
29 Practice one's lines
33 "Amen!"
34 180-degree maneuver
35 Burritos' kin
37 Explosive letters
38 __ Free
39 Four-door car
40 Morning fog
41 Auctioneer's quest
42 More pristine
43 Erie or Suez
44 French president's palace
46 Make over
48 Esteem
49 Greek portico
50 Topple
52 Changed direction
57 Oprah's production company
59 "Flip my lid!"
62 Poet Nash
63 Moises of baseball
64 Gymnast Korbut
65 Actors Stephen and William
66 Coarse file
67 Leery

DOWN

1 Twofold
2 Back then
3 Shiny mineral
4 "Halt!"
5 Ship's steerer
6 Whitney or Wallach
7 Yoko __
8 Beach surface
9 Inner-city sections
10 Self-centered person
11 "Squeeze me!"
12 Malay isthmus
13 Airline to Stockholm
18 Daughter of Lear
22 Director Welles
24 Fall flower
25 Some school books
27 Attacks
28 Pay up
29 Eraser material
30 Star: Fr.
31 "I'm cranky!"
32 Fish-eating bird
36 Insertion mark
39 "Blue __ Shoes"
40 West of Hollywood
42 Missing __ bureau
43 Diet guru Jenny
45 Drained
47 Snuggle
51 Ski lift
53 Get taller
54 Elaborate party
55 RR driver
56 June 6, 1944
57 Prefix for goblin
58 "Long __ and Far Away"
60 Menu phrase
61 Derek and Jackson

BARNYARD LANGUAGE

by Norma Steinberg

ACROSS
1 Thick slice
5 Nautical steering wheel
9 Whirlpool competitor
14 Bye-bye, in Bristol
15 Toast topping
16 Shade of purple
17 Author unknown: Abbr.
18 Be in front
19 Frankie or Cleo
20 Nestling's comment?
23 Arm of the sea
24 Unvoiced
25 Arnold's wife
27 Film holders
30 Up until now
33 __ room
36 Photo processing products
38 Heed
39 Parcel out
41 Done __ turn
42 Harsh light
43 Down in the dumps
44 Extreme fright
46 Pitch in
47 Leave the group
49 Musical sounds
51 Makes booties
53 Churchill successor
57 Noah's boat

59 Pessimistic horses?
62 Shoe material
64 Novelist Gould
65 Camera part
66 The Yokum lad
67 *The King* __
68 A Great Lake
69 "For __ sake!"
70 Observes
71 Recolors

DOWN
1 RBI, ERA, etc.
2 Hawaiian patio
3 Coral island
4 Treasurer
5 Carrying case
6 Util. bill
7 Wife of Jacob

8 Internet connection need
9 Honor for a footballer
10 Actress Sara
11 Arabian ram?
12 The Darlings' dog
13 __-deucey
21 Bumbling
22 Grub
26 Role model
28 Lo-cal
29 Sound of derision
31 Actress Hatcher
32 Checked out
33 Tatters
34 Model Macpherson

35 Super Chicken's alter ego?
37 Poi ingredient
40 Augury
42 Garbo of film
44 Head: Fr.
45 Greek tycoon
48 Roadside restaurants
50 Arranged, as hair
52 __ *Marner*
54 Suspicious
55 Bert's pal
56 Curved letters
57 Now!
58 Cartoonist Goldberg
60 Auctioneer's call
61 Put out of sight
63 Billy __ Williams

T CROSSINGS

by Fred Piscop

ACROSS

1 Not busy, at work
5 Mgr.'s helper
9 Slender-waisted insect
13 Nash's "one-L __"
14 Tennis star Gerulaitis
16 Buffalo's lake
17 *Lucky Jim* novelist
18 Have __ up one's sleeve
19 Land measure
20 Socializing
23 Lauder of cosmetics
24 Volcanic fallout
25 Ruination
27 Obey the coxswain
29 Socialite Mesta
33 "Toodles!"
35 Bernanke's group, for short
37 Iranian currency
38 Jolson number
41 From the top
42 Homer Simpson exclamation
43 Range of influence
44 Returned to session
46 Boars and bulls
48 Nights, poetically
49 Tot's break
51 Practices with a pug
53 Occurring after about 1685, in England
60 Branding tool
61 Pre-fight psych job
62 Cold capital
63 El __, TX
64 Like Cheerios
65 Change the decor of
66 Piggy-bank opening
67 Second to none
68 Like a lamb

DOWN

1 Smeltery waste
2 Like some excuses
3 Leave out
4 Thrifty maxim
5 __-garde
6 Band's front man
7 Governor's speech
8 Snack in a shell
9 Tough it out
10 Eyebrow shape
11 Farm father
12 Juror, in theory
15 Nintendo competitor
21 __ *a Letter to My Love* (Signoret film)
22 Paranormal power: Abbr.
25 Memorable trailblazer
26 Emollient-yielding plants
28 Sodden
30 Up and about
31 Places to hibernate
32 Gen. Robert __
33 Walk of Fame embedment
34 "What hath __ wrought"
36 Windows precursor
39 "Isn't that nice!"
40 Wagnerian work
45 Roofer's gunk
47 Allergens for some
50 Mexicali moolah
52 Do not exist
53 Spots on a deuce
54 Nonwritten test
55 Middling
56 Shot in the dark
57 "Understood!"
58 Shoppe sign word
59 Cozy corner

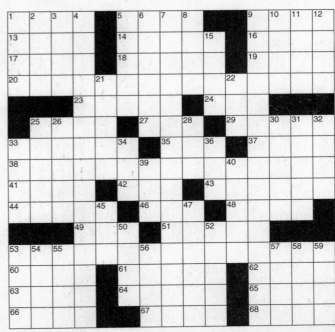

78 STRAIGHT ADVICE

by Lee Weaver

ACROSS

1 Got taller
5 5.5 yards
8 Single-cell organism
13 Préval of Haiti
14 Debtor's letters
15 Charm
17 Start of a quip
19 Hot-dog topper
20 Social occasion
21 Part 2 of quip
23 Small combos
25 Grassy field
26 Zilch
27 City served by Gardermoen Airport
28 Environmental sci.
31 Sensible
32 In a tizzy
34 Makes very happy
36 Part 3 of quip
39 Pays for one's pals
40 Of some use
41 Fix in the mind
42 Bear in the sky
43 Centers of power
47 NYC opera house
48 Trade-unions org.
50 *Don Juan* writer
51 Part 4 of quip
56 Arctic assistant
57 Fierce speech
58 End of quip
60 Acted as usher
61 Sundown, to Shelley
62 Coconut husk fiber
63 Speaks unclearly
64 XL squared
65 Wallet fillers

DOWN

1 Cavelike shrine
2 Alludes (to)
3 Bring into play
4 Like Willie Winkie
5 Sacred ceremony
6 Sounds of awe
7 Song for two
8 __-la-Vallée (EuroDisney site)
9 Greek letter
10 __ and void
11 Make hostile
12 Sets apart for a purpose
16 Gunwale fulcrums
18 Weights-and-measures agcy.
22 100%
24 Tuba sound
28 Slugger Slaughter
29 Spy org.
30 Take place
31 Without danger
33 Paintings, e.g.
34 Director Kazan
35 __ *Abner*
36 Blood vessels
37 Chest-related
38 Altitudes: Abbr.
39 Leads astray, perhaps
42 Einstein's birthplace
44 Eugene's home
45 Herding dog
46 Deduces
48 Birch family member
49 Nourishes
50 Ram's remark
52 __ Khan (Golden Horde leader)
53 Flower stalk
54 Made angry
55 Coordination
59 Sgt. or cpl.

ACROSS

1 Letter additions: Abbr.
4 Actress Maples
9 Paula of pop
14 Part of CPA
15 Sea
16 Bullwinkle, for one
17 Full-house letters
18 Expanse of land
19 Church instrument
20 Go ballistic
23 French girlfriend
24 Jekyll's counterpart
25 Part of a flock
28 Militaristic Greek city-state
31 Seized control of
34 Meal
37 Impolite looks
38 Be very anxious
41 Catch some Z's
42 Córdoba coin
43 Two bits
45 Campaign event
49 No longer working: Abbr.
50 Peachy-keen
53 Deep black
54 Speaks at length
59 *Fargo* creators Ethan and Joel
61 Sorbonne student
62 Attorney's org.
63 Swagger
64 Basketballers Archibald and Thurmond
65 Scott Joplin piece
66 Gaping pit
67 Ivan and Nicholas
68 HST's successor

DOWN

1 Turkish titles
2 Cut corners
3 Nova __, Canada
4 Butterfly relative
5 Land measure
6 Within __ (close by)
7 Cagney's partner
8 Counteragents
9 Mine, to Mimi
10 "__ to Run" (Springsteen song)
11 Silly poetry
12 UN Security Council member
13 Spy writer Deighton
21 Airedale, for one
22 *My Name Is Asher* __
26 Big fights
27 Coast Guard officer: Abbr.
29 Entice
30 NYPD call
32 Bring joy to
33 Change a tag
35 Right now
36 Pronoun for a boat
38 Hint
39 Reminiscent of cowhide
40 Tie the knot
41 Not rnd.
44 Terminal
46 On the train
47 "What a shame!"
48 Make angry
51 Traveler's reference
52 Iota preceder
55 Responsibility
56 WWII transports
57 Continually
58 Admit, with "up"
59 Civil War initials
60 Horseplayer's haunt, for short

80 ROUGH STUFF

by Fred Piscop

ACROSS

1 Theater awards
6 Papal proclamation
11 Cleveland hoopster, for short
14 Kidney-related
15 Poet Federico García __
16 Blow away, so to speak
17 Dieter's nosh
19 Put a strain on
20 Long Island university
21 Apparition, to a Brit
23 Do KP work
25 Lubricated
26 Come to pass
30 Show clearly
33 Like Wrigley Field's walls
34 Blazing
35 After-school org.
38 Nintendo competitor
39 "__ luck!"
40 Throat trouble
41 __ Lanka
42 Skater Henie
43 River to the Rhone
44 Sartre novel
46 Mull over
47 Liszt or Kafka
49 Whirring sound
51 They return to bad habits
54 Prom-night presentation
59 Blood-typing letters
60 Court woe

62 Shoot the breeze
63 Poke fun at
64 "Mule Train" singer
65 Fr. holy woman
66 Mystery writers' award
67 *Inside the Third Reich* author

DOWN

1 Killer whale
2 Bit of a necklace
3 Concerning, to a lawyer
4 Viscount's superior
5 Fed, as hogs
6 Corporate cow
7 i topper

8 Spring bloom
9 Letters on *Sputnik*
10 Free sample come-on
11 Cowpuncher's device
12 In the know
13 Perturbed
18 "In that case . . ."
22 Pres., to the military
24 Boxer's blow
26 Serenade the villain
27 State surely
28 Risky purchase
29 Potpie spheroid
31 Traveler's need
32 Lyricist Gershwin
34 Topnotch
36 Vocal quality

37 Maturing agent
39 __ Alamos, NM
40 Admirer
42 Crêpe __
43 Brownish horses
45 Ques. response
46 Old hands
47 Criticizes severely
48 Morocco's capital
50 More slippery
52 Sax player's buy
53 Hosiery woe
55 Duel precursor, perhaps
56 Irish Rose lover
57 Auctioneer's cry
58 Basin accessory
61 Code-breaking org.

ACROSS

1 Nautical "stop"
6 Ribbon ornament
13 Tattletale
14 Spaniard, for one
15 Self-satisfying act
17 Roofed porch
18 Express disbelief
20 Cooked in oil
21 Anti-Prohibitionists
22 Young seal
25 Sensible
26 Give a party for
27 Rental contract
29 Family supporter
31 Lassie, for one
35 Created first
36 Illusion of a sort
40 Fireplace residue
41 Mayberry kid
42 Boston orchestra
46 Sun. talk
47 Tizzy
48 Eagle's nest
49 "Nothing to it!"
52 Theft
55 __ spoon (kitchen utensil)
56 Bird's feathers
57 Utility-room appliances
58 Made unyielding
59 Mails (out)

DOWN

1 Exotic cat
2 Perlman's instrument
3 '40s British prime minister
4 Cape Cod entree
5 Sparse
6 Held firmly
7 Minds Mama
8 Dried out
9 Historic periods
10 Sardine holder
11 Lincoln son
12 Bambi's aunt
13 Feudal farmers
16 Flycatching bird
19 __ good example
22 Window glass
23 Takes advantage of
24 Full of zip
26 Guitar ridge
27 Easter flower
28 Pass catcher
29 Storage boxes
30 Answered the alarm
31 No. crunchers
32 Seine tributary
33 Glassmaking oven
34 Golf ball's position
37 Sweetened
38 DeMille genre
39 House lots
42 Jelly ingredient
43 Stood on a soapbox
44 Pennypinchers
45 Watermelon features
47 Burn slightly
48 Prefix for mentioned
49 Wile E. Coyote's supplier
50 Church-bell sound
51 Automotive pioneer
52 '60s records
53 Hgt.
54 Feel remorse about

82 FOUNDERS' DAY

by Bob Frank

ACROSS

1 Good, slangily
4 Four six-packs
8 Flapjack-chain letters
12 Understanding words
14 Rara avis
15 Designates
17 Microsoft founder
19 Drum attachment
20 On an even keel
21 Filet __
22 Make a doily
23 ". . . and the world will __ path . . ."
25 Three-toed ungulate
28 CNN founder
32 Robin portrayer in '38
33 Blue-pencil
34 Keats creation
35 ". . . and the __ defeat"
37 Acted devilishly
40 Arcing pitch
41 Not at all exciting
43 O. Henry specialty
44 Apple Computer founder
47 Minister's home
48 Church shouts
49 Popular
50 __ water (cologne)
53 Kitchen fixtures
58 Like a bucket of song
59 Wal-Mart founder
60 Gallup finding
61 Slapstick ammo
62 "Outer" word form
63 Act the wisenheimer
64 Diarist Frank
65 Chop a yew

DOWN

1 Lettuce variety
2 Tibet's locale
3 Gateway competitor
4 Do in unison
5 Up-front money
6 Place of development
7 Hosp. sections
8 At the original locale
9 Plane home
10 Yemen neighbor
11 But: Sp.
13 High spirits
16 Sun Yat-__
18 Bent and twisted, as a tree
21 Unglossy finish
24 Head and Wharton
25 Colorful ducks
26 Vernacular
27 Research project
28 Kitchen coating
29 "__ a bet!"
30 Lost paradises
31 Change color again
36 __ d'art
38 Brunch beverage
39 Babble on and on
42 Voluntarily refrain
45 "La Bamba" singer
46 Corrects text
49 Boat bow's anchor hole
50 Youngster
51 Rowboat duo
52 Name in Scandinavian furniture
54 Writing on the wall
55 Make a deep impression
56 Non-mnemonic method
57 Skiers' base
59 Mineral spring

83 ONLY 15 AWAY

by A.J. Santora

ACROSS

1 Kiss
6 Dallas player, for short
9 Frighten
14 Lily plant
15 Dig this
16 Gripper of a sort
17 March award
18 Orange kin
20 With 56 Across, game show
22 Ullmann or Tyler
23 High crag
24 Performing
28 Ooze
30 Do the case over
32 Shea player
33 Pacific island
35 Bouquet
37 Key phrase on 20 Across
40 Word game
42 Jungle vine
43 Legal hurdle?
44 Sheikdom of song
46 Science class adjuncts
50 Type of pipe connection
53 Baton Rouge sch.
55 Same-old-same-old
56 See 20 Across
59 *Late Late Show* viewer, maybe
62 Duplicate
63 Tentative
64 Moose relative
65 Successful dieter
66 Clark's partner
67 Castaway's call
68 Water pitchers

DOWN

1 Unwelcome looks
2 Five-iron
3 Nook
4 Hammer part
5 Gold measure
6 Expos' home
7 Father of Phobos
8 Airplane's path
9 Tries
10 Insertion mark
11 Ring name
12 Rum, in Rioja
13 Wind dir.
19 Stylish
21 Bellini opera
25 Cupid's alias
26 Bijou
27 Airport abbr.
29 Greek letters
31 Flippant phrase
34 Hill builder
35 Bristle
36 Honest-to-goodness
37 __ song (cheaply)
38 Nine-irons
39 Authority
40 *Saint Joan* initials
41 Yes, in Japan
44 M __ "Meredith"
45 Banks (on)
47 Melodic
48 Range device
49 Takes the tiller
51 New Zealand native
52 TV awards
54 Cry of defeat
57 *Le roi d'Ys* composer
58 In the hold
59 Inauspicious
60 Bridal-notice word
61 Insure, with "up"

84 WHITEWASH

by Fred Piscop

ACROSS

1 Lacking politeness
6 It's a long story
10 Gondola propeller
14 __ yoga
15 __ monde (high society)
16 Biblical brother
17 West African nation
19 Yemeni money
20 Highly original and influential
21 Cyberspace nuisances
23 Fictional work
25 Middling grade
26 Cow or sow
28 Early-morning vehicle
33 Helix
36 Poor, as excuses
37 Nutritional initials
38 "Alley __!"
39 Yank's foe
41 Kids' card game
42 Not 'neath
43 Soda __
44 Biblical prophet
46 Deny
48 Arctic bird
51 Slithery fish
52 Darlin'
53 Latin music
56 Containing element #5
60 "__ Porgie"
64 Kazakhstan sea
65 It's often wiped clean
67 Daily delivery
68 Icicle site
69 Zhou __

70 One on your side
71 "Never mind!" to an editor
72 Pee Wee of baseball

DOWN

1 Greek letters
2 Great review
3 Physicist's study
4 Conventioneer in a fez
5 Turn down, with "to"
6 Author Asch
7 Small battery size
8 Flow like oil, perhaps
9 Offense player in lacrosse
10 Actress Sarah Jessica __
11 Theater award
12 TV producer Norman
13 Some pipe joints
18 Cleveland cager, for short
22 Et __
24 __ Abner
26 Soup utensil
27 Zoo heavyweight
29 Dershowitz's field
30 Cropped up
31 Utopian
32 __ a soul (no one)
33 Absorbs, with "up"
34 Region of Spain

35 Sweet summer snack
40 Derisive cry
45 Flat-tire sound
47 The very beginning
49 100%
50 Aerie hatchling
54 Albanian currency
55 Sensible
56 Tuscaloosa school, for short
57 Evangelist Roberts
58 Racetrack boundary
59 Friendly talk
61 Strong wind
62 401(k) cousins
63 Falco of *The Sopranos*
66 St. crosser

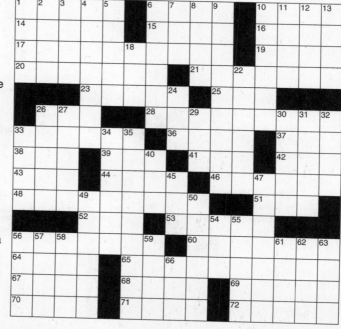

ACROSS

1 Soccer score
5 Bar bills
9 Call to mind
14 *The King and I* character
15 First name in scat
16 Green carvings
17 '60s sitcom mom
18 Fossil fuel
19 Upscale
20 Make peace
23 Digging tool
24 Facts
25 Incite to action
29 Manhattan, for one
33 Madrid Mrs.
36 *The Chosen* author
38 In __ of (rather than)
39 Make peace
43 Golden-__ (senior citizen)
44 Mennonite group
45 W.C. Fields persona
46 Curator employer
49 March honoree, for short
51 Starting with
53 Army weapon
57 Make peace
62 Cutting tool
63 Rookie
64 "Too bad!"
65 Acquire, as debts
66 Petroleum grp.
67 Campbell of *Scream*
68 Film units
69 Luxurious
70 Fr. holy women

DOWN

1 Modes of dress
2 Get the better of
3 "It's the end of __!"
4 Memorable bride of '81
5 Georgia __ University
6 Sunblock ingredient
7 Uninteresting
8 Course with greens
9 Throws out
10 Odin's hall
11 Garfield's foil
12 Etta of comics
13 Compass pt.
21 Metronome setting
22 Skater Babilonia
26 Sound of a punch
27 Erupter of 1992
28 Weaving machines
30 Ventilates
31 Verne captain
32 Coating to clean off
33 Close loudly
34 Prego competitor
35 Affirmative votes
37 Work with yarn
40 Extremely bad
41 Sixth sense
42 Puppeteer Lewis
47 Flashlight carriers
48 It's heard in a herd
50 Giants
52 Photographer's setting
54 __ mignon
55 Depart
56 Curvy letters
57 Feminine ending
58 Riviera resort
59 Editor's find
60 Angers
61 __ Ness
62 Cassis-flavored apéritif

86 "GIRL" SINGERS

by Bob Frank

ACROSS

1 Leftover
6 Saintly symbol
10 "Get outta here!"
14 Hilo hello
15 Words to Brutus
16 "This can't be!"
17 "Maggie May" singer
19 Air bag?
20 Get mellow
21 Eye drop
22 Disorderly disturbance
24 Portrait medium
25 Chronometer
26 Furry slinkers
29 Sugar pills
32 Levels (up)
33 *Mourning Becomes Electra* character
34 Repairman's fig.
35 Start over
36 Verge
37 Soft cheese
38 Furthermore
39 CPA's record
40 Electrician, at times
41 Not at all long-term
44 "And __ off!"
45 Parka parts
46 Bearing
47 Performing company
49 Seaside soarer
50 Actress Gardner
53 Assistance

54 "Clementine" singer
57 Club Med locale
58 Bangkok resident
59 Legal
60 Eye annoyance
61 For a __ (cheaply)
62 Cow of commercials

DOWN

1 Gilbert of *Roseanne*
2 Pipe problem
3 Went piggyback
4 Sighs of content
5 Peppermint candies
6 "__ chubby and plump, a right jolly old elf"
7 Perfume oil: Var.
8 Wd. part
9 Get around, militarily
10 Comfort
11 "Maybellene" singer
12 __ *Karenina*
13 Clothes
18 Snakelike fish
23 Mythical bird
24 Substitute spread
25 Dirty Harry portrayer
26 Valuable violin
27 Sports site
28 "Peggy Sue" singer

29 Quite expensive
30 Willow twig
31 Cubic meter
33 Killer whales
36 Certain write-offs
37 Well, in Nice
40 Cajole
42 Pate topper
43 "Alley __!"
44 Mite-sized
46 Top man
47 "Memories Are Made of __"
48 Take five
49 Abba of Israel
50 Pendulum paths
51 Clock numeral
52 Start the pot
55 "You sly one, you!"
56 Be unwell

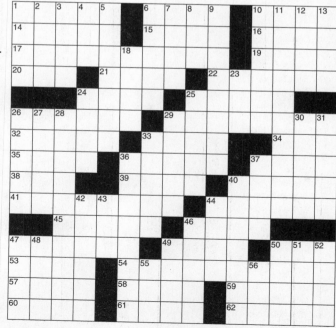

87 THEY'RE ALL WET

by A.J. Santora

ACROSS

1 __ buco
5 Packs (away)
10 Worry
14 Wagon-__ (sleeping cars)
15 Gluck opera character
16 Emanation
17 Adored one
18 "Suddenly" singer
20 *I Married a Witch* star
22 Merino mama
23 Self-importance
24 Drinks noisily
28 Occupied
30 Faucet
33 Vertical, at sea
34 Where Aden is
36 Multitude
38 __ Khan
39 *The Member of the Wedding* actress
43 Vain fellow
45 Chamomile, e.g.
46 Elite group
48 Stagehands
51 Nautical dir.
53 Pumpkin kin
55 Diamond units
57 Dernier __ (latest fashion)
59 Actress Charlotte
60 Dixieland clarinetist
64 "Can we talk?" comic
67 One opposed
68 Coastal flyer
69 Rental contract
70 Sgts., e.g.
71 Go like the wind
72 __ Park, CO
73 *Power* star

DOWN

1 Fake pearl
2 Indirect
3 Country merchant
4 Fjord city
5 Ferber novel
6 Knit fabric
7 *Man __ Mancha*
8 Healthy
9 Bean plants
10 Showing, as a card
11 Regret
12 Clemens stat.
13 Cure hides
19 Kans. neighbor
21 Singer Cherry
25 Confidence-building words
26 Buddy
27 Wild blue yonder
29 CPR giver
31 Egyptian dam
32 Green shade
35 Profit
37 __ glance
40 Sheltered side
41 Hoopster Baylor
42 Carnival locale
43 Govt. airwaves board
44 Mouths: Lat.
47 Turncoat
49 *People's Court* judge
50 Suffix for drag
52 City near Detroit
54 Poet Levertov
56 Sort of stairway
58 Tricks
61 Pre-holiday times
62 Accomplishment
63 Sharp taste
64 Deep black
65 Lode load
66 Santa __, CA

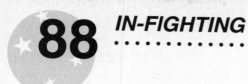

by Merle Baker

ACROSS

1 Bad-service result
6 Immigration Museum island
11 Not masc.
14 Proverb
15 Show surprise
16 Skeletal start
17 Excessive admiration
19 "__ lazy river . . ."
20 Darn
21 Extension
23 Yodeler's range
26 Needle
27 Author Umberto
28 Med. school subject
31 __ *Three Lives*
32 Singer Morissette
36 Hairnet
38 Chance on
40 45 Down resident
44 Terrier type
46 Takes care of
47 Fill fully
50 Restraint
52 Bud's buddy
53 Publish
55 Driver of the desert
59 Monteverdi opera
60 Spanish inn
61 Campy sound of discomfort
62 Chicago School architects' products
67 Memo letters
68 Protozoan propellers
69 Thought-provoking
70 Heir, often
71 Close, in poesy
72 Pivoted

DOWN

1 Slangy denial
2 Lyric poem
3 Sailor
4 Stravinsky et al.
5 Small bird
6 Early-edition insert
7 Wounds
8 Bolger costar
9 Here, in France
10 3/17 honoree
11 Of serfs and vassals
12 Tabloid shocker
13 Lamented
18 Choose
22 Soap actress Hall
23 Timidity
24 Legal rights org.
25 Bank offering
29 Mandela's grp.
30 1992 Robin Williams film
33 Christian creed
34 Tempest __ teapot
35 Agitate
37 Unfold, in verse
39 Bauxite, for one
41 Tropical spot
42 Western Indian
43 Inspection trip
45 Mediterranean capital
47 Parodies
48 Gorge
49 Luncheon, in London
51 Daytona 500 org.
54 Puccini work
56 Damage
57 Red-coated cheeses
58 Pin place
60 Nabors role
63 Relatives
64 __ de Cologne
65 Map abbr.
66 Chaplin brother

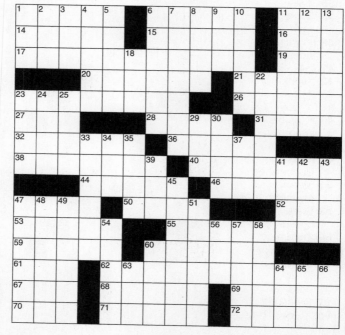

by Richard Silvestri

ACROSS

1 M*A*S*H star
5 Male deer
9 Dan of Laugh-In
14 Furnace fodder
15 Skyscraping
16 Deliver an address
17 Harvard and Yale's group
19 "Ditto!"
20 Sandy expanse
21 I Remember __
23 Shore eagle
24 Vittles
26 Landed estate
28 Aardvark
32 Unanimously
35 Head Stooge
36 Nullify
38 Good-deed doer
39 Impressionist painter
41 In the past
42 Spoof
43 Forever __ day
44 Paris-based intl. agency
46 PC key
47 Actor Liam
49 Unpunished
51 Send payment
53 State confidently
54 Third man in the ring
56 Etc. kin
58 Make possible
62 Coral reef
64 Atrium
66 Kitchen appliance
67 Concerning
68 The Time Machine race
69 Small: Fr.
70 Minister to
71 Bumper bruise

DOWN

1 Litmus reddener
2 Zero, in tennis
3 "Those Were the __"
4 Assert without proof
5 Regulation
6 Kids' game
7 Graduate, for short
8 Flash of light
9 Italian cheese
10 Smeltery input
11 Utility measurer
12 Comment ending
13 Light gas
18 Wandering
22 Spouse
25 Started
27 Diamond Head's home
28 Jordan's capital
29 Nary a soul
30 Novice Boy Scout
31 Goes ballistic
33 Got up
34 Time being
37 Puccini opera
40 Comfort
42 Packing a punch
44 Module
45 Like Old West wagons
48 Brunch entrée
50 Worn at the edges
52 Not spelled out
54 Sound hoarse
55 Diminutive ending
57 Solitary
59 Farm bundle
60 Writer Hubbard
61 Mark up manuscripts
63 Roman 56
65 Coffee server

DAIRY CASE

by Fred Piscop

ACROSS

1 Dry run
5 Attire
9 Go by bike
14 Pro __ (proportionally)
15 Aroma
16 Wagnerian work
17 Lay __ thick
18 Actress Turner
19 Imitate
20 Patent medicine
23 Tough to climb
24 Angelic topper
25 Copy, for short
29 Vintage Ford
33 Stubborn equine
36 Fictional Lorna
38 Author Levin et al.
39 Crooks' cry of old
43 Harpo or Chico
44 Kind of paint
45 Mach 1 breaker
46 Makes into law
49 Settle accounts
51 Novelist Ambler
53 Conduits
57 A-one stuff
62 Riyadh resident
63 Have the courage
64 *Out of the Inkwell* clown
65 Pilgrim John
66 Gung-ho
67 Water pitcher
68 Iditarod vehicles
69 Alluring
70 Lacoste of tennis

DOWN

1 Removes the fat from
2 Yankovic song parody
3 Plagiarized
4 Ship of fuels
5 Tiger's game
6 Genesis figure
7 Barrett of gossip
8 "Erin go __!"
9 Grapefruit kin
10 Like soap operas
11 Actress Moore
12 Scotto solo
13 Fond du __, WI
21 Commentators' pages
22 Where many vets served
26 "Annabel Lee" writer
27 Stir up
28 Ready to pour
30 Love god
31 Swimmer's measures
32 Mgr.'s aide
33 High point
34 Writer Eda Le__
35 Blood fluids
37 Sundance's girlfriend
40 Went over
41 "Yo!"
42 Radiate, as charm
47 Prepares, as an athlete
48 Actor Alastair
50 React to a lemon
52 Musical postscripts
54 Russell of *The Insider*
55 Straphanger's buy
56 Mushroom-to-be
57 Poker action
58 Lacking couth
59 Top pick, slangily
60 Kids' cereal
61 Lamarr of Hollywood
62 KLM rival

CAR TUNES

by Bob Frank

ACROSS

1 Rowing equipment
5 *Spaceballs* princess
10 Polite address
14 High-school dance
15 Egg-shaped
16 Jamaican fruit
17 Press for
18 Slow tempo
19 Achievement
20 1969 Young-Holt Unlimited tune
23 Shoelace hole
24 Literary postscript
28 Brillo rival
29 Weightroom users
33 Pizarro's quest
34 Hand-___ (decorated)
35 Piece of cake
36 1969 Blood, Sweat and Tears tune
40 Chagall or Antony
41 Female fowl
42 In the past
43 Air passage
45 Tax expert: Abbr.
48 Personnel listing
50 Bolivian bouquet
52 1984 Jacksons tune
56 Hemingway sobriquet
59 ___ Haute, IN
60 Open ___ of worms
61 Skunk's defense
62 Playful sea critter
63 City near Lake Tahoe
64 Website address parts
65 Staggers
66 Helper: Abbr.

DOWN

1 Musical works
2 River gulch
3 Scoundrels
4 One of the senses
5 Spiraled shape
6 Daredevil Knievel
7 Some business partners
8 Actor Brad
9 Idolizer
10 Civilian clothes
11 AARP membership determinant
12 Fla. neighbor
13 With, in Bonn
21 Serious criminal
22 Increases, as the ante
25 Isolated
26 Unwritten exam
27 Lott's grp.
30 Somersaults
31 Article of faith
32 Bergen or Degas
34 ___-tac-toe
35 D.C. VIP
36 Type of palm tree
37 Cons' adversaries
38 Strikeout victims
39 "___ bells!"
40 Scratch up
43 Fishing need
44 Speechifier
45 "Time in a Bottle" singer's family
46 Texas nuts
47 "___ what your country . . ."
49 Russian royals
51 Leigh role
53 French head
54 Art Deco artist
55 Hurler Hershiser
56 Pea holder
57 Commotion
58 Poker prize

by Norma Steinberg

ACROSS

1 Prize benefactor
6 Big party
10 What *id* means
14 *Amo*, in America
15 Writer Wiesel
16 Stockings
17 Dressed to the __
18 Role for Calista
19 Artist née Romain de Tirtoff
20 Raggedy Andy's girlfriend
21 Actress in the Mediterranean?
24 __ and blood
26 Commands
27 Mongolians, e.g.
29 Hawaiian island
31 Pronoun on a towel
32 Brigham's destination
34 South American dance
39 Iowa city
40 New York Indians
42 Equipment
43 Animal on a nickel
45 __ mater
46 Land measurement
47 Money machines: Abbr.
49 Choir members
51 Homer's partner
55 Italian lady
56 Arts in India?
59 Trouble
62 *Uncle Remus* epithet
63 Kitchen worker
64 Keens
66 Withstand
67 Pro golfer Irwin
68 Donkeys
69 LL.D. holder
70 Concludes
71 "Whoopee!"

DOWN

1 Columbus' smallest ship
2 Actress Lena
3 German blazes?
4 Seth's mother
5 Abate
6 *Baywatch* setting
7 "__ want is a room somewhere . . ."
8 Window ledge
9 "Psst!"
10 "__ never believe me . . ."
11 Steed
12 Fur tycoon
13 Adolescents
22 Magazine edition
23 Speaker of baseball
25 Will Rogers prop
27 Jezebel's husband
28 Large truck
29 Posts
30 Sound for attention
33 Trolley
35 "Encore!"
36 Saudi Arabian fantasy?
37 Unadorned
38 God of war
41 Enjoy greatly
44 Antidrug cop
48 Word of acknowledgment
50 Words on an arrow
51 __ the Hutt
52 Long-legged bird
53 Halloween option
54 Ike's predecessor
55 Fists
57 Temporary gift
58 Snitched
60 Toast topping
61 Antique road sign
65 Simile words

93 FAUX VACATIONS

by A.J. Santora

ACROSS

1 Sesame Street grouch
6 Camel attribute
10 Free ticket
14 Esther of *Good Times*
15 Way off
16 On __ with
17 Short vacation?
20 Solo in space
21 Roofing goo
22 Straw for hats
23 Bother
24 Some races
27 Chemical suffix
28 Lowercase-letter part
31 Poetic tributes
32 Paul, in *Exodus*
33 Capp and Capone
35 Auto-body woe
36 Vacationing alone?
39 Told, as a tale
41 Wildebeest
42 Rocker Brian
43 Affected
44 Facial appearances
49 Male turkey
50 "The Toastmaster General"
52 Actress Arthur
53 Footless
55 San Juan aunt
57 Scale notes
58 Summer bummer?
62 Donna __ (Don Juan's mother)
63 Threesome
64 That: Fr.
65 Yield
66 Looked at
67 Bandage

DOWN

1 Greenhouse plant
2 ". . . __ as a day in June"
3 Blockheads
4 Spinks defeater
5 Relax
6 Animus
7 *X-Files* subject
8 Chess piece
9 Dull, as writing
10 Lyricist Sammy
11 Bloomed
12 "Tell it to the __!"
13 Advance trial
18 Taking home
19 Unseld of the NBA
25 Alliances
26 Alice's Restaurant patron
29 Astute
30 Historical period
31 Mythical hunter
34 Rainbow trout
36 Passé
37 Loose matters?
38 Single-stranded molecule
39 Rushdie's __ *Verses*
40 Tell to a judge
45 Systematic plan
46 Layperson
47 Shies away, perhaps
48 Window frames
50 Blue bird
51 Make happy
54 Stun
56 Kid's song start
59 Taste
60 Get even with
61 Auction finish

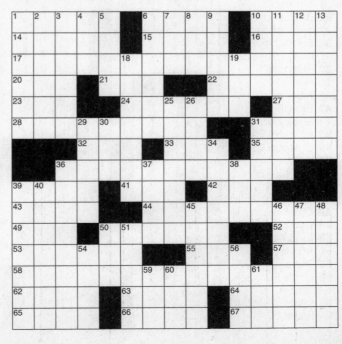

94 HEAD DOWN

by Fred Piscop

ACROSS
1 "Ah, me!"
5 Casino game
9 Airplane tracker
14 __ of the above
15 Actor Baldwin
16 Grinding material
17 Evade the ticket-taker
19 English coins
20 Magazine employee
21 Inert gas
23 Military scout's job, for short
24 Sign of sorrow
28 Upperclassmen: Abbr.
29 Clotheshorse
32 Elevator alternative
33 Tenor Enrico
36 Redcap's burdens
37 Teapot Dome figure
40 Pinnacle
42 Plaza Hotel imp
43 Pago Pago native
46 Phone no. add-on
47 Cry of discovery
50 Place to empty a pail
53 Indy 500 and others
55 John Jacob __
56 Sea rays
57 Italian staple
60 Corner bar, perhaps
62 Video-game name
63 Bartlett's abbr.
64 Fifty-fifty
65 Word before code or colony
66 *Nautilus* skipper
67 E-mailed

DOWN
1 Riles
2 Stevedore
3 High jinks
4 Take care of
5 Klinger player
6 According to
7 Returned to session
8 Earth hue
9 School assignment
10 Like our Constitution
11 Reading room
12 Pendulum's path
13 Pumpernickel alternative
18 Casual talk
22 Fossil fuel
25 Iranian money
26 Association: Abbr.
27 Ltr. addenda
30 Crude metal
31 24-karat
33 Antony's love
34 NL Central team
35 Wind instrument
37 Bullets
38 Difficult spot
39 Of the stars
40 Chucklehead
41 "Silent" president
44 Attack violently
45 Prefix for picker
47 On the roster
48 Supreme happiness
49 Concurrence
51 Fireballer Ryan
52 Danish money
54 Lake Titicaca's locale
56 "Look __ hands!"
57 Mushy food
58 Gulped down
59 __ Bernardino
61 Net address suffix

WELL IN HAND

by Merle Baker

ACROSS

1 Like a flapper's hair
7 Get better
14 Baltimore baseballer
15 *Lo's Diary* author
16 Blame
18 Suffix for billion
19 Ford and Pyle
21 "Blame __ the Bossa Nova"
24 Outback birds
27 Frozen treats
28 Blue jeans
30 Region including Lebanon
33 Acquiesce
36 USN VIP
37 Fix a squeak
38 ". . . __ daily bread"
39 Actress Farrow
42 Bribery
45 Cole and Wood
48 Mother-of-pearl
49 Pod denizens
50 Parkway exit
53 Placed down
54 Perches
57 Obi-Wan portrayer
59 One way to stand out
65 Cyber-names
66 Lack of purpose
67 Application of an astringent
68 First *Family Feud* host

DOWN

1 Jazz style
2 Tulsa school: Abbr.
3 Small amount
4 Pertaining to plants
5 K-12, scholastically
6 Plow pioneer
7 Sch. in Troy, NY
8 German article
9 Teller's post
10 Abbr. on a phone
11 French mathematician
12 Beethoven's third symphony
13 Hindu princesses
17 Gram. designation
20 Air France plane
21 Actress Chase
22 Incline
23 Egg cell
25 Former leader of Burma
26 Sir, in Spain
29 Toast word
31 Together, musically
32 Showed again
34 Leslie Caron role
35 Bugs hunter
39 Thin-layered mineral
40 Cross inscription
41 Matured
42 Maid's need
43 Govt. property overseer
44 Skating jump
45 Noncommercial news source: Abbr.
46 Greek wind god
47 Follower of Lao-tzu
51 Deface
52 Beg
55 Maryland collegian
56 *Je ne __ quoi*
58 Active volcano
60 Anti-ICBM plan
61 CIA forerunner
62 Syllables of hesitation
63 *"O Sole __"*
64 Hoss' father

96 TO A PULP

by Nelson Hardy

ACROSS

1 Rumba relative
6 Pitfall, perhaps
11 Rock band accessory, for short
14 Birdlike
15 E-mail forerunner
16 With 70 Across, prehensile-tailed animal
17 Perennial Halloween tune
19 Basketball position: Abbr.
20 Contra- relative
21 Cupboard part
22 Under way
24 Hartford's home: Abbr.
26 A "cocktail" was named for him
28 "It's clear now!"
31 Droning musician
33 Rodeo rope
35 WWII craft
36 Imperfection
40 Yellowish vegetable
44 "Don't move, Spot!"
45 1952 election monogram
46 Togetherness
47 Infamous WWI figure
51 Bob and Mohawk
52 Aromatic evergreen
55 Patsy
57 Disney mermaid
58 __ M for Murder
60 Totally absorbed
64 Opposite of max.
65 Popular soft drink

68 Ingest
69 Sign on an entrance ramp
70 See 16 Across
71 "Keep it down!"
72 Prepares pies
73 All worked up

DOWN

1 Nursery cry
2 Stratford's river
3 Make cents
4 No-frills
5 Ottawa's prov.
6 Like some odors
7 Verne captain
8 Chicken Little, for one
9 Home: Abbr.
10 Blow out
11 Fancy neckwear
12 "I agree!"

13 Fourth sequel
18 Journalist Buchanan
23 As a joke
25 Clarinet cousin
27 Withdraws, with "out"
28 Priests' robes
29 __ monde (high society)
30 *The Thin Man* terrier
32 Like some carpeting
34 Throw for a loop
37 Put down, as carpet
38 Concerning
39 Reporters' questions
41 Give a number to
42 Time just before nightfall

43 Words from a wit
48 Poise
49 "Money isn't everything" et al.
50 Run the realm
52 Actor Woods
53 Dickensian clerk
54 Last inning, usually
56 Miscue
59 *Bus Stop* playwright
61 Star's mystique
62 Attention-getting whisper
63 What "you" used to be
66 Stephen of *The Crying Game*
67 Frat letter

97 OFF ON THE RIGHT FOOT

by Paul MacNamara

ACROSS
1 Wears a long face
6 Welcome giver
9 Brown ermine
14 __ Rogers St. Johns
15 Abbr. on toothpaste boxes
16 Winter quaff
17 Sub detector
18 Hoopster, at times
20 Aspirator
22 Telephonic 6
23 Gen. Robert __
24 Bottom line
25 Part of NB
27 __-crab soup
29 City in *Italia*
32 Atty.'s title
35 Up to
38 Crucifix
39 Bullheaded
43 Salty droplet
44 Deeply felt
45 Sunbather's goal
46 Quilts
49 Tie the knot
51 Narrative
52 "Get it?"
54 Toward sunup
58 "The Greatest"
60 Stretchy stuff
63 Many a campaign worker
65 Hosiery shade
66 Like Humpty Dumpty
67 Hill dweller

68 Analyze ore
69 Pokes around
70 "Yay team!"
71 Loaf ends

DOWN
1 Billiards shot
2 Lefty of baseball
3 Pound parts
4 Sends to cloud nine
5 Delhi dress
6 French river
7 Skillful
8 Verboten: Var.
9 Lethargy
10 Won __ soup
11 One not fitting in
12 Mideast's Gulf of __
13 Newbie
19 Prefix for present
21 Bridge bid, for short
26 Designate
28 Center of activity
29 Custard treat
30 *Nana* author
31 Place of temptation
32 Ballpark figs.
33 Plan part
34 Test-result groupings
36 Cobb contemporary Speaker
37 *Newhart* setting

40 La __ Tar Pits
41 Norton's workplace
42 "You __ here"
47 Trues up
48 Soup-can flaw
50 Lower in quality
52 Tuscan city
53 Solar orbiter
55 Treat badly
56 Flower part
57 Poker cards
58 Bard's river
59 Timber wolf
61 Letter opener
62 Four Corners state
64 Avail oneself of

98 ANIMAL ACTS

by Richard Silvestri

ACROSS

1 Shoot the breeze
5 Lose traction
9 Garbed like Ginsburg
14 Venerable historian
15 The O'Hara place
16 Shade of blue
17 Makeup, e.g.
18 Eden's earldom
19 Mochrie of *Whose Line Is It Anyway?*
20 Sheep beeping?
22 Small bay
23 They may be knotted or broken
24 Lend an ear
25 Fireplace tool
28 Viking of the comics
31 Kimono closer
34 Skips over
36 Spoil
37 Alphabet finaliser
38 Ancient
39 Unquestionable
42 Down with a bug
43 *Delta of Venus* author
44 Joplin specialty
45 1964 Hitchcock movie
47 Nay canceler
48 Rage
50 Ale alternative
51 Overly proper
53 List extender
55 Gimme on the green
57 Sick donkey?
62 Cordial flavoring
63 __ Bator
64 Psychic's words
65 Copier additive
66 Gave an account
67 School on the Thames
68 Peeved
69 Toe the mark
70 Ready to eat

DOWN

1 Trucker with a handle
2 Twice tri-
3 Second sinner
4 Played the siren
5 Show place
6 Extravagant
7 Mill material
8 Attack of remorse
9 More indelicate
10 Endangered layer
11 Bovine asleep?
12 Great Lakes port
13 Bad impression
21 Went public with
24 Sultan's spouses
25 State flower of Indiana
26 Stan's partner
27 Young goat off guard?
29 Pal
30 Wander about
32 Prove false
33 Do-nothing
35 It's in your blood
40 One for the road
41 __ Lama
46 Came from behind
48 Sunday clothes
49 Flea-market transaction
52 Tread's mate
54 *Driving Miss Daisy* Oscar winner
55 "Cheerio!"
56 In a while
57 Self starter?
58 Oscar Madison, for one
59 Ratio phrase
60 Light stuff
61 Trait carrier

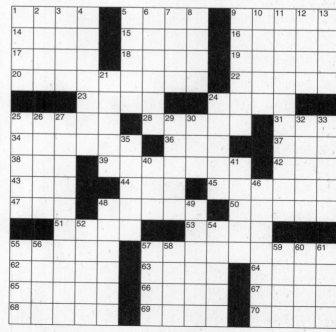

by Fred Piscop

ACROSS

1 Fire truck
7 Family group
11 Singing syllable
14 Hawaii senator Daniel
15 Boxcar rider
16 Above, poetically
17 Musical extravaganza
19 Bub
20 For the asking
21 *CHiPs* star Erik
23 Fla. neighbor
26 *Platoon* setting
28 Like some arguments
29 Trump or Duck
32 Kimono accessory
34 Had on
35 "I __!" ("Search me!")
36 Punished, Biblically
38 Spiderlike critter
42 Broadcasts again
43 Actor Cheech
45 Mediocre
48 Highway: Abbr.
49 Ravel classic
50 Loosen up
52 Costa __ Sol
54 Freshly painted
55 Least bouncy, as a tennis ball
57 Come down hard
60 Fall from grace
61 Sweet little Mary's location, in a kids' song

66 Fraternal fellow
67 Balm ingredient
68 Puts into words
69 Full of guile
70 For fear that
71 Sticky note

DOWN

1 Doozy
2 Numero __
3 Thick mane
4 Huff's partner
5 Watchful one
6 Mail again
7 Greek X
8 Jennifer __ Hewitt
9 Embarrassing
10 Nick of *Cape Fear*
11 Salad ingredient
12 "See Spot run" book
13 Skee-Ball site
18 Afternoon social
22 Short end of the stick
23 Tack on
24 Boisterous
25 Soprano Moffo
27 Went for a drive
30 Man-machine
31 Ore source
33 __ mots (witticisms)
36 Use a letter opener
37 Sailors' saint
39 Place for bargains
40 Sprouted
41 Farm father
44 Petal plucker's word

45 Washes with detergent
46 Former House Speaker
47 Very elegant
49 Enlarge, as a photo
51 Himalayan monarchy
53 Emissions-watching org.
56 "__ company, three's a crowd"
58 Capable of
59 Charlie Brown expletive
62 Hamster or hound
63 Hanoi holiday
64 Dernier __
65 "The buck stops here" monogram

100 EYES FOR YOU

by R.J. Hartman

ACROSS

1 St. Louis hrs.
4 O'Hare runways
11 Swelled head
14 Taunting cry
15 Ring-shaped
16 Right away
17 Home of William Faulkner
19 Water-temperature tester
20 Shakespeare sprite
21 Squealer
22 Comedian Foxx
23 Attacked from the air
26 Bedspread
28 Warlike
32 Train stop: Abbr.
35 *Peter Pan* dog
36 Desist
37 Volcano output
39 *The Count of __ Cristo*
42 Cultivate
43 Battle site of 1836
45 36 inches
47 New Jersey cager
48 Slander
52 Playing marble
53 Betrothed
57 James Bond foe
59 Matterhorn, for one
61 Blacksmith's workshop
62 Sinbad's bird
63 Peoria resident
66 Fire residue
67 Nursery supply
68 NFL scores
69 Spelling event
70 Owl cry
71 Wind dir.

DOWN

1 Deep sleeps
2 Collared garment
3 __ *With Love*
4 Fender feature
5 Reply: Abbr.
6 ER workers
7 Naturalist John
8 Llama cousin
9 Hostage holder
10 __ Lanka
11 Amuse
12 Admirable
13 Had markers out
18 Clothing connector
22 Bowling-lane button
24 Oater actor Jack
25 Hollywood producer de Laurentiis
27 Old __ (London theatre)
29 Country singer Tucker
30 Man or Wight
31 Welshman
32 Belgrade native
33 Anklebones
34 Himalayan danger
38 Baja buddy
40 *Little Man __* (Foster film)
41 Land of the leprechauns
44 "Son __ gun!"
46 Small shark
49 Slanted type style
50 Last place, in sports
51 Greek temple
54 Macon breakfast
55 "Goodness gracious!"
56 Thick as a brick
57 Dreary
58 Ascended
60 Meerschaum, e.g.
63 Freudian topics
64 Once called
65 Whale-like animal

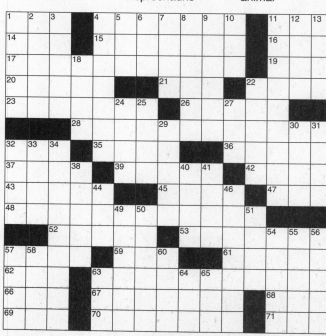

ANSWERS

1

C	O	M	P		M	E	A	N	S		W	A	W	A
O	D	O	R		A	T	B	A	T		I	N	O	N
T	I	N	Y		S	T	I	N	E		S	T	E	T
	C	A	N	Y	O	U	T	O	P	T	H	I	S	
		N	A	N				S	O	L				
E	D	S	E	L		A	R	S		W	I	N	C	E
M	O	P		I	N	T	A	K	E		S	E	L	L
I	L	I	K	E	I	T	L	I	K	E	T	H	A	T
L	O	R	I		T	I	L	L	E	R		R	I	O
E	R	E	C	T		C	Y	L		U	T	U	R	N
			K	O	A				S	P	A			
	O	N	E	O	R	T	H	E	O	T	H	E	R	
A	W	E	D		A	R	I	E	L		I	R	O	N
D	E	M	I		B	O	Y	L	E		T	I	M	E
A	N	O	N		S	T	A	Y	S		I	C	E	D

2

C	A	B	I	N		H	A	H	A		I	D	L	E
O	P	I	N	E		E	T	O	N		S	H	E	S
L	E	O	T	O	L	S	T	O	Y		A	L	A	S
E	D	G	E		A	I	N	T		T	I	A	R	A
			R	E	S	T		S	C	R	A	W	N	Y
T	A	J	M	A	H	A	L		B	O	H	R		
A	W	A	I	T		T	A	P	E	D		E	S	T
M	A	N	X		C	E	D	A	R		E	N	T	O
E	Y	E		O	R	D	E	R		L	U	C	I	E
	A	U	R	A		S	C	R	A	P	E	R	S	
T	S	U	N	A	M	I		H	U	G	H			
B	A	S	I	N		S	E	M	I		O	A	T	S
I	T	T	O		A	L	L	E	N	D	R	U	R	Y
L	I	E	N		R	E	I	N		A	I	D	E	S
L	E	N	S		S	T	A	T		W	A	I	S	T

3

T	O	G	O		A	M	O	S			C	A	S	T	E
E	M	I	R		M	E	N	U			A	L	T	O	S
N	A	V	E		E	R	I	C			R	I	A	T	A
T	H	E	O	N	L	Y	T	H	I	N	G	Y	O	U	
H	A	S		O	I	L			R	E	N				
	A	L	V	A		D	R	E	S	S	A	G	E		
S	H	O	E		I	R	O	N			N	O	R		
S	H	O	U	L	D	D	O	B	E	H	I	N	D	A	
M	O	O		A	L	I	S		I	V	E	S			
U	P	T	U	R	N	E	D		S	T	Y	X			
	L	I	Z		T	A	U		A	M	A				
M	A	N	S	B	A	C	K	I	S	P	A	T	I	T	
A	N	I	T	A		A	N	T	S		G	I	N	S	
Y	O	K	E	L		S	O	L	E		R	O	S	E	
S	N	E	R	D		A	W	E	D		A	N	K	A	

4

A	L	I	B	I		U	N	T	O		P	I	L	E
R	E	B	A	R		N	E	E	R		A	S	E	A
M	A	M	B	O		V	A	S	T		T	S	A	R
		U	N	D	E	R	T	H	E	S	U	N		
A	S	S	I	S	I			A	Y	E	S			
I	N	T	H	E	C	L	O	U	D	S				
C	O	R	K	S		U	N	I	T		T	I	N	
O	D	E	A		K	I	T	E	S		M	A	N	E
N	E	W		A	I	D	E		P	U	R	S	E	
			S	T	A	R	C	R	O	S	S	E	D	
S	P	C	A			O	U	T	H	I	T			
M	O	O	N	L	I	G	H	T	E	R				
O	L	L		O	L	E	O		N	O	T	C	H	
E	K	E	D		U	S	E	R		C	O	A	T	I
L	E	S	S		P	A	S	T		E	M	I	R	S

5

M	A	T	E	S		B	A	L		S	H	O	A	L
A	D	A	N	O		O	N	O		T	E	R	R	A
N	A	P	O	L	E	O	N	S		E	D	A	M	S
A	P	P	L	E	C	H	E	E	K	E	D			
G	T	E		D	U	O		E	L	A	T	E	D	
E	S	T	A		O	S	S	A			I	V	E	
			S	A	M		W	A	T	T	A	G	E	S
S	P	R	U	C	E	G	O	O	S	E				
O	N	E	S	I	D	E	D		N	O	S			
D	E	E		D	E	E	M		T	H	A	T		
D	O	R	S	A	L		A	A	A		I	D	O	
		C	H	E	R	R	Y	P	I	C	K	E	R	
C	A	N	O	E		H	E	A	R	T	I	E	S	T
A	R	E	N	A		E	E	N		C	A	R	T	E
M	E	W	E	D		A	D	S		H	O	S	E	S

6

P	A	C		D	I	G	I	T		S	E	A	M	S
R	E	O		A	M	O	C	O		T	U	N	E	R
E	R	N	O	R	U	B	I	K		P	R	A	D	O
	A	C	M	E	S		E	E	R		O	L	D	
S	T	A	N			E	R	N	I	E	P	Y	L	E
N	O	V	I	S	A	D		O	N	E	S	E	C	
O	R	E		T	R	E	A	D		F	A	T	S	O
			E	R	I	N	M	O	R	A	N			
I	P	A	N	A		S	C	I	O	N		O	V	O
T	O	M	A	T	O		N	O	T	E	P	A	D	
E	R	I	C	A	J	O	N	G			L	I	R	E
S	S	T		S	L	O		S	U	S	A	N		
A	C	T	I	I		E	R	I	K	S	A	T	I	E
S	H	A	N	K		A	G	R	E	E		E	S	P
S	E	D	G	E		N	E	E	D	S		S	H	A

7

S	T	I	R		S	T	E	A	M		A	L	M	A
T	O	N	I		S	E	L	M	A		S	E	A	L
R	A	P	S	E	S	S	I	O	N		H	A	L	L
I	D	L	E	S		H	O	R		S	E	T	T	O
F	I	A	S	C	O		T	A	L	K	S	H	O	W
E	S	C		E	T	A		L	A	I		E	S	E
S	H	E	A		H	M	O		R	E	A	R	E	D
			S	P	E	A	K	E	A	S	Y			
V	E	S	S	E	L		S	A	M		E	S	S	E
I	N	T		A	L	P		R	I	M		L	O	X
C	H	A	T	R	O	O	M		E	A	S	E	U	P
T	A	M	E	S		T	O	E		D	E	E	R	E
U	N	I	T		J	A	W	B	R	E	A	K	E	R
A	C	N	E		A	T	E	A	M		T	E	S	T
L	E	A	S		M	O	R	N	S		O	R	T	S

8

L	E	V	I		A	L	M	S		E	A	R	P
I	R	A	N		T	O	I	L		S	N	E	R	D
P	A	L	L		T	U	N	A		P	O	L	A	R
	H	A	M	U	N	I	V	E	R	S	I	T	Y	
C	L	A	W	I	N	G			P	I	E	C	E	S
L	I	L		N	E	E	D	N	O	T				
A	T	L	A	S		I	O	C		A	S	O	F	
S	H	A	C	K	A	N	D	S	H	A	C	K	I	I
P	E	S	T		L	E	N		S	E	A	L	S	
	L	I	E	T	E	S	T		T	E	T			
B	A	R	T	A	B		D	A	R	T	E	R	S	
A	B	E	I	N	I	L	L	I	N	O	I	S		
B	L	A	N	C		E	A	S	E		B	O	O	S
S	E	D	G	E		A	M	O	S		I	F	F	Y
R	Y	E	S		D	E	N	T		A	F	A	R	

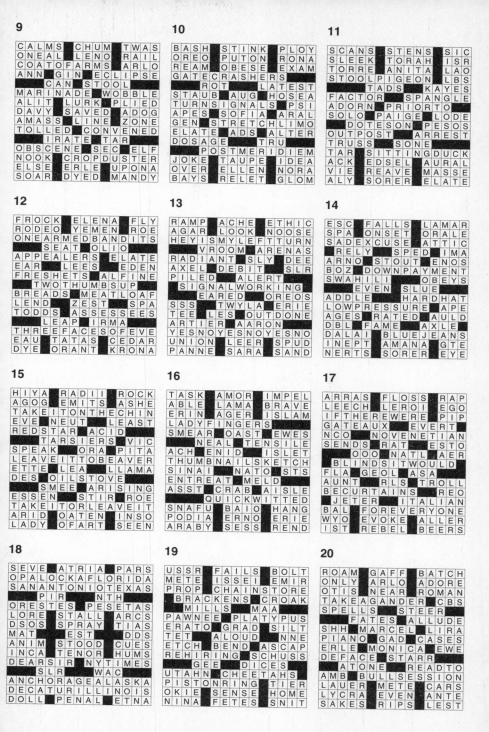

9

```
CALMS  CHUM   TWAS
ONEAL  LENO   RAIL
COATOFARMS    ARLO
ANN   GIN   ECLIPSE
    CAN    STOOL
MARINADE    WOBBLE
ALIT   LURK   PLIED
DAVY   SAVED   ADOG
AMASS   LINE   ZONE
TOLLED   CONVENED
    IRATE   TAR
OBSCENE   SEC   ELF
NOOK   CROPDUSTER
ELSE   ERLE   UPONA
SOAR   DYED   MANDY
```

10

```
BASH   STINK   PLOY
OREO   PUTON   RONA
REAM   OBESE   EXAM
GATECRASHERS
    ROT    LATEST
STAUB   AUG   HOSEA
TURNSIGNALS    PSI
APES   SOFIA   ARAL
GEN   STRETCHLIMO
ELATE   ADS   ALTER
DOSAGE    TRU
    POSTMERIDIEM
JOKE   TAUPE   IDEA
OVER   ELLEN   NORA
BAYS   RELET   GLOM
```

11

```
SCANS   STENS   SIC
SLEEK   TORAH   ISR
TORRE   ANITA   LAO
STOOLPIGEON    LBS
    TADS    KAYES
FACTOR   SPANGLE
ADORN   PRIORTO
SOLO   PAIGE   LODE
DOTESON    PESOS
OUTPOST   ARREST
TRUSS    SONE
TAR   SITTINGDUCK
ACK   EDSEL   AURAL
VIE   REAVE   MASSE
ALY   SORER   ELATE
```

12

```
FROCK   ELENA   FLY
RODEO   YEMEN   ROE
ONEARMEDBANDITS
    SEAT   OLIO
APPEALERS   ELATE
EAR   LEES   EDEN
FRESHETS   ALFINE
    TWOTHUMBSUP
BREADS   MEATLOAF
LEND   ZEST   SPA
TODDS   ASSESSEES
    LEAP   IRMA
THREEFACESOFEVE
EAU   TATAS   CEDAR
DYE   ORANT   KRONA
```

13

```
RAMP   ACHE   ETHIC
AGAR   LOOK   NOOSE
HEYISMYLEFTTURN
    VROOM   ARENAS
RADIANT   SLY   DEE
AXEL   DEBIT   SLR
PILED    ALERT
SIGNALWORKING
    EARED   OREOS
SSS   TWYLA   ERIE
TEE   LES   OUTDONE
ARTIER   AARON
YESNOYESNOYESNO
UNION   LEER   SPUD
PANNE   SARA   SAND
```

14

```
ESC   FALLS   LAMAR
SPA   ONSET   ORALE
SADEXCUSE   ATTIC
RELY   SPED   IMA
ARNO   STOUT   ENOS
BOZ   DOWNPAYMENT
SWAHILI    OBEYS
    EVEN   SLUE
ADDLE   HARDHAT
LOWPRESSURE   APE
AGES   RATED   AULD
DBL   FAME   AXLE
DALAI   BLUEJEANS
INEPT   AMANA   GTE
NERTS   SORER   EYE
```

15

```
HIYA   RADII   ROCK
AGOG   EMITS   ASHE
TAKEITONTHECHIN
EVE   NEUT   LEAST
REDSTAR    ACID
    TARSIERS   VIC
SPEAK   ORA   PITA
LEAVEITTOBEAVER
ETTE   LEA   LLAMA
DES   OILSTOVE
    SMEE   ARISING
ESSEN   STIR   ROE
TAKEITORLEAVEIT
ARID   OATEN   INSO
LADY   OFART   SEEN
```

16

```
TASK   AMOR   IMPEL
ABLE   LAMA   BRAVE
ERIN   AGER   ISLAM
LADYFINGERS
SMEAR   OAST   EWES
    NEAL   TENSILE
ACH   ENID   ISLET
THUMBNAILSKETCH
SINAI   NATO   STS
ENTREAT   MELD
ASST   CRAB   AISLE
    QUICKWITTED
SNAFU   BAIO   HANG
PODIA   ERNO   ERIE
ARABY   SESS   REND
```

17

```
ARRAS   FLOSS   RAP
LEECH   LEROI   EGO
IFTHEREWERE    PIP
GATEAUX    EVERT
NCO   NOVENETIAN
SENDS   RAT   ESTO
OOO   NATL   AER
BLINDSITWOULD
FLA   GEOL   ASA
AUNT   RLS   TROLL
BECURTAINS    REO
JETER   ITALIAN
BAL   FOREVERYONE
WYO   EVOKE   ALLER
IST   REBEL   BEERS
```

18

```
SEVE   ATRIA   PARS
OPALOCKAFLORIDA
SANANTONIOTEXAS
    PIR    NTH
ORESTES   PESETAS
LORE   STALL   ARCS
DSOS   SPRAY   TIAS
MAT   EST   DDS
ANIM   STOOD   CUES
INCA   TENOR   HUMS
DEARSIR   NYTIMES
    SLR   WAC
ANCHORAGEALASKA
DECATURILLINOIS
DOLL   PENAL   ETNA
```

19

```
USSR   FAILS   BOLT
METE   ISSEI   EMIR
PROP   CHAINSTORE
BRACKENS   CROAK
    MILLS    MAA
PAWNEE   PLATYPUS
ERATO   GRAD   SILT
TET   ALOUD   NNE
ETCH   BEND   ASCAP
REHIRING   SCHUSS
    GEE    DICES
UTAHN   CHEETAHS
PISTONRING   TIER
OKIE   SENSE   HOME
NINA   FETES   SNIT
```

20

```
ROAM   GAFF   BATCH
ONLY   ARLO   ADORE
OTIS   NEAR   ROMAN
TAKEAGANDER    CBS
SPELLS    STEER
    FATES   ALLUDE
SHH   MARCEL   LIRA
PIANO   GAD   CASES
ERLE   MONICA   EWE
DEFACE    STARR
    ATONE   READTO
AMB   BULLSESSION
LAUER   METE   CARS
LYCRA   EVEN   ANTE
SAKES   RIPS   LEST
```

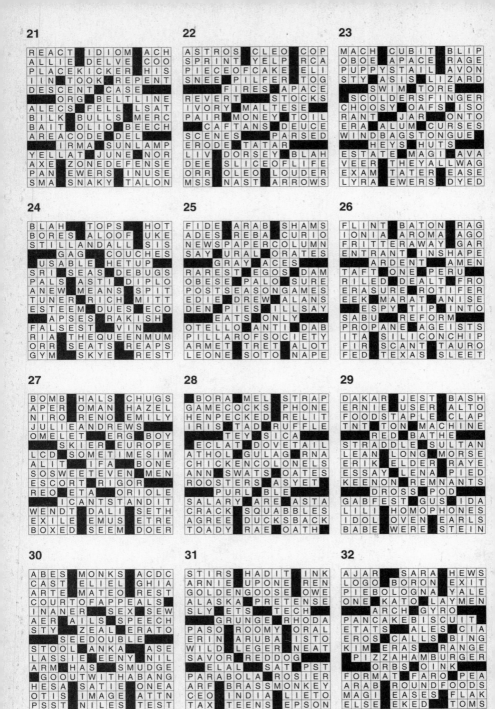

21

```
R E A C T   I D I O M   A C H
A L L I E   D E L V E   C O O
P L A C E K I C K E R   H I S
I I N   T O O K   R E P E N T
D E S C E N T   C A S E
    O R G   B E L T L I N E
A L E C S   F E L L   L S A T
B I L K   B U L L S   M E R C
B A I T   O L I O   B E E C H
A R E A C O D E   D E L
    I R M A   S U N L A M P
Y E L L A T   J U N E   N O R
A X E   Z O N E D E F E N S E
P A N   E W E R S   I N U S E
S M A   S N A K Y   T A L O N
```

22

```
A S T R O S   C L E O   C O P
S P R I N T   Y E L P   R C A
P I E C E O F C A K E   E L I
S N E E   P I L F E R   T O G
    F I R E S   A P A C E
R E V E R T   S T O C K S
I V O R Y   M A L T E S E
P A I R   M O N E Y   T O I L
    C A F T A N S   D E U C E
S C E N E S   P A R S E D
E R O D E   T A T A R
L I V   D O R S E Y   B L A H
D E E   S L I C E O F L I F E
O R R   O L E O   L O U D E R
M S S   N A S T   A R R O W S
```

23

```
M A C H   C U B I T   B L I P
O B O E   A P A C E   R A G E
P U P P Y S T A I L   A V O N
S T Y   A S I S   L I Z A R D
    S W I M   T O R E
S C O L D E R S F I N G E R
C H O O S Y   O A F S   I S O
R A N T   J A R   O N T O
E R A   A L U M   C U R S E S
W I N D B A G S T O N G U E
    H E Y S   H U T S
E S T A T E   M A G I   A V A
V E E R   T H E Y A L L W A G
E X A M   T A T E R   E A S E
L Y R A   E W E R S   D Y E D
```

24

```
B L A H   T O P S   H O T
B O R E S   A L O O F   U K E
S T I L L A N D A L L   S I S
    G A G   C O U C H E S
U S A B L E   H E T U P
S R I   S E A S   D E B U G S
P A L S   A S T I   D I P L O
A N E W   M E A N S   S P I T
T U N E R   R I C H   M I T T
E S T E E M   D U E S   E C O
    A P S E S   R A K I S H
F A L S E S T   V I N
R I A   T H E Q U E E N M U M
O R R   S E A T S   R E A P S
G Y M   S K Y E   R E S T
```

25

```
F I D E   A R A B   S H A M S
A D E S   R E B A   C U R I O
N E W S P A P E R C O L U M N
S A Y   U R A L   O R A T E S
    G R A Y   A C E S
R A R E S T   E G O S   D A M
O B E S E   P A L O   S U R E
P O S T S E A S O N G A M E S
E D I E   D R E W   A L A N S
D E N   P I E S   I L L S A Y
    E A T S   O N L Y
O T E L L O   A N T I   D A B
P I L L A R O F S O C I E T Y
A R M E T   T R E T   A L O T
L E O N E   S O T O   N A P E
```

26

```
F L I N T   B A T O N   R A G
I O N I A   A R O M A   A G O
F R I T T E R A W A Y   G A R
E N T R A N T   I N S H A P E
    A R D E N T   A M E N
T A F T   O N E   P E R U
R I L E D   D E A L T   F R O
E R A S U R E   R O T I F E R
E E K   M A R A T   A N I S E
E S P Y   T I P   I N T O
S A B U   R E F O R M
P R O P A N E   A G E I S T S
I T A   S I L I C O N C H I P
F I R   S C A N T   T A U R O
F E D   T E X A S   S L E E T
```

27

```
B O M B   H A L S   C H U G S
A P E R   O M A N   H A Z E L
N I R O   R E N O   E M I L Y
J U L I E A N D R E W S
O M E L E T   E R G   B O Y
S K I E R   E U R O P E
L C D   S O M E T I M E S I M
A L I T   I F A   B O N E
S O S W E E T E V E N   M E N
E S C O R T   R I G O R
R E O   E T A   O R I O L E
    I C A N T S T A N D I T
W E N D T   D A L I   S E T H
E X I L E   E M U S   E T R E
B O X E D   S E E M   D O E R
```

28

```
B O R A   M E L   S T R A P
G A M E C O C K S   P H O N E
H E N P E C K E D   R E L I T
I R I S   T A D   R U F F L E
    T E Y   S I C A
E C L A T   D O V E T A I L
A T H O L   G U L A G   R N A
C H I C K E N C O L O N E L S
A N N   S W A T S   O A T E S
R O O S T E R S   A S Y E T
    P U R L   B L E
S A L A R Y   A R E   A S T A
C R A C K   S Q U A B B L E S
A G R E E   D U C K S B A C K
T O A D Y   R A E   O A T H
```

29

```
D A K A R   J E S T   B A S H
E R N I E   U S E R   A L T O
F O O D S T A P L E   C L A P
T N T   T O N   M A C H I N E
    R E D   B A T H E
S T R A D D L E   S U L T A N
L E A N   L O N G   M O R S E
E R I K   E L D E R   R A Y E
E S S A Y   L E N A   P I E D
K E E N O N   R E M N A N T S
    D R O S S   P O D
G A B F E S T   G U S   I D A
L I L I   H O M O P H O N E S
I D O L   O V E N   E A R L S
B A B E   W E R E   S T E I N
```

30

```
A B E S   M O N K S   A C D C
C A S T   E L I E L   G H I A
A R T E   M A T E O   R E S T
C O U R T O F A P P E A L S
I N A N E R   S E X   S E W
A E R   A I L S   S P E E C H
S T Y   Z E A L   E R A T O
    S E E D O U B L E
S T O O L   A N K A   A S E
L A S S I E   E E N Y   N I L
A R M   H A S   S M U D G E
G O O U T W I T H A B A N G
H E S A   S A T I E   O N E A
O T I S   I M A G E   A T T N
P S S T   N I L E S   T E S T
```

31

```
S T I R S   H A D I T   I N K
A R N I E   U P O N E   R E N
G O L D E N G O O S E   O W E
A L A S K A   P R E T E N S E
S L Y   E T S   T E C H
    G R U N G E   R H O D A
P A S O   R O O M Y   O R A L
E R I N   A R U B A   I S T O
W I L D   L E G E R   N E A T
S A V O R   R E D D O G
    E L A L   S A T   P S T
P A R A B O L A   R O S I E R
A R F   B R A S S M O N K E Y
C E O   I N D I A   L I E T O
T A X   T E E N S   E P S O N
```

32

```
A J A R   S A R A   H E W S
L O G O   B O R O N   E X I T
P I E B O L O G N A   Y A L E
O N E   K A T O   L A Y M E N
    A R C H   G Y R O
P A N C A K E B I S C U I T
E T A T S   A L E S   C I A
E R O S   C A L L S   B I N G
K I M   E R A S   R A N G E
P I Z Z A H A M B U R G E R
    O R B S   O I N K
F O R M A T   F A R O   P E A
A R A B   R O U N D F O O D S
M A G I   E A S E S   F L A K
E L S E   E K E D   T O M S
```

33

```
HUGS   GETS   BORGE
ETAS   INON   ULCER
ITSWHATYOULEARN
RET ANI    OSLO
ERR  STRETCH  CPA
SLOTH  ENS  OGRES
SYNE  TLC  ARROWS
   ONCEYOUKNOW
BEMOAN  RNA  ONED
ALERT  BED  AMPLE
GIS  CHASERS  RES
   GAIT  ROT ICI
ITALLTHATCOUNTS
REPEL  EWOK  SCOT
SATES  DEWY  SERS
```

34

```
NOTICE  ALF  ATME
EMOTER  LEI  SEAT
WATERMELON  TALE
THEREIN  SALUTES
SAD  ANDS   NATO
   ALEUT  CHEWER
JAMBS  RAWER  ETA
ERIC  MOTHS  SLUG
ELL  BASIE  SUSIE
POKIES  ORSON
GRAS  NEER   DBL
HOLIDAY  ONTARIO
ALAS  COFFEECAKE
RISE  RUE  CREPES
MOSS  ERE  ASSESS
```

35

```
IRR  LAVA  TEMPTS
CEE  IRES  OJIBWA
IMA  GILT  WESSON
EARTHSCIENCE
SKEETER  RETREAD
TERM   OPA   YALE
   PUP  ESSO  REW
WORLDSERIES
RNA  NYET   ALL
PERP   NYE   IAGO
MATISSE  NUZZLED
GLOBETHEATRE
MEMOIR  BRUT  HAS
CLAUDE  RARA  ELS
SITTER  OPUS  ADA
```

36

```
YETI  FLAMER  MGS
AMAN  RELATE  ART
PUBCRAWLING  GAR
AYN   NATALIE
ACCRA  LGE  CINE
GREENTEA  LATEST
TOR   RADIATE
WALKINGTHEDOG
LOOSEST   VAT
ANNALS  TAILPIPE
BEAM  SST  OLDEN
ASTAIRE   ONO
STU  RUNNINGWILD
EER  ASTUTE  ERIE
DDE  STATES  DELE
```

37

```
SHOW  CPAS  UMASS
CAVE  ALSO  PARTY
ORAL  LUIS  TRIED
WILLIAMSAROYAN
TRIP   ODS
CANOES  ATTA  POD
ACED  ELIOT  ABA
THEODOREDREISER
COD  JUICY  NEST
HOY  ITES  PEKOES
ABE   SERB
HONOREDEBALZAC
PERDU  VERB  OEIL
ALERT  EVIL  TADA
NISEI  SAFE  SLED
```

38

```
BRATS   SCI  LST
WRITER  AMOR  ITE
HIGHROLLERS  TEA
ANILE  OLLA  ITEM
MEDES  BILLFOLDS
TAI   ASONE
BABE  DEER  SAJAK
OIL  BOXCARS  ONO
KRAAL  TOTE  FEEL
CRUOR   PAR
POKERFACE  LEAST
RAJA  NCAA  ISSUE
ATA  POTATOCHIPS
DEC  ATEN  WILDES
ORK  WED  LAYER
```

39

```
FEAT   MASH   TAP
OGLED  BATHE  OAR
ROLLOVERBAR  ARE
RADIAL   ASPS
STAIN   STOPIT
CHASSIS  MIDMAY
ARKS  TOAD  PEALE
TIE  CYCLOPS  SPA
ENTRE  KIRI  OTIS
REHASH  PREVENT
ESTATE   AWARE
BACH   REMOTE
ERA  CRACKERJACK
ELK  RISES  SADIE
FOE  ISEE   BODY
```

40

```
MAPS  CAPS  SLURP
ALOE  HEEP  TOTER
CAMERAREADYCOPY
ANODE   PHILIP
WINESAP  NEE  ITS
SAD  DIS   PAUL
PANTS   VINNY
WEAIMTOPLEASE
RANGE   ARRAY
INDO  YES   BOG
PEZ  ASI  ETHANES
OUGHTA   ARENA
PONTIACFIREBIRD
ONEAL  HALO  IDEA
MOSHE  YRLY  EAST
```

41

```
MASTS  DAIS  MESA
SPYRI  ECRU  AMEN
STRINGBEAN  TENS
CERISE   ATRIA
BABYSIT  IVEGOT
TALC  TSETSE  ERE
URALS   MANNA
HEADLETTUCE
SCREE   EQUIP
LIL  HEARST  URNS
ABATED  TAPIOCA
BERET   CLAIRE
ERIE  NOODLESOUP
LIAM  AMOI  SCRAP
SATS  BETA  SEERS
```

42

```
ATRIP  SPA  SITON
PRADO  TRU  TROUT
PICTUREOFHEALTH
AVIATOR   SWELL
LING  ONSITE  FIT
LAG  AFOUL  DARNS
PUT  MIA   SEEK
BOOKOFMATCHES
ELKS  PLO   HAY
RULER  ENDIT  INA
REA  ERASER  ONES
CHAFE   TSETSES
SHOWOFGRATITUDE
TIMER  OBI  ROLLS
SPASM  DIN  ESTES
```

43

```
CHAT  ALE  ARABIC
IONE  COM  DELANO
TAKESTWOTOTANGO
ERASE  ETON  NEAT
UTA   IRISH
PAPALOVESMAMBO
NAH  APE  ILIAD
AGOUTIS  INTENSE
TAMPA  PRO   ITS
ONESTEPATATIME
TAMER   HOG
THEA  ANAT  ONSET
WALTZINGMATILDA
ATHEEL  OAT  TOIL
SHIRES  NNE  EPEE
```

44

```
ERAS  REPAST  IDA
LASH  ANISLE  NIX
URSA  BOTTOM  TEE
DEEPDISHAPPLE
ESTEE   RETIRED
STS  LAST  SACRE
HELLENE  NOEL
BOSTONCREAM
FAIR  ABSORBS
ARRAS  ESSO  RTE
REDCAPS  LEERY
LEMONMERINGUE
TEA  ORIOLE  ONEL
ANN  ATTEST  LATE
JED  NESTED  ALOT
```

45

```
A G A R   E L B A   W A D E D
M A L I   R O A D   A R O M A
B I L L Y R O S E   L E N I N
I T A L I A N S   O R A C L E
    S H E E N   O N R U S H
    L T D   A R S   E R G
A C R I D   R E M I   C R A M
S H I N   T A P I N   O R C A
T A C K   E G A N   D O Y E N
A R K   A P O   G S A
    I N T E N D   C I G A R
D I L A T E   R E A L I Z E D
E V A D E   H A R R Y R U B Y
S A K E S   A P S E   T R E E
I N E R T   W E E D   H E L D
```

46

```
H U M I D   M E S A   O B A D
A T O N E   A G E R   W O R E
S A N D B A G G E R   E R I C
T H A I   T A S T E S   N S A
    L A P A Z   H A Y S E E D
U R I   O L I V E R S T O N E
P A S A D E N A   S T U
S N A G   E S S   M E R E
    E A R   E Q U I P P E D
C H A N N E L S U R F   H M S
R E D T A P E   A I S L E
A R E   T A T T L E   A M E S
Y E L L   S H E L L S T E A K
O B I E   T A R E   T E R R A
N Y E T   S L I D   E X A L T
```

47

```
S T E T   S E L L S   S C A T
L O P E   T R E A T   E A V E
A N I N V E N T I O N U S E D
V I C T I M   G R O U S E R S
      H O W S O   G A S S Y
D O M   L A P   G E N
O B E Y   R I F E   C H A S E
T O W A K E T H O S E O F U S
S E L M A   E A R L   T A M P
      H O D   G U S   R O Y
T O A L L   V E G A S
S A N G U I N E   A G A T H A
W H O H A V E N O B A B I E S
I O N A   E X U D E   L E A K
T E E S   S T E E D   E R R S
```

48

```
A N D Y   F L I C   C U D
L Y R I C   A S C U S   U N O
A C U P U N C T U R E   R T E
M T M   C O E S   R A P T O R
B I S C U I T   P I L E A
    U M A   A L E   C I N E
S O R B   C U R C U L I O
B O C C E   G U M   U L E N E
C U C U R B I T   R I D E
S L U M   E R E   A L A
    P A P A L   C U I R A S S
E R A S E R   N U N C   B A H
T O N   A C C U L T U R A T E
C U T   S U E D E   E A S E D
H E S   B E E T   M E S S
```

49

```
A L T O   B A W L   G I N
B O O E D   A E R I E   A D O
E X P R E S S L I N E   R E O
    B A I L E D   S D A K
    B J O R N   S L U I C E
G R A N A D A   P R A N C E
R E B A   R U D E   A N S E L
A M B   W A N N A B E   T A D
P E E V E   T A T A   E A S E
E N R O L L   S T A R T E R
    W I D E N S   T R E E S
S H O D   G O A T E E
H O C   H A S F I N A L S A Y
I R K   S T E E P   S A U C E
P A Y   T O S S   B E T S
```

50

```
C O U C H   S E R A C   B B S
A L P H A   A R E N A   O L E
P A P E R P R O F I T   R A W
E V E   B E G S   A M A Z E
    R H O N E   R E L A X E D
T S H I R T   R E D Y E
U L A N   O A S E S   S A S
B I N D I N G C O N T R A C T
A D D   C A R E W   A N N E
    F E T E D   R A I S E R
A P R O P O S   B O N D S
A R U B A   P U T T   E O N
R I P   C O V E R C H A R G E
O D E   K N A C K   E X I L E
N E E   S E N S E   R E F E R
```

51

```
S C A D S   S P A   S T R E W
T O N E R   T A B   T R U L Y
E N D P A P E R S   R I N S E
P E S O   A R C   D O D G E S
    S I R E E   I V E
L I N C O L N C E N T E R
B L U T O   S O T   T O R E
E E R   N O G   R A E   R I A
E V E S   W A S   L A T E R
F I S H I N G T A C K L E
    A D E   R E B E L
B A N T E R   A R E   E L M O
E V I T A   G U A R D R A I L
N O N E T   E S T   A G I L E
S N O R E   T S E   G Y R O S
```

52

```
P A N D A   P A N G   G M E N
A L I E N   I S E E   R O L E
S P L A T   A T I T   U R S A
T H E L I O N I N W I N T E R
    O N O   O A T
T H E I C E S T O R M   D A B
E A R T H   H R S   L U G E
N I N E   S P R E E   O B I T
S L I M   C O O   S C A R E
E S E   T H E B I G C H I L L
    A I M   R A H
C O L D C O M F O R T F A R M
A R E A   O R A N   I O N I A
S C A M   Z E R O   C R O N Y
H A N S   E D E N   K A N G A
```

53

```
A T I T   F A R A D   I M U S
F A R R   A L A M O   N A N O
T Y R U S R A Y M O N D C O B
E L E C T   R E A D E   L I B
R O G E R   N A M   A L E
S R S   O M I T   H O L I E R
    E L I S H A   A N D
    W I L L I E M A I Z E
    P A R   S T E R N E
A R L E N E   A N T S   G B S
P U T   E L I   I D I O T
A D Z   H A N G S   D O N H O
T H E L I T T L E K E R N E L
H O R A   E R E C T   M I M I
Y E S M   D O N T S   S E E D
```

54

```
P E S C I   A S A P   T V A D
E V I L S   B E R T   H O M E
Z E T A S   B L A B   E G O S
    R U N O F B A D L U C K
O I L I E S T   R O M E O S
A V O N   A T L A N T A
T I M E D   A G U E   S A S
H E A T O F T H E M O M E N T
S S N   M O O T   N I N N Y
    B I O N I C S   S O I L
C L I E N T   O A K T R E E
D A S H O F P E P P E R
R U L E   A L T O   A I D E S
O R E S   L I E U   T A I N T
M A S T   L E S T   S L E D S
```

55

```
S T O A S   H A R M   G R A D
A E R I E   O N E A   R O V E
G R A D E A M I L K   A M E N
E R N   D U E T   E A T E R Y
R A G G E D   A F O R E
    E R I C   T R I D E N T
D O I N   S C A R   E M C E E
O S H E A   L B O   L O C U S
W H A R F   A T O P   V E N T
D A D A I S M   P E R I
    T R A P P   D E E P E N
D A N I E L   A L A N   R E O
O L E O   M O D E L T F O R D
O M A N   O D D S   A R N I E
M A R X   N A Y S   L O G E S
```

56

```
I D L E   B A T H   B A D
N O O N   E R R O R   T I L E
C O O D E G R A C E   W A V E
A M P   R E A P   C A E S A R
    C I T Y   B E T E
S A S H E S   S I D E T R I P
O B O E S   M A D E   H I D E
F A D E   C A V E D   E D E N
A S A P   O M E N   S A G A N
R E S T O R E D   P U R E L Y
    R U S T   L A S T
T A H I T I   A U R A   W O O
E R I C   C O M M O N C A W S
L I N K   A R I E L   P I L L
L A D   G E N E   A L S O
```

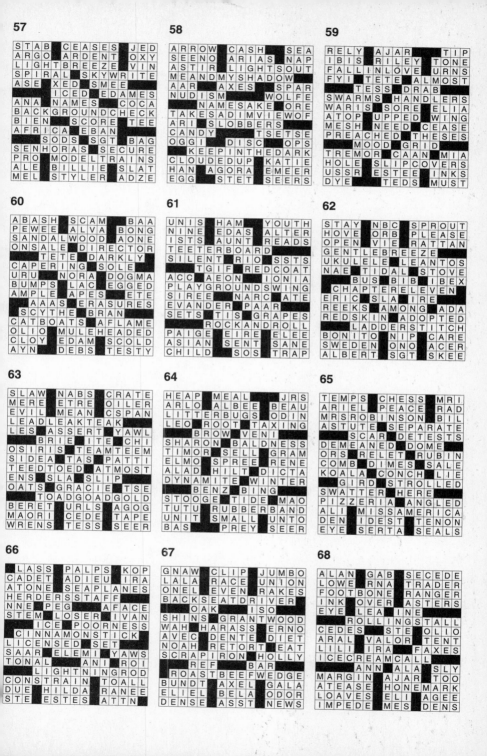

57

```
STAB  CEASES  JED
ARGO  ARDENT  OXY
LIGHTBREEZE   VIN
SPIRAL  SKYWRITE
ASE  XED    SMEE
     ICED  EDAMES
ANA  NAMES   COCA
BACKGROUNDCHECK
BIEN   SCORE   TEE
AFRICA   EBAN
  SODS   SGT  BAG
SENHORAS  SECURE
PRO  MODELTRAINS
ALE  BILLIE  SLAT
MEL  STYLER  ADZE
```

58

```
ARROW  CASH    SEA
SEENO  ARIAS   NAP
ASTIR  LIGHTSOUT
MEANDMYSHADOW
AAR   AXES    SPAR
NUDISM      WOLFE
  NAMESAKE   ORE
TAKESADIMVIEWOF
ARI   SLOBBERS
CANDY      TSETSE
OGGI   DISC   OPS
  KEEPINTHEDARK
CLOUDEDUP   KATIE
HAN  AGORA  EMEER
EGG   STET  SEERS
```

59

```
RELY  AJAR     TIP
IBIS  RILEY   TONE
FALLINLOVE   URNS
FYI   TETE  ALMOST
     TESS   DRAB
SWARMS   HANDLERS
WARIS  SORE   ELIA
ATOP  UPPED   WING
MESH  NEED   CEASE
PREACHED   THESES
     MOOD   GRID
TREMOR  CAAN   MIA
HOLE  SLIPCOVERS
USSR  ESTEE   INKS
DYE   TEDS    MUST
```

60

```
ABASH  SCAM     BAA
PEWEE  ALVA    BONG
SANDALWOOD    AONE
ONSALE  DIRECTOR
  TETE    DARKLY
CAPERING    SOLE
URU   NORA   DOGMA
BUMPS  LAC   EGGED
AMPLE  APES    ETE
  AAAS   ERASURES
SCYTHE     BRAN
CATBOATS   AFLAME
OLIO  MULEHEADED
CLOY  EDAM   SCOLD
AYN   DEBS   TESTY
```

61

```
UNIS  HAM    YOUTH
NINE  EDAS   ALTER
ISTS  AUNT   READS
TEETERBOARD
SILENT  RIO   SSTS
   TGIF   REDCOAT
ACC  AEON   IONIA
PLAYGROUNDSWING
SIREE  NARC    ATE
EVANDER    PAAR
SETS  TIS   GRAPES
  ROCKANDROLL
PAIGE  EIRE   ELEE
ASIAN  SENT   SANE
CHILD  SOS    TRAP
```

62

```
STAY  NBC   SPROUT
HOVE  ORB   PLEASE
OPEN  VIE   RATTAN
GENTLEBREEZE
UKULELE    LEANTOS
NAE   TIDAL  STOVE
   BUS   BIB   IBEX
CHAPTERELEVEN
ERIC   SLA    IRE
REEKS  AMONG   ADA
REDSKIN   ADOPTED
LADDERSTITCH
BONITO  NIP   CARE
SWEDEN  ONO   ACER
ALBERT  SGT   SKEE
```

63

```
SLAW  NABS   CRATE
MERE  ETRE   OILER
EVIL  MEAN   CSPAN
LEADLEAKTEAK
LES   ASSERT  YAWL
   BRIE   ITE   CHI
OSIRIS   TEAMTEEM
SIDEA  TAS   PATTI
TEEDTOED   ATMOST
ENS   SLA    SLIP
OATS  GRACIE   TSE
  TOADGOADGOLD
BERET  URLS   AGOG
MAORI  CEDE   TAPE
WRENS  TESS   SEER
```

64

```
HEAP  MEAL     JRS
ARLO  ALBEE   BEAU
LITTERBUGS   ODIN
LEO   ROOT  TAXING
   BROW    VENI
SHARON   BALDNESS
TIMOR  SELL   GRAM
ELMO  SPREE   RENE
ALAD  HILT   DICTA
DYNAMITE   WINTER
   BENZ    BING
STOOGE  TIDE   MAO
TUTU  RUBBERBAND
UNIT  SMALL   UNTO
BAS   PREY    SEER
```

65

```
TEMPS  CHESS   MRI
ARIEL  PEACE   RAD
MRSROBINSON   BIL
ASTUTE   SEPARATE
   SCAR    DETESTS
DEMEANED     DOME
ORS   RELET  RUBIN
COMB  DIMES   SALE
KOALA  CONCH   LIE
   GIRD   STROLLED
SWATTER     HERE
PIZZERIA   ANGLED
ALI   MISSAMERICA
DEN   IDEST  TENON
EYE   SERTA  SEALS
```

66

```
  LASS  PALPS   KOP
CADET  ADIEU   IRA
ATONE  SEAPLANES
HERDERSSTAFF
NNE   PEG    AFACE
STEM  LOSER   IVAN
  ICE    POORNESS
CINNAMONSTICK
LICENSED     SET
SAAR  ELEMI   YAWS
TONAL   ANI    ROI
   LIGHTNINGROD
CONSTRAIN   TOALL
DUE   HILDA  RANEE
STE   ESTES   ATTN
```

67

```
GNAW  CLIP   JUMBO
LALA  RACE   UNION
ONEL  EVEN   RAKES
BACKSEATDRIVER
   OAK        ISO
SHINS   GRANTWOOD
WAH   HARASS  ERNO
AVEC  DENTE   DIET
NOAH  RETORT   EAT
SCRAPIRON   HOLLY
   REF        BAR
ROASTBEEFWEDGE
BUNDT  AXEL   GALA
ELIEL  BELA   ODOR
DENSE  ASST   NEWS
```

68

```
ALAN  GAB   SECEDE
LOWE  RNA   TRADER
FOOTBONE   RANGER
INK   OVER  ASTERS
EYE   LEA      INE
ROLLINGSTALL
CEDES   STE    OLIO
ARAL  VALOR   TENT
LILI   IRA   FAXES
ICECREAMCALL
   ANN    ALA   SLY
MARGIN  AJAR   TOO
ATEASE  HONEMARK
LOAVES  ELI   AGEE
IMPEDE  MES   DENS
```

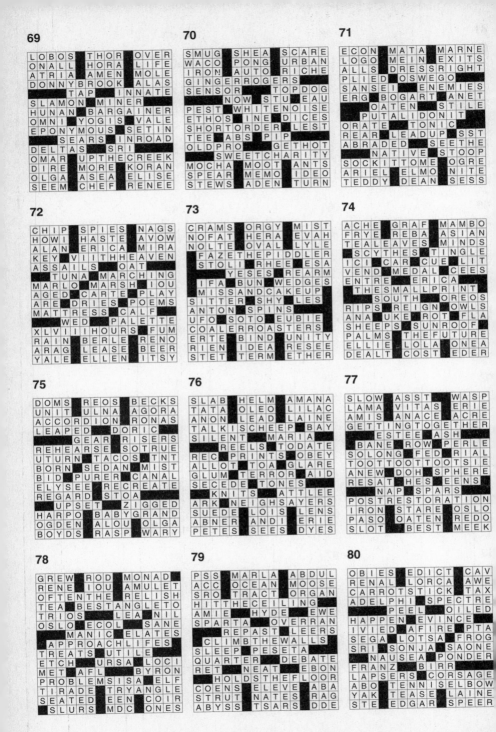

69

L	O	B	O	S		T	H	O	R		O	V	E	R
O	N	A	L	L		H	O	R	A		L	I	F	E
A	T	R	I	A		A	M	E	N		M	O	L	E
D	O	N	N	Y	B	R	O	O	K		A	L	A	S
			T	A	P			I	N	N	A	T	E	
S	L	A	M	O	N		M	I	N	E	R			
H	U	N	A	N		B	A	R	G	A	I	N	E	R
O	M	N	I		Y	O	G	I	S		V	A	L	E
E	P	O	N	Y	M	O	U	S		S	E	T	I	N
			S	E	A	R	S		I	N	R	O	A	D
D	E	L	T	A	S			S	R	I				
O	M	A	R		U	P	T	H	E	C	R	E	E	K
D	I	R	E		M	O	R	E		K	O	R	A	N
O	L	G	A		A	S	E	A		E	L	I	S	E
S	E	E	M		C	H	E	F		R	E	N	E	E

70

S	M	U	G		S	H	E	A		S	C	A	R	E
W	A	C	O		P	O	N	G		U	R	B	A	N
I	R	O	N		A	U	T	O		R	I	C	H	E
G	I	N	G	E	R	R	O	G	E	R	S			
S	E	N	S	O	R			T	O	P	D	O	G	
			N	O	W		S	T	U		E	A	U	
P	E	S	T		W	H	I	T	E	N	O	I	S	E
E	T	H	O	S		I	N	E		D	I	C	E	S
S	H	O	R	T	O	R	D	E	R		L	E	S	T
T	E	E		A	B	S		P	I	P				
O	L	D	P	R	O		G	E	T	H	O	T		
			S	W	E	E	T	C	H	A	R	I	T	Y
M	O	C	H	A		M	O	O	T		A	N	T	S
S	P	E	A	R		M	E	M	O		I	D	E	O
S	T	E	W	S		A	D	E	N		T	U	R	N

71

E	C	O	N		M	A	T	A		M	A	R	N	E
L	O	G	O		M	E	I	N		E	X	I	T	S
A	L	L	S		D	R	E	S	S	R	I	G	H	T
P	L	I	E	D			O	S	W	E	G	O		
S	A	N	S	E	I				E	N	E	M	I	E	S
E	R	G		B	O	G	A	R	T		A	N	E	T
			O	A	T	E	N			S	T	I	L	E
		P	U	T	A	L	I	D	O	N	I	T		
O	R	A	T	E			T	O	N	I	C			
R	E	A	R		L	E	A	D	U	P		S	S	T
A	B	R	A	D	E	D			S	E	E	T	H	E
			N	A	T	I	V	E			S	T	O	O	P
S	O	C	K	I	T	T	O	M	E			O	G	R	E
A	R	I	E	L		E	L	M	O		N	I	T	E
T	E	D	D	Y		D	E	A	N		S	E	S	S

72

C	H	I	P		S	P	I	E	S		N	A	G	S
H	O	W	I		H	A	S	T	E		A	V	O	W
A	L	A	N		E	R	I	C	A		M	I	R	A
K	E	Y		V	I	I	I	T	H	H	E	A	V	E	N
A	S	S	A	I	L	S			O	A	T			
			T	U	N	A		M	A	R	C	H	I	N	G
M	A	R	L	O		M	A	R	S	H		I	O	U
A	G	E	D		C	A	R	T	E		P	L	A	Y
A	R	E		D	R	I	E	S		P	O	E	M	S
M	A	T	T	R	E	S	S		C	A	L	F		
			W	E	D		P	A	L	E	T	T	E	
X	L	V	I	I	I	H	O	U	R	S		F	U	M
R	A	I	N		B	E	R	L	E		R	E	N	O
A	R	A	G		L	E	A	S	E		B	E	E	R
Y	A	L	E		E	L	L	E	N		I	T	S	Y

73

C	R	A	M	S		O	R	G	Y		M	I	S	T
N	O	F	A	T		H	E	R	A		E	V	A	H
N	O	L	T	E		O	V	A	L		L	Y	L	E
F	A	Z	E	T	H	E	P	I	D	D	L	E	R	
S	T	O	L	I		R	H	E	E		E	S	A	
				Y	E	S	E	S		R	E	A	R	M
I	F	A		B	U	N		W	E	D	G	E	S	
M	I	S	S	A	N	D	C	A	K	E	U	P		
	S	I	T	T	E	R		S	H	Y		L	E	S
A	N	T	O	N		S	P	I	N	S				
U	F	O		S	O	T	O		E	U	B	I	E	
C	O	A	L	E	R	R	O	A	S	T	E	R	S	
E	R	T	E		B	I	N	D		U	N	I	T	Y
R	I	E	N		I	D	E	A		R	E	S	E	E
S	T	E	T		T	E	R	M		E	T	H	E	R

74

A	C	H	E		G	R	A	F		M	A	M	B	O
F	R	Y	E		R	E	B	A		A	S	I	A	N
T	E	A	L	E	A	V	E	S		M	I	N	D	S
S	C	Y	T	H	E	S		T	I	N	G	L	E	
I	C	I		C	A	R		C	U	E		L	I	T
V	E	N	D		M	E	D	A	L		C	E	E	S
E	N	T	R	E			E	R	I	C	A			
			T	H	E	S	M	A	L	L	P	R	I	N	T
		S	O	U	T	H				O	R	E	O	S
R	I	P	S		R	E	I	G	N		O	W	L	S
A	N	A		U	K	E		R	O	T		F	L	A
S	H	E	E	P	S		S	U	N	R	O	O	F	
P	A	L	M	S		T	H	E	F	U	T	U	R	E
E	L	L	I	E		L	O	L	A		O	N	E	A
D	E	A	L	T		C	O	S	T		E	D	E	R

75

D	O	M	S		R	E	O	S		B	E	C	K	S
U	N	I	T		U	L	N	A		A	G	O	R	A
A	C	C	O	R	D	I	O	N		R	O	N	A	S
L	E	A	P	E	D		D	O	R	I	C			
			G	E	A	R		R	I	S	E	R	S	
R	E	H	E	A	R	S	E		S	O	T	R	U	E
U	T	U	R	N		T	A	C	O	S		T	N	T
B	O	R	N		S	E	D	A	N		M	I	S	T
B	I	D		P	U	R	E	R		C	A	N	A	L
E	L	Y	S	E	E		R	E	C	R	E	A	T	E
R	E	G	A	R	D			S	T	O	A			
			U	P	S	E	T		Z	I	G	G	E	D
H	A	R	P	O		B	A	B	Y	G	R	A	N	D
O	G	D	E	N		A	L	O	U		O	L	G	A
B	O	Y	D	S		R	A	S	P		W	A	R	Y

76

S	L	A	B		H	E	L	M		A	M	A	N	A
T	A	T	A		O	L	E	O		L	I	L	A	C
A	N	O	N		L	E	A	D		L	A	I	N	E
T	A	L	K	I	S	C	H	E	E	P		B	A	Y
S	I	L	E	N	T		M	A	R	I	A			
			R	E	E	L	S		T	O	D	A	T	E
R	E	C		P	R	I	N	T	S		O	B	E	Y
A	L	L	O	T		T	O	A		G	L	A	R	E
G	L	U	M		T	E	R	R	O	R		A	I	D
S	E	C	E	D	E		T	O	N	E	S			
			K	N	I	T	S		A	T	T	L	E	E
A	R	K		N	E	I	G	H	S	A	Y	E	R	S
S	U	E	D	E		L	O	I	S		L	E	N	S
A	B	N	E	R		A	N	D	I		E	R	I	E
P	E	T	E	S		S	E	E	S		D	Y	E	S

77

S	L	O	W		A	S	S	T		W	A	S	P
L	A	M	A		V	I	T	A	S		E	R	I	E
A	M	I	S		A	N	A	C	E		A	C	R	E
G	E	T	T	I	N	G	T	O	G	E	T	H	E	R
			E	S	T	E	E			A	S	H		
B	A	N	E		R	O	W		P	E	R	L	E
S	O	L	O	N	G		F	E	D		R	I	A	L
T	O	O	T	T	O	O	T	T	O	O	T	S	I	E
A	N	E	W		D	O	H		S	P	H	E	R	E
R	E	S	A	T		H	E	S		E	E	N	S	
			N	A	P		S	P	A	R	S			
P	O	S	T	R	E	S	T	O	R	A	T	I	O	N
I	R	O	N		S	T	A	R	E		O	S	L	O
P	A	S	O		O	A	T	E	N		R	E	D	O
S	L	O	T			B	E	S	T		M	E	E	K

78

G	R	E	W		R	O	D		M	O	N	A	D
R	E	N	E		I	O	U		A	M	U	L	E	T
O	F	T	E	N	T	H	E		R	E	L	I	S	H
T	E	A		B	E	S	T	A	N	G	L	E	T	O
T	R	I	O	S			L	E	A		N	I	L	
O	S	L	O		E	C	O	L		S	A	N	E	
			M	A	N	I	C		E	L	A	T	E	S
A	P	P	R	O	A	C	H	L	I	F	E	S		
T	R	E	A	T	S			U	T	I	L	E		
E	T	C	H		U	R	S	A		L	O	C	I	
	M	E	T		A	F	L		B	Y	R	O	N	
P	R	O	B	L	E	M	S	I	S	A		E	L	F
T	I	R	A	D	E		T	R	Y	A	N	G	L	E
S	E	A	T	E	D		E	E	N		C	O	I	R
	S	L	U	R	S		M	D	C		O	N	E	S

79

P	S	S		M	A	R	L	A		A	B	D	U	L
A	C	C		O	C	E	A	N		M	O	O	S	E
S	R	O		T	R	A	C	T		O	R	G	A	N
H	I	T	T	H	E	C	E	I	L	I	N	G		
A	M	I	E		H	Y	D	E			E	W	E	
S	P	A	R	T	A			O	V	E	R	R	A	N
			R	E	P	A	S	T		L	E	E	R	S
		C	L	I	M	B	T	H	E	W	A	L	L	S
S	L	E	E	P		P	E	S	E	T	A			
Q	U	A	R	T	E	R		D	E	B	A	T	E	
R	E	T		N	E	A	T		E	B	O	N		
		H	O	L	D	S	T	H	E	F	L	O	O	R
C	O	E	N	S		E	L	E	V	E		A	B	A
S	T	R	U	T		N	A	T	E	S		R	A	G
A	B	Y	S	S		T	S	A	R	S		D	D	E

80

O	B	I	E	S		E	D	I	C	T		C	A	V
R	E	N	A	L		L	O	R	C	A		A	W	E
C	A	R	R	O	T	S	T	I	C	K		T	A	X
A	D	E	L	P	H	I		S	P	E	C	T	R	E
				P	E	E	L			O	I	L	E	D
H	A	P	P	E	N		E	V	I	N	C	E		
I	V	I	E	D		A	F	I	R	E		P	T	A
S	E	G	A		L	O	T	S	A		F	R	O	G
S	R	I		S	O	N	J	A		S	A	O	N	E
			N	A	U	S	E	A		P	O	N	D	E	R
F	R	A	N	Z				B	I	R	R			
L	A	P	S	E	R	S		C	O	R	S	A	G	E
A	B	O		T	E	N	N	I	S	E	L	B	O	W
Y	A	K		T	E	A	S	E			L	A	I	N	E
S	T	E		E	D	G	A	R			S	P	E	E	R

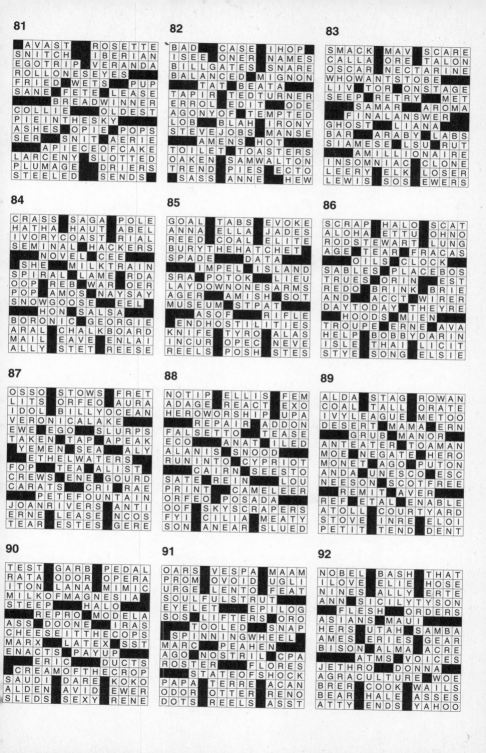

81

```
A V A S T # # R O S E T T E
S N I T C H # I B E R I A N
E G O T R I P # V E R A N D A
R O L L O N E S E Y E S # # #
F R I E D # W E T S # # P U P
S A N E # F E T E # L E A S E
# # B R E A D W I N N E R # #
C O L L I E # # O L D E S T #
P I E I N T H E S K Y # # # #
A S H E S # O P I E # P O P S
S E R # S N I T # A E R I E #
# # A P I E C E O F C A K E #
L A R C E N Y # S L O T T E D
P L U M A G E # D R I E R S #
S T E E L E D # # S E N D S #
```

82

```
B A D # C A S E # I H O P #
I S E E # O N E R # N A M E S
B I L L G A T E S # S N A R E
B A L A N C E D # M I G N O N
# # # T A T # B E A T A # # #
T A P I R # T E D T U R N E R
E R R O L # E D I T # # O D E
A G O N Y O F # T E M P T E D
L O B # B L A H # I R O N Y #
S T E V E J O B S # M A N S E
# # # A M E N S # H O T # # #
T O I L E T # T O A S T E R S
O A K E N # S A M W A L T O N
T R E N D # P I E S # E C T O
# S A S S # A N N E # H E W #
```

83

```
S M A C K # M A V # S C A R E
C A L L A # O R E # T A L O N
O S C A R # N E C T A R I N E
W H O W A N T S T O B E # # #
L I V # T O R # O N S T A G E
S E E P # R E T R Y # # M E T
# # # S A M A R # # A R O M A
# F I N A L A N S W E R # # #
G H O S T # # L I A N A # # #
B A R # A R A B Y # # L A B S
S I A M E S E # L S U # R U T
# # # A M I L L I O N A I R E
I N S O M N I A C # C L O N E
L E E R Y # E L K # L O S E R
L E W I S # S O S # E W E R S
```

84

```
C R A S S # S A G A # P O L E
H A T H A # H A U T # A B E L
I V O R Y C O A S T # R I A L
S E M I N A L # H A C K E R S
# # N O V E L # C E E # # # #
# S H E # M I L K T R A I N #
S P I R A L # L A M E # R D A
O O P # R E B # W A R # O E R
P O P # A M O S # N A Y S A Y
# S N O W G O O S E # E E L #
# # # # H O N # S A L S A # #
B O R O N I C # G E O R G I E
A R A L # C H A L K B O A R D
M A I L # E A V E # E N L A I
A L L Y # S T E T # R E E S E
```

85

```
G O A L # T A B S # E V O K E
A N N A # E L L A # J A D E S
R E E D # C O A L # E L I T E
B U R Y T H E H A T C H E T #
S P A D E # # # D A T A # # #
# # I M P E L # I S L A N D #
S R A # P O T O K # L I E U #
L A Y D O W N O N E S A R M S
A G E R # A M I S H # S O T #
M U S E U M # S T P A T # # #
# # A S O F # # # R I F L E #
# E N D H O S T I L I T I E S
K N I F E # T Y R O # A L A S
I N C U R # O P E C # N E V E
R E E L S # P O S H # S T E S
```

86

```
S C R A P # H A L O # S C A T
A L O H A # E T T U # O H N O
R O D S T E W A R T # L U N G
A G E # T E A R # F R A C A S
# # # O I L S # C L O C K # #
S A B L E S # P L A C E B O S
T R U E S # O R I N # # E S T
R E D O # B R I N K # B R I E
A N D # A C C T # W I R E R #
D A Y T O D A Y # T H E Y R E
# # H O O D S # M I E N # # #
T R O U P E # E R N E # A V A
H E L P # B O B B Y D A R I N
I S L E # T H A I # L I C I T
S T Y E # S O N G # E L S I E
```

87

```
O S S O # S T O W S # F R E T
L I T S # O R F E O # A U R A
I D O L # B I L L Y O C E A N
V E R O N I C A L A K E # # #
E W E # E G O # S L U R P S #
T A K E N # T A P # A P E A K
# Y E M E N # S E A # A L Y #
# # E T H E L W A T E R S # #
# F O P # T E A # A L I S T #
C R E W S # E N E # G O U R D
C A R A T S # C R I # R A E #
# # # P E T E F O U N T A I N
J O A N R I V E R S # A N T I
E R N E # L E A S E # N C O S
T E A R # E S T E S # G E R E
```

88

```
N O T I P # E L L I S # F E M
A D A G E # R E A C T # E X O
H E R O W O R S H I P # U P A
# # R E P A I R # A D D O N #
F A L S E T T O # T E A S E #
E C O # A N A T # I L E D # #
A L A N I S # S N O O D # # #
R U N I N T O # C Y P R I O T
# # C A I R N # S E E S T O #
S A T E # R E I N # L O U # #
P R I N T # C A M E L E E R #
O R F E O # P O S A D A # # #
O O F # S K Y S C R A P E R S
F Y I # C I L I A # M E A T Y
S O N # A N E A R # S L U E D
```

89

```
A L D A # S T A G # R O W A N
C O A L # T A L L # O R A T E
I V Y L E A G U E # M E T O O
D E S E R T # M A M A # E R N
# # # G R U B # M A N O R # #
A N T E A T E R # T O A M A N
M O E # N E G A T E # H E R O
M O N E T # A G O # P U T O N
A N D A # U N E S C O # E S C
N E E S O N # S C O T F R E E
# # R E M I T # A V E R # # #
R E F # E T A L # E N A B L E
A T O L L # C O U R T Y A R D
S T O V E # I N R E # E L O I
P E T I T # T E N D # D E N T
```

90

```
T E S T # G A R B # P E D A L
R A T A # O D O R # O P E R A
I T O N # L A N A # M I M I C
M I L K O F M A G N E S I A #
S T E E P # # # H A L O # # #
# # # R E P R O # M O D E L A
A S S # D O O N E # I R A S #
C H E E S E I T T H E C O P S
M A R X # L A T E X # S S T #
E N A C T S # P A Y U P # # #
# # E R I C # D U C T S # # #
C R E A M O F T H E C R O P #
S A U D I # D A R E # K O K O
A L D E N # A V I D # E W E R
S L E D S # S E X Y # R E N E
```

91

```
O A R S # V E S P A # M A A M
P R O M # O V O I D # U G L I
U R G E # L E N T O # F E A T
S O U L F U L S T R U T # # #
E Y E L E T # # # E P I L O G
S O S # L I F T E R S # O R O
# # T O O L E D # S N A P # #
# S P I N N I N G W H E E L #
M A R C # P E A H E N # # # #
A G O # N O S T R I L # C P A
R O S T E R # # # F L O R E S
# # # S T A T E O F S H O C K
P A P A # T E R R E # A C A N
O D O R # O T T E R # R E N O
D O T S # R E E L S # A S S T
```

92

```
N O B E L # B A S H # T H A T
I L O V E # E L I E # H O S E
N I N E S # A L L Y # E R T E
A N N # S I C I L Y T Y S O N
# # F L E S H # # # O R D E R S
A S I A N S # M A U I # # # #
H E R S # U T A H # S A M B A
A M E S # E R I E S # G E A R
B I S O N # A L M A # A C R E
# # # A T M S # V O I C E S #
J E T H R O # D O N N A # # #
A G R A C U L T U R E # W O E
B R E R # C O O K # W A I L S
B E A R # H A L E # A S S E S
A T T Y # E N D S # Y A H O O
```

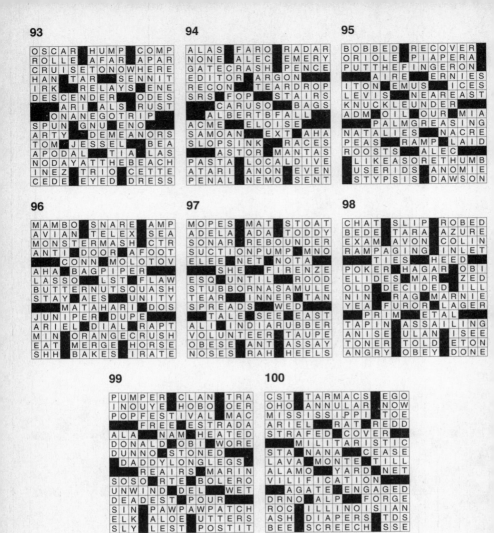

93

O	S	C	A	R		H	U	M	P		C	O	M	P
R	O	L	L	E		A	F	A	R		A	P	A	R
C	R	U	I	S	E	T	O	N	O	W	H	E	R	E
H	A	N		T	A	R			S	E	N	N	I	T
I	R	K		R	E	L	A	Y	S		E	N	E	
D	E	S	C	E	N	D	E	R		O	D	E	S	
			A	R	I		A	L	S			R	U	S	T
	O	N	A	N	E	G	O	T	R	I	P			
S	P	U	N		G	N	U		E	N	O			
A	R	T	Y			D	E	M	E	A	N	O	R	S
T	O	M		J	E	S	S	E	L		B	E	A	
A	P	O	D	A	L			T	I	A		L	A	S
N	O	D	A	Y	A	T	T	H	E	B	E	A	C	H
I	N	E	Z		T	R	I	O		C	E	T	T	E
C	E	D	E		E	Y	E	D		D	R	E	S	S

94

A	L	A	S		F	A	R	O		R	A	D	A	R
N	O	N	E		A	L	E	C		E	M	E	R	Y
G	A	T	E	C	R	A	S	H		P	E	N	C	E
E	D	I	T	O	R		A	R	G	O	N			
R	E	C	O	N		T	E	A	R	D	R	O	P	
S	R	S		F	O	P		S	T	A	I	R	S	
			C	A	R	U	S	O			B	A	G	S
	A	L	B	E	R	T	B	F	A	L	L			
A	C	M	E		E	L	O	I	S	E				
S	A	M	O	A	N		E	X	T		A	H	A	
S	L	O	P	S	I	N	K		R	A	C	E	S	
A	S	T	O	R		M	A	N	T	A	S			
P	A	S	T	A		L	O	C	A	L	D	I	V	E
A	T	A	R	I		A	N	O	N		E	V	E	N
P	E	N	A	L		N	E	M	O		S	E	N	T

95

B	O	B	B	E	D		R	E	C	O	V	E	R
O	R	I	O	L	E		P	I	A	P	E	R	A
P	U	T	T	H	E	F	I	N	G	E	R	O	N
	A	I	R	E					E	R	N	I	E	S
I	T	O	N		E	M	U	S			I	C	E	S
L	E	V	I	S		N	E	A	R	E	A	S	T	
K	N	U	C	K	L	E	U	N	D	E	R			
A	D	M		O	I	L		O	U	R		M	I	A
			P	A	L	M	G	R	E	A	S	I	N	G
N	A	T	A	L	I	E	S			N	A	C	R	E
P	E	A	S			R	A	M	P		L	A	I	D
R	O	O	S	T	S			A	L	E	C			
L	I	K	E	A	S	O	R	E	T	H	U	M	B
U	S	E	R	I	D	S		A	N	O	M	I	E
S	T	Y	P	S	I	S		D	A	W	S	O	N

96

M	A	M	B	O		S	N	A	R	E		A	M	P
A	V	I	A	N		T	E	L	E	X		S	E	A
M	O	N	S	T	E	R	M	A	S	H		C	T	R
A	N	T	I		D	O	O	R		A	F	O	O	T
			C	O	N	N		M	O	L	O	T	O	V
A	H	A		B	A	G	P	I	P	E	R			
L	A	S	S	O			L	S	T		F	L	A	W
B	U	T	T	E	R	N	U	T	S	Q	U	A	S	H
A	E	S			U	N	I	T	Y					
			M	A	T	A	H	A	R	I		D	O	S
J	U	N	I	P	E	R			D	U	P	E		
A	R	I	E	L			D	I	A	L		R	A	P	T
M	I	N		O	R	A	N	G	E	C	R	U	S	H
E	A	T		M	E	R	G	E		H	O	R	S	E
S	H	H		B	A	K	E	S		I	R	A	T	E

97

M	O	P	E	S		M	A	T		S	T	O	A	T
A	D	E	L	A		A	D	A		T	O	D	D	Y
S	O	N	A	R		R	E	B	O	U	N	D	E	R
S	U	C	T	I	O	N	P	U	M	P		M	N	O
E	L	E	E		N	E	T		N	O	T	A		
			S	H	E		F	I	R	E	N	Z	E	
E	S	Q		U	N	T	I	L		R	O	O	D	
S	T	U	B	B	O	R	N	A	S	A	M	U	L	E
T	E	A	R		I	N	N	E	R			T	A	N
S	P	R	E	A	D	S			W	E	D			
			T	A	L	E		S	E	E		E	A	S	T
A	L	I		I	N	D	I	A	R	U	B	B	E	R
V	O	L	U	N	T	E	E	R		T	A	U	P	E
O	B	E	S	E		A	N	T		A	S	S	A	Y
N	O	S	E	S		R	A	H		H	E	E	L	S

98

C	H	A	T		S	L	I	P		R	O	B	E	D
B	E	D	E		T	A	R	A		A	Z	U	R	E
E	X	A	M		A	V	O	N		C	O	L	I	N
R	A	M	P	A	G	I	N	G			I	N	L	E	T
			T	I	E	S			H	E	E	D		
P	O	K	E	R			H	A	G	A	R		O	B	I
E	L	I	D	E	S		M	A	R			Z	E	D
O	L	D		D	E	C	I	D	E	D		I	L	L
N	I	N			R	A	G			M	A	R	N	I	E
Y	E	A		F	U	R	O	R		L	A	G	E	R
			P	R	I	M			E	T	A	L		
T	A	P	I	N			A	S	S	A	I	L	I	N	G
A	N	I	S	E		U	L	A	N		I	S	E	E
T	O	N	E	R		T	O	L	D		E	T	O	N
A	N	G	R	Y		O	B	E	Y		D	O	N	E

99

P	U	M	P	E	R		C	L	A	N		T	R	A
I	N	O	U	Y	E		H	O	B	O		O	E	R
P	O	P	F	E	S	T	I	V	A	L		M	A	C
			F	R	E	E		E	S	T	R	A	D	A
A	L	A			N	A	M		H	E	A	T	E	D
D	O	N	A	L	D		O	B	I		W	O	R	E
D	U	N	N	O		S	T	O	N	E	D			
			D	A	D	D	Y	L	O	N	G	L	E	G	S
R	E	A	I	R	S			M	A	R	I	N		
S	O	S	O		R	T	E		B	O	L	E	R	O
U	N	W	I	N	D		D	E	L			W	E	T
D	E	A	D	E	S	T		P	O	U	R			
S	I	N		P	A	W	P	A	W	P	A	T	C	H
E	L	K		A	L	O	E		U	T	T	E	R	S
S	L	Y		L	E	S	T		P	O	S	T	I	T

100

C	S	T		T	A	R	M	A	C	S		E	G	O
O	H	O		A	N	N	U	L	A	R		N	O	W
M	I	S	S	I	S	S	I	P	P	I		T	O	E
A	R	I	E	L		R	A	T		R	E	D	D	
S	T	R	A	F	E	D		C	O	V	E	R		
			M	I	L	I	T	A	R	I	S	T	I	C
S	T	A		N	A	N	A		C	E	A	S	E	
L	A	V	A		M	O	N	T	E		T	I	L	L
A	L	A	M	O		Y	A	R	D		N	E	T	
V	I	L	I	F	I	C	A	T	I	O	N			
	A	G	A	T	E		E	N	G	A	G	E	D	
D	R	N	O		A	L	P			F	O	R	G	E
R	O	C		I	L	L	I	N	O	I	S	I	A	N
A	S	H		D	I	A	P	E	R	S		T	D	S
B	E	E		S	C	R	E	E	C	H		S	S	E

SATOSHI WAGAHARA
ILLUSTRATED BY 029 (ONIKU)

YEN ON
NEW YORK

THE DEVIL IS A PART-TIMER!, Volume 16
SATOSHI WAGAHARA, ILLUSTRATION BY 029 (ONIKU)

Translation by Kevin Gifford
Cover art by 029 (oniku)

HATARAKU MAOUSAMA!, Volume 16
© Satoshi Wagahara 2016
Edited by Dengeki Bunko
First published in Japan in 2016 by KADOKAWA CORPORATION, Tokyo.
English translation rights arranged with KADOKAWA CORPORATION,
Tokyo, through TUTTLE-MORI AGENCY, INC., Tokyo.

English translation © 2020 by Yen Press, LLC

Yen On
150 West 30th Street, 19th Floor
New York, NY 10001

Visit us at yenpress.com
facebook.com/yenpress
twitter.com/yenpress
yenpress.tumblr.com
instagram.com/yenpress

First Yen On Edition: April 2020

Yen On is an imprint of Yen Press, LLC.
The Yen On name and logo are trademarks of Yen Press, LLC.

The publisher is not responsible for websites (or their
content) that are not owned by the publisher.

Library of Congress Cataloging-in-Publication Data
Names: Wagahara, Satoshi. | 029 (Light novel illustrator)
illustrator. | Gifford, Kevin, translator. | Steinbach, Kevin,
translator.
Title: The devil is a part-timer! / Satoshi Wagahara ;
illustration by 029 (oniku) ; translation by Kevin Gifford.
translation by Kevin Steinbach.
Other titles: Hataraku Maousama! English
Description: First Yen On edition. | New York, NY :
Yen On, 2015–
Identifiers: LCCN 2015028390 |
ISBN 9780316383127 (v. 1 : pbk.) |
ISBN 9780316385015 (v. 2 : pbk.) |
ISBN 9780316385022 (v. 3 : pbk.) |
ISBN 9780316385039 (v. 4 : pbk.) |
ISBN 9780316385046 (v. 5 : pbk.) |
ISBN 9780316385060 (v. 6 : pbk.) |
ISBN 9780316469364 (v. 7 : pbk.) |
ISBN 9780316473910 (v. 8 : pbk.) |
ISBN 9780316474184 (v. 9 : pbk.) |
ISBN 9780316474207 (v. 10 : pbk.) |
ISBN 9780316474238 (v. 11 : pbk.) |
ISBN 9780316474252 (v. 12 : pbk.) |
ISBN 9780316474252 (v. 13 : pbk.) |
ISBN 9780316474252 (v. 13 : pbk.) |
ISBN 9781975302658 (v. 14 : pbk.) |
ISBN 9781975302672 (v. 15 : pbk.) |
ISBN 9781975302696 (v. 15 : pbk.) |
ISBN 9781975302719 (v. 16 : pbk.)
Subjects: CYAC: Fantasy.
Classification: LCC PZ7.1.W34 Ha 2015 | DDC
[Fic]—dc23
LC record available at
http://lccn.loc.gov/2015028390

ISBNs: 978-1-9753-0271-9 (paperback)
978-1-9753-0272-6 (ebook)

1 3 5 7 9 10 8 6 4 2

LSC-C

Printed in the United States of America

THE DEVIL
KING GETS
SENTIMENTAL

From somewhere in the distance, a dog's howl ripped through the shadowy night.

Only a few cars passed down that way, with almost no human figures to be found—not even a stray cat crossing the street.

Step into a side alley from here, and the ambient light visibly dims, the nearby stoplights cycling through their lonely red-yellow-green routine to an empty audience.

At one in the morning, the neighborhood of Sasazuka, in the Shibuya ward of Tokyo, was slowly putting the previous day behind it, settling down to sleep and preparing for the new, upcoming day.

But in the midst of this, a lone figure was crouched over his bicycle, pedaling with an unsteady pace, as if feebly pursuing the past.

He was clearly exhausted, body and soul. Along with that howling dog, the horns from the cars traversing the Koshu-Kaido road, and the knifelike breeze of cold air that dominated the city, the only sounds occupying the night were this man's breathing, the chain of his bike, and the occasional screeching of his rear disc brake.

He took no notice of those sources of noise, even though they were clearly there; but each obstacle stood boldly before him, sapping his already-drained will to continue.

Through it all, the man discovered his home looming ahead

in the darkness, drumming up what little spirit he had left as he pushed down on the pedals. The building was like a shadow itself, completely bereft of human activity, but it was nonetheless his lone island of solace.

He stopped his bike, his breath forming wild, wispy curls in the air, and forced his already-spent body to climb up the building's outdoor staircase. The handrail felt like a cylinder of ice on this cold winter's night, as did the doorknob that greeted him at the top. It felt like winter was designed from start to finish to rob this man of any strength he dared keep for himself.

Now in the hallway, the only sound was the buzzing of a fluorescent light about to breathe its last. Nobody but him was there, and nobody else was beyond any of the doors that lined the walls in greeting.

His numb hands fumbled the key to Room 201 several times before he finally succeeded on getting it into the lock.

The room beyond, as illuminated by the hallway light, was barren. No furniture or fixtures of any sort were visible. The man pulled the cord dangling from the lone light upon the ceiling. It revealed a single pile of clothing in the corner, neatly folded up for him.

"One AM, huh…"

The man looked down at his watch as he removed it, then glanced further, toward the center of the floor. He quickly averted his eyes.

"Let's just sleep. Tomorrow's gonna suck."

He placed the watch into his pocket, then removed his coat and hung it off a hanger set on the windowsill. He shivered a bit, the indoor temperature not much higher than outside, and began to disrobe, changing into a set of sweats he used as pajamas, as quickly as he possibly could.

"Ugh, it's freezing," he muttered to himself as he plugged his phone into its charger. Taking a few steps over to the decrepit-looking kitchen area, he filled a well-worn kettle with water and turned on one of the gas burners. Then, from next to the sink, he picked up something that resembled a tortoise shell. Its lid twisted off. It was a

Japanese hot-water bottle, and once the water was heated up enough, the man quickly filled up the container.

"Oops..."

Wiping away the steaming water that had spilled out from the lip, the man closed the bottle and tucked it inside a handmade-looking cloth pouch.

"This is the only thing saving me right now..."

With that, he unfolded and laid out his futon. A full futon. Not the simple sheets he had been using all summer. An actual mattress, a blanket, even a full-on duvet!

"Nnnhh...... Ahhh...mmph..."

Clutching the hot-water bottle close, the man moaned in pleasure as he burrowed deep inside the brand-new bedding. The fabric of the futon was just as frigid as the air temperature, but between the bottle and his own heat, it ever-so-gradually began to grow warm. However, as much as that combined heat loosened up his body, it could do nothing to open up his tightly wound heart.

Not long ago—not very long at all—this apartment room had been bustling with bright activity. The man had had roommates to live with, a litany of guests to entertain, and between them all, he always had a crowd to deal with around the dinner table. They didn't need a gas heater; the place always felt perfectly warm and cozy to him.

Now, though, he was alone. The table they all gathered around was gone, as were any utensils he could cook with. The refrigerator contained some cucumbers, a cube of *konnyaku* gel, a container of milk, and little else; it was actually colder outside the fridge than inside it, so the man kept it running mainly to keep the milk from freezing.

Nearly everything that had kept this room a warm place in the past was now far, far away. In exchange, the man got this futon.

He had prepared himself for this state of affairs, or so he thought, but now, he could physically feel precisely how unprepared he really was. Nobody was coming to visit. Nobody was waiting up for him. Nobody was cooking. Nobody was calling his name. Everything that was here, only a moment ago—gone.

"Ashiya," the man whispered. "Urushihara. Emi, Alas Ramus, Suzuno."

Only the man himself, curled up in his bedding, could hear his voice.

"Chi..."

The sigh, formed just as his body was warm enough to be comfortable, puffed out into a small, white cloud before dissipating.

"...I might be a little lonely."

The man would have a battle to fight soon. A battle to earn the birthday present he felt he owed his daughter. There would be a god to slay for that, and to prepare accordingly, most of his friends and acquaintances, along with nearly everything he owned, had been transported to Ente Isla, the Land of the Holy Cross. And now that it was all said and done, Sadao Maou was beginning to feel seriously lonesome.

✳

The future of mankind, the fate of the world—none of that mattered more than a lone request from their daughter. Such was the judgment of Sadao Maou and Emi Yusa.

Back when they were strictly the Devil King and the Hero, two presences that could never coexist in harmony, they were greeted with Alas Ramus, a "daughter" who nestled in right between them. The three of them weren't related by blood, and "Mommy" and "Daddy" didn't exactly have the healthiest of relationships, but the bond between parent and child was real nonetheless.

The potential fall of Ente Isla, a destiny that the archangel Laila had spent the past few centuries (a millennium, even) laying the groundwork to prevent, was something that made neither Maou nor Emi bat an eye. Maou, being a demon, had no motivation for rescuing mankind, and apart from being called a Hero in her past, Emi had no duty to play the savior once again. The people around them—those who treasured Emi and Maou in their lives anyway—fully understood that. But no matter what Laila said in a vain attempt to convince them, no matter how much Gabriel (connected to Laila behind the scenes in complicated ways) pushed them in her direction, neither Maou nor Emi felt the need to step up and defend Ente Isla's people. Not the two of them, not Shirou Ashiya, not Hanzou Urushihara, not Suzuno Kamazuki, not even Chiho Sasaki.

But in the end, even after finding this safe, pleasant home in Japan after days of blood, pain, and fighting, all of them (Chiho included) had resolved to throw themselves into the fray, to defeat a figure that was the closest Ente Isla had to a god and also, oh yes, save the planet as a result. There was no lofty ideal behind this, no noble drive to step up and save the world. They had decided to fight strictly because of a single, forlorn little girl, and the simple, modest hope she had for her life:

"I want to see Malkuth. I want to see everyone."

As Alas Ramus was revving up for her first Christmas in Japan, Maou talked with his acquaintances about what to give her as a present. But all she wanted was to see the people from her past again—her old comrades, the friends she held dear, the family she loved. And as a Sephirah, born from the Tree of Sephirot that protected all humanity on Ente Isla, the "everyone" Alas Ramus wanted to see was connected to the battle Laila and Gabriel wanted to wage.

Now all of them—the Devil King, the Hero, and all their friends—were united under a single goal. They had to make the girl's wish come true. They were all ready to risk their lives once again, on a stage with world-changing consequences, all for the sake of Alas Ramus.

✳

"I *do* intend to risk my life for this. Even now."

The shallow light of a winter's morning hit Maou's face through the window, waking him up. His watch told him it was half past six. The sunrises were starting to come earlier again, but the chill he faced outside his futon was still bracing. Because he'd purchased a full futon set, something he swore he would never invest in, the pain of getting *out* of that warm sanctuary every day was beyond description. He had forbidden himself from buying a futon because he feared doing so would root him in Japan too much to return to Ente Isla; now, ironically enough, he was forced into buying one just as he was forced to go back. Abandoning this warm abode and exposing himself to the freezing air surrounding him took an astonishing amount of resolve and courage.

"I'm never gonna get breakfast if I stay in here… Dahhh! Oof!"

Maou was still balled up in the futon, whining to himself, but it was almost time for work. Struggling to find any willpower at all to muster up, he leaped out of the futon.

"Ahhhhh, it's freezing, it's freezing, ugghhh, I'm gonna diiieeee…"

The fatigue, like an aura of haze around him, quickly vanished, but in its place was a sudden rise in blood pressure that made him wonder if heat shock was on the horizon for him. Fumbling around at six in the morning wasn't going to make a heater show up in this apartment, though, so he filled his kettle once more, cupping his hands in front of it as he patiently waited for a fresh hot-water supply.

"I'm sorry, Alas Ramus," he admitted to a daughter who wasn't there. "I think I'm losing my enthusiasm…"

Rubbing his hands and legs against each other, he looked around the empty, almost cavernous-looking apartment, reflecting on how this all happened.

It all began with Ignora, the leader of the angels and the "god" who ruled over heaven, or at least, heaven as pictured on Ente Isla. Reaching her would involve traveling up there, of course, but—due to reasons that still remained murky—heaven was not currently accessible by a direct Gate jump. It wasn't clear whether this was a two-way restriction or only applied when going from a mortal plane to heaven, but it meant the only way to reach the blue orb the angels called their home base was to physically travel there from Ente Isla.

They would need a spaceship, in other words—and this existed in the form of Devil's Castle, the vast edifice built by Maou in the middle of the Central Continent and where he engineered the invasion

of Ente Isla. However, as they recently found, restoring Devil's Castle to spaceworthy shape would require replacing a few parts.

These parts were the so-called relics left by the Devil Overlord Satan. The relics were, in no particular order: the Nothung, a fabled magical sword; the Spear of Adramelechinus, wielded by the late Great Demon General Adramelech; the Sorcery of the False Gold, a tome of forbidden magic; and the Astral Gem, a crystal of concentrated energy whose manufacturing method was lost to time.

Together, they were called the Noah Gears, and Maou's group needed to track down all of them—but apart from knowing that everything except the Spear was in the demon realm, they had zero leads. Camio, Maou's regent who was currently ruling there, was combing every inch of demon land in search of the sword, the tome, and the energy gem, but it would clearly take time to see results.

Meanwhile, over on Ente Isla, a combined team of humans and demons was working to prepare Devil's Castle for launch, as well as search for demon survivors from the war before any hostile humans unwittingly killed them. The human side was led by General Hazel Rumack, hailed as the most influential Western Island leader outside the imperial court of Saint Aile; and Albert Ende, former companion of the Hero. The demons, meanwhile, answered to the young Malebranche tribal leader Farfarello—connected to the Sephirah children, aware of Maou's presence in Japan, and on astonishingly friendly terms with the human Chiho.

Under this trio, the army was working to prepare for this human-demon tandem effort to slay their own "god," under the guise of dismantling Devil's Castle and wiping out the remaining demonic forces. The two species joining hands like this, even if it was just partially and provisionally, would have been impossible to imagine a scant few years ago; seeing it unfold like this indicated what kind of crosstribal peace Ente Isla enjoyed at the moment.

But this peace was both heavily limited and built off extremely personality-driven reasons; just a tiny sliver of nations and people knew the reasons behind it, and spreading the word far and wide would never convince everyone else of its validity. Unless they defeated the god who lived up on her moon world, the holy force that enveloped this world would disappear before long, wiping out humanity. It was far too outlandish a story to swallow in one gulp. Attempting to explain that an angel who appeared in holy scripture had learned of this world's potential end, and that the Hero and the Devil King were working together to help everyone after they had been blown into another world, would make most people wonder about your sanity.

Ente Isla was in the "post-Devil King" era. The rebuilding process was well underway, and every nation was engaged in a power struggle over who'd gain the most advantageous positions in the new world order. If this operation was revealed to anyone not currently a part of it, more than one national power would take it as *humans colluding with demons*—and the fallout would spread worldwide like a flash flood. There were already people who saw the Hero's existence as too much to bear; they already tried to betray her once.

For now, they had enough commanders to work with, considering Ashiya, Urushihara, Suzuno, and Emeralda were all ensuring things went smoothly between humans and demons. The chain of command was working flawlessly as a result, and even if the heavens staged an attack, they had Gabriel and Laila on tap—as well as Ashiya and Urushihara, who had full access to their demonic powers in Ente Isla.

The result of all this was that Sadao Maou and Emi Yusa weren't needed on-site, and therefore unwelcome. Gathering so many powerful figures in a single place tended to attract attention, after all.

Maou had been personally involved with the Western Island's leaders, and with Ashiya's Eastern Island connections, many people from that continent had also joined the army. For similar reasons, Hazel Rumack, head of Saint Aile's palace guard and general commander of the Federated Order, would never want Albert Ende and Emeralda Etuva, the Hero's closest friends, on the Central Continent without good reason. Add the elite troops from the Eastern Island's Knights of the Eight Scarves, and the whole area was already sticking out like a sore thumb.

At the moment, the Eastern and Western Islands were in deliberations, seeking common ground over the East's meddling in the

Central Continent. The Northern and Southern Islands, alongside the numerous smaller nations on the Western one, believed in that pretext—but to avoid attracting curious eyes, Rumack, Albert, Emeralda, and the Eastern knight leaders had taken pains to rotate their schedules, making sure their stays in the Central Continent didn't overlap too closely with one another.

After all, besides the crossplanetary travelers in Suzuno and Emeralda's party, the only people from the East who were in on the story were the Azure Emperor and a handful of generals among the Eight Great Scarves forces who served him. In the Western lands, that group consisted of the palace guards under Rumack, the sorcerers in the Holy Magic Administrative Institute, and a few clerics with the Reconciliation Panel; it didn't include the leader or crown prince of Saint Aile, or any of the Six Archbishops, who wielded decision-making power in the Church. The Northern and Southern Islands, meanwhile, were completely out of the loop.

In this situation, having someone like Emi (whose face was too well-known) or Maou (who'd have hordes of demons falling to their knees in supplication whenever he passed by) hanging out there would simply get in the way. As Suzuno Kamazuki, chief logistics lady at the site and a woman who had clout with the East, the West, humans, and demons, put it: "I will call for you when I need you. Until then, live in Japan as you always do. Chiho has college examinations awaiting her next year; this is a vital time for her. To a high school senior, a round trip of one hour and twenty minutes is nothing to sniff at. We cannot afford to make her travel away from her school and her job too frequently. I will not demand she stop visiting, but as it was in Room 201, there is a certain line that needs to be maintained. Plus…"

She gave Maou a smile, one that seemed to chide him despite the gloomy air surrounding it.

"I am sure you being in Japan would help calm Chiho."

Maou wanted to say a lot about that but couldn't find the words to counter her. He was, at first, reluctant to have Chiho come to Ente Isla to back him and Emi up. She was certainly involved with Ente Isla now, of course, but Chiho lacked the strength to fight, and the idea of taking a high school teen to a battle that could decide the fate of worlds filled him with anxiety. What surprised him, though, was how no one was against Chiho making the trip. If anything, they welcomed her.

"I wanted to have her come here sooner or later!" Emi effused.

"Indeed," Suzuno replied. "I was hoping I could give her a tour of my hometown."

"If we have the tiiime, she simply muuust see the imperial seat of Saint Aiiile, too…"

Ashiya, standing alongside Urushihara, shrugged. "Well, why not? Apart from the angels, there is no one on Ente Isla who would wish harm upon her. As long as she doesn't stray too far from Devil's Castle, we and the Malebranche can keep her safe enough."

"Yeah, what's the big deal, dude?" Urushihara chimed in. "It's not like Chiho Sasaki's stupid or anything. If we tell her *Don't go anywhere dangerous*, she'd be smart enough to follow that."

In fact, it turned out that Maou had nothing to worry about. Once he'd brought the Earthling to Ente Isla, Hazel Rumack had made sure Chiho always had a guard with her—a suggestion from Emeralda, perhaps. Even Farfarello was eager to bodyguard her, for reasons that Maou assumed he hadn't been around to witness. In a way, all this attention almost made Chiho a tad uncomfortable. Plus, in the end, Emi's need to keep her identity on the down-low meant she was often working alongside Chiho anyway. The girl didn't have just an iron wall of protection; it was more like a full-on fallout shelter.

By this time, Chiho had fallen into a regular routine—crossing worlds via Room 201 with some food and other provisions; chatting with the demons and humans she was close with, then returning to Sasazuka before it grew too late. It was really Maou who had problems to deal with. The main one: that forty-minute-long journey each way that Suzuno mentioned. With Maou's current living situation, it was a pretty big burden.

"Maybe I better head back for today… My shift ends at six…but, ah, if I go to the bathhouse and stuff, it could wind up being more like nine…"

Emi had always been living by herself in Eifukucho, as did Suzuno in Room 202. But Maou had roomed with Ashiya since the very start, splitting up chore duties in Japan under a system designed with perfect precision by Ashiya. At the moment, Ashiya was busy leading the demons and Eight Great Scarves knights in Ente Isla, and his base of operations was there anyway, so if Maou wanted any domestic contribution from him, he'd have to travel to his apartment from work, then take the forty-minute journey across the Gate. With as many acquaintances around Sasazuka as he had now, Maou couldn't say who might see him if he opened a Gate in the middle of town instead of returning home first.

This made Maou's schedule maddeningly complex. The journey between his job at the MgRonald near Hatagaya Station and Villa Rosa Sasazuka was five or six minutes by bike, fifteen on foot—fairly close, and Maou structured his work shifts to take advantage of this. It let him pull off power moves like back-to-back closing and opening shifts. But when another forty minutes of commuting was added to this, then suddenly, the schedule turned into a gauntlet.

If Maou was closing at MgRonald, the absolute earliest he could reach his apartment was twelve forty at night. If he went on a Gate cruise, he'd be at Ente Isla at one twenty AM Japan time—and presuming he ate dinner and so on, he'd likely get to sleep around two. But if he was opening the next day, he had to be at MgRonald no later than six thirty. It meant he'd have to sleep at two, then wake up at five if he wanted time to eat breakfast and make the long Gate crossing. What's worse, being a demon (which he was, regardless of whatever human form he took on Earth), he couldn't rely on an angel's feather pen to open a Gate, like Chiho and Rika could. If that feather pen allowed them a first-class bullet-train seat to Ente Isla, Maou had to take the highway route on a rickety old beater car—and much like driving a car, he had to stay alert while the Gate spell was active. No napping was possible on the way.

So basically, there were dates on Maou's schedule that made it all but impossible to return to Ente Isla between shifts. On nights like those, if he wanted to eat dinner, he'd have to use the MgRonald employee discount, grab something from the twenty-four-hour convenience store, or use the few cooking tools that hadn't been taken to Ente Isla and attempt to cobble something together.

"I've got so much laundry to do…" Maou sized up the pile of clothes on the floor, then he checked the clock as he recalled the current contents of his wallet. "Crap. I don't want to waste the money, but I guess I gotta hit the Laundromat…"

Ashiya's absence didn't just affect his daily habits; it made every chore impossible to organize.

Maou had planned to clean when the place screamed for it, but since work and Ente Isla came first, it wasn't long before a fine layer of dust had settled on the bathroom floor, the windowsills, and the spaces between the kitchen's wood paneling. Thanks to his long shifts, it was hard to find the time to dry the laundry at home, too, so he had come to rely on the dryers at the Laundromat once the pile grew impossible to tame.

He knew from his early days in Japan that this was a decadent luxury; he could practically hear Ashiya admonishing him with every 100-yen coin he tossed into the dryer.

Emi, his rival, was less of a threat now. No human or angel could best him, and he had fully regained his demonic force. To Satan, the Devil King, the world was his oyster—but to Sadao Maou, the human being, life felt oppressively constricted.

But what was Chiho doing? Chiho, a girl he figured would help out on the food and cleaning front? Maou had actually forbidden her from hanging out at Room 201, apart from when she used the Gate. The reason, of course, was that Maou's residence was a literal man cave.

Chiho had become a frequent visitor, motivated by her feelings for Maou, after Urushihara and Suzuno moved in. To her, Room 201 was not just Maou's home, but also the place where a lot of her friends hung out, which was the main reason she was there all the time. Now that it was Maou and Maou alone, things were different. Room 201 had always been an entirely male domain, but Suzuno had been right next door, and the paper-thin walls ensured she could hear everything. Now, however, Maou was usually the only person in the entire building—and having a teenager in a high school uniform regularly visiting a part-timer living alone in his crappy apartment was not really something modern society would smile upon. She had, in fact, already been called to task about this, based on the sensibilities that ruled in modern Japan.

Thus, whenever Maou was forced to let Chiho head to Ente Isla, he established the rather mean-spirited condition that the two of them should never be alone together in Room 201. If she had to use a Gate, she could either work with Suzuno and Emi to make one in Villa Rosa Sasazuka or do it in her own room instead. This exasperated their friend circle—why *that* attitude, at *this* point?—but Maou doubled down on it, and Chiho had meekly accepted it.

"I guess it's important, huh? Making…distinctions like that."

The statement, delivered with a straightforward smile, gave Maou a guilty conscience—perhaps because he never got around to making the "distinctions" he should have made a long time ago.

Still, it wasn't like he was totally cut off from Ashiya, Urushihara, Suzuno, Nord, or Laila. Ashiya had too many responsibilities to come home very easily, but Suzuno and Urushihara swapped taking trips back to Earth every two or three days. She had even begun setting up a vegetable garden in the backyard, when he wasn't paying attention. Suzuno or Nord would also come home to babysit Alas Ramus whenever Emi—now a prime contributor to MgRonald at Hatagaya, despite cutting down her hours a bit—had a particularly long shift.

But despite that, Maou was now facing many more days than before where he never talked to anyone outside the restaurant. It made him realize all the more exactly how blessed he had been, with all the kindness his friends gave him.

And so morning came, about a month into this new life of living alone, incomparably quieter and more barren than his life before.

"Maou! Maou! Heeyyyy!!"

"…" Maou winced at the merciless knocking on the front door, cursing it in his mind.

"You are going to the training again in afternoon, no? Starting when?!"

"...I'm working through the lunch rush, so one PM."

He had half muttered the words, but the woman on the other side had superhearing at times like these.

"Yahoo! If I ask Mikitty for early lunch, I have enough time! Today, I go to new all-you-can-eat restaurant!"

"...Yeah, great."

"See ya!"

The presence in the hallway loudly drifted off, never getting to see how badly Maou twisted up his face.

"I seriously wanna punch the dude who created this whole 'latent force' system."

Thanks to assorted circumstances, there was one person who still loomed just as large in Maou's life—Acieth Alla, a woman who didn't have the words *modesty* or *concern* in her dictionary. He could imagine her briskly smiling, imagining the culinary delights waiting at this new eatery. He hadn't eaten anything yet, but his stomach already felt heavy.

Upon finishing his MgRonald shift at one, Maou took the Keio Line to Shinjuku, in the heart of Tokyo. As he walked to the site for his full-time staffer training, he spoke up to Acieth, who was fused back inside him.

"So how was the all-you-can-eat place?"

"Huh? You will take me to it again?"

Maou still had trouble grappling with Acieth's leaps in logic. It was usually Miki Shiba, landlord of the Villa Rosa Sasazuka he stayed at, who took her around—why was it "again" for him?

"..."

"Just kidding! Come on, I am just the kidding! Maou! You need broader heart!"

Acieth must have picked up on how frayed his heart was, because she tried (and failed) to make up for her words quicker than usual. She was, after all, one of the biggest reasons why he couldn't keep a broader heart. She was as gluttonous as always, she never demonstrated a care in the world about him, she didn't try to hide her conniving side, and it was impossible to tell what she'd do next.

Waging this god-slaying battle to make Alas Ramus's dream come true was a good thing for Acieth as well, being Alas Ramus's younger sister. But Maou was stressed out. If it was Acieth who had crashed into his yard in that golden apple instead of Alas Ramus, he doubted he'd ever have adopted a father-daughter relationship with her, much less accept Laila's plea. Apart from their faces, there was nothing alike about the two sisters.

"*So you know, the restaurant, it was mainly about the meats.*"

"An all-you-can-eat meat deal? Wait, did you go to a *yakiniku* place for lunch?"

Fused like this, Acieth's voice could be heard only in Maou's mind and to nobody else. Maou, meanwhile, had to actually speak to get his words across, so an impartial observer could marvel at the disturbing sight of a young man in business attire mumbling incoherently to himself.

Maou's face had taken on a dour look as of late, besides. If he didn't have his phone to his ear like he did now, pretending to talk to someone, he'd likely be put in a facility long before the police got involved.

"*Uh-uh. The all-you-can-eat* yakiniku *near us, they say I eat too much. They ban me.*"

"Seriously?"

Maou wasn't aware of this, but whenever Acieth joined Amane Ohguro (her usual caretaker at the moment) at a place like that, the manager would usually have to intervene once she started treating it like an eating contest on TV. If someone with Acieth's voracious appetite went all-out at a *yakiniku*, Maou couldn't blame the place for booting her.

"*Mostly, they have big metal skillet, and they cook the steak and the sirloin. If you pay more, then drinks and salads and soups and curries and desserts, they are all free.*"

"Wow, not only drinks and soups but all that, too? That's brave of them. Do they give you any rice?"

"*Oh, yes! All-you-can-eat rice.*"

"Huh. Remember the name of the place?"

"The name? Um, what was it? It was maybe Big Guy? Or Giant Boy? *...But why you ask so sudden? Normally, when I eat, you say, 'Oh, it is the bad manners, it is bad for wallet.'"*

"Just one second."

Maou lowered his phone and used it to search for the place Acieth mentioned, relying on her vague memory of the all-you-can-eat curry location for his keywords. He found the chain restaurant in short order.

"Oh, here? So if you pay extra, you get free drinks and an all-you-can-eat buffet for salad, the soup of the day, curry, and desserts. Hmm... Too bad. I like the price, but this is more a diner than anything."

"What is it you mean?"

"A few people in my training program are talking about a get-together sometime soon. We haven't settled on a date yet, but we're starting to toss candidates for a location around, so I'm looking for places we can go to."

"Eww." Acieth sounded disgusted. *"Too much work. A get-together like that, it is all* Oh, pour beer for boss, Oh, let boss berate you in front of friend, Oh, let coworkers who are only good at the sucking-up-to-boss run all over you, *then* Oh, blackout on the sake you can't drink, *and then coworker says* Oh, you are the wimp *the next day, yes? It is the waste of precious time, yes?"*

"Where did you take all that from?" Maou shook his head, the pace of his walk slowing down. "Stop sounding like Urushihara if you don't even know what you're talking about. Get-togethers like this, you never know how they might help you out down the line. I might wind up sharing office space with some of these guys later on, so unless you wanna get on their bad side, it never hurts to hang out and have a drink."

"It is what you say, but you are not so, ah, enthusiastic, yes?"

"...I'll partly admit that."

It was rare to hear Maou sound unmotivated about work. He knew that, in this fused state, Acieth could partially pick up on what he felt, although it wasn't some kind of full-on telepathy trick.

"I mean, you see lots of different trainees attend these classes. You got people with customer-facing jobs like me, you have people from the bun manufacturing plants, you got hires from other companies, and you got brand-new guys brought on to lead new locations, which means I have to do a bunch of on-location training, even though I know it by heart. So we're all talking about going out some evening."

"*Hmm.*"

"And I do want to talk to people from our rival chains and the processing plants. One of 'em used to serve in the Japan Self-Defense Forces, and he's still young, but I'm kinda curious about what his life's been like. But... I dunno. I think this get-together isn't gonna work like that."

"*Why not?*"

"Well, the guy who suggested it is this dude in his midtwenties, from a region the Hatagaya location isn't part of, and it's like...he's not really hiding it, you know?"

"*No? You are being the not very specific. It is strange.*"

"I mean, you can tell he's aching for a fast-track career. He's always one of the first to speak up in when working in a group. It's like he wants to lead, and everyone else needs to follow. And he suggested this meetup, too, even though we've only shared a classroom a few times and the attendee list changes a lot. I guess what I'm saying is... for all the bark he gives you, there's not a lot of bite, you know?"

That was just it. This man had a tendency to act like the able leader in any group he was in, even though his skills were decidedly on the average side. People were already starting to shun him a little for that, and even Maou had to admit he wasn't too good with that type of person. But he wasn't *incompetent.* As Maou's beloved boss, Mayumi Kisaki, put it, "A salaried employee is asked for more than merely their strengths on the front lines." Here he was, after all, trying to break the ice and help all these trainees from different regions and professions to work together. The larger the firm you worked for, the more vital those kinds of skills became.

"*So what is big problem with it? You understand his reasons, yes?*"

"Sure. Assuming breaking the ice really is his sole motivation."

"*Huh?*"

"There's someone else in our group. A sort of young girl. You've seen her a few times..."

"*Whaaa?! You found another of the sacrifice for you, Maou?!*"

"*...*"

"*...Oh, don't be mean,*" Acieth sulked. "*I know. It was Kusunoki, or Masashige, or something close.*"

"Kusuda. Her name's Kusuda."

Being fused with Maou during training, Acieth was at least casually familiar with everyone Maou met there.

"It's totally obvious this guy, our team leader, wants to get closer to Kusuda. Like, when we're working in a group and stuff, he's practically stuck to her like glue."

"*Oh, so that man organizing party, he likes this Kusuda? Who was he? Ashikaga, or Godaigo, or something?*"

"...Nitta. His name's Nitta. If you don't know someone's name, don't go spitting out anything that comes to mind."

Acieth's suggestions sounded a lot like the names of famous old samurai. Maou began to wonder what kind of media she consumed at Shiba's place all day.

"*Well, Nitta, he is poor judge of women! I can tell, that Kusuda, she plays poor, innocent little girl type! You first look at her, she is kind of mature, like Chiho, but she is just good at the buttering-up of you! You know, I saw Kusuda in training center bathroom, and she was giving someone the bad mouth in there! Chiho, she never does that!*"

"You saw her *where?*" Maou was taken aback. Several major revelations were packed into that statement.

"*You know, the second class! You say 'Oh, I cannot concentrate when you do this carrying on,' so we separate. Then, you give me money to go eat. So I walked around training center a little...*"

"Why did you do *that*...?"

He did vaguely remember something like that. They were holding staff interviews that day, way up in the same building Maou took his MgRonald Barista training in. It was the kind of place filled with nothing but salarymen in business suits, so a silver-haired, violet-eyed preteen was going to stand out a bit.

"Right, well, between this, that, and the other thing, I'm not too enthusiastic about the meetup, no. I feel like it's all just a pretext, you know?"

"But you say it is vital, no? Because you do not want to be the bad side with them, and all?"

"…Kinda." Maou shrugged at having his words bounced back at him.

"But you know what it is, Maou?"

"What?"

"If you are the talking to me about all of it, it must bother you great deal, huh?"

"…!"

Maou stopped. He was at the west exit of JR Shinjuku Station in the afternoon, a fairly crowded place to stand motionless. Several passersby gave him dirty looks as they shoved their way around his side.

"Emi and Chiho, they don't come to apartment too much lately, and Ashiya and Lucifer and Suzuno, they don't come back much, either. You are that lonely?"

Had he weakened to the point that even Acieth was pointing it out to him? Was it that bleedingly obvious? Or could you describe this as being "weakened" at all?

To be sure, Maou's life had changed a lot, starting around the new year. People and things he normally took for granted were gone from sight. But as Acieth just hinted at, they hadn't completely vanished. He saw Emi and Chiho all the time at work, Urushihara and Suzuno came home on regular occasions, and he maintained close contact with Ashiya. Sometimes, Maou went over to Ente Isla himself, even. Things had only been like this for about a month—but did Acieth really feel *that* compelled to speak up after looking at his work and his personal feelings? It seemed impossible to imagine.

"…Well…"

"Mm?"

"To be honest, I'm getting pretty sick of takeout."

"Oh, be more honest!"

Acieth seemed to almost enjoy the desperately bold front Maou attempted to put up. These changes were, frankly, tiny in the great scheme of things. Compared to the first few days after losing to Emi and getting thrown into Japan, they were nothing. But it was only human to feel stressed out over sudden environmental changes.

Maou had put a firm deadline of "Alas Ramus's birthday" on their god-slaying battle. It was already early February. If things went the way Maou pictured them, it'd all be settled in less than five months. Of course, that was a lofty goal; they hadn't found any Devil Overlord relics yet, and once they reached heaven, there was a long hit list of targets up there. Nobody had any idea what kind of battle awaited. But Maou had promised his "daughter" that the Christmas present he couldn't obtain would be her birthday present instead.

So with all that fighting to do and promises to keep, why was he letting *this* run him down?

"You are no good as Devil King."

"Stop talking to me like you're reading my mind," Maou said as he began to walk again. "But I guess I am overreacting a little. Sorry."

"Well, I feel fine, and Mikitty, she lets me eat lots of the delicious things, so I never get sick of takeout. But..."

"Mm?"

"Don't you think your guard, it is being let down too much?"

"My guard?"

"Yes! I know that everyone, they work at Ente Isla, and you and Emi are on standby here, but the angels, none of them said Oh, we will be doing the nothing, *yes?"*

"Well, yeah, but..."

"Mikitty and Amane, they are strong, so maybe the angels do something under the covers, hiding from them? You know, those little stinkers!"

After learning the whole story behind them, Maou knew full well that Acieth's negative assessment of the angels was absolutely right. It chagrined him a little.

"And you know, Suzuno, she is not home very often. Are you think-ing about safety of Chiho? You cannot trust words of Gabriel, ever!"

"We're all good there. I had him tell me about the security net built around Chi's place. If she's around there or in Sasahata North High School, and a non-Earth-based source of holy or demonic force appears, the net sends out a distress sonar that covers a radius of over a mile. Me, Emi, and Amane have worked things out so at least one of us is always in the area. If something goes awry, we can respond in a flash."

"A sonar with a radius of over a mile? Won't that annoy neighbors?"

"Nah, it's not at a frequency that normal people can hear. It's basi-cally a big barrier—a simple reactionary sonar, so even if it goes off, it'll be kind of like a buzzing sound to Chi. And if she's out of range, I told her to let me, Emi, Suzuno, or Amane know first."

"...Hmm."

"What? You got a problem with that?"

"No," a dubious Acieth replied, looking more dissatisfied every second. *"If you and Chi are okay, then hunky-dory, but..."* She began to choose her words more carefully. *"But I wonder, is Chi really okay with it?"*

"She said it'd put her mind at ease."

"Oh, no, no good."

"What do you mean by that?!"

"I mean just what I say. We are close to destination, yes? I am full for today, so I will nap and be quiet, okay? See ya!"

"Wh-whoa! Acieth! What are you talking about...? Hey, are you really asleep?"

Maou could sense Acieth's presence vanish, like a snap of one's fingers. He flipped shut his phone, which had never been on a call anyway, and sighed.

"...Come on."

He didn't need it spelled out for him. He knew full well: Laila said it, Ashiya said it, and Suzuno thrust it in front of his face. Plus, Chiho herself said it to him again. But he didn't know how to give an answer, and that made everything he did with her seem vague, and not quite fully there. Or was it? He didn't know.

Going back to the previous example, there really weren't many methods Maou had at hand to guarantee Chiho's safety at the moment. The best he could do was have a system where he'd receive instant alerts if something came up, but he knew that wasn't what Acieth meant—and having Acieth doubt him only made him angrier.

"You say that, but…what am I supposed to do…?"

The moment Chiho first admitted her love for him, Maou managed to keep his cool under the hot summer sun. Internally, he was torn, but Chiho had nothing but love to offer him, nevertheless.

And as he stewed over this, a man and a woman passed him by, holding hands. Lovers, no doubt, in the midst of a relationship. He had thought, at one point, that going around together like that was what Chiho pictured for the two of them. The past few months, however, had dissuaded him of that. Simply building a close kinship with Maou was not enough to satisfy Chiho. It wasn't that she *didn't* want such a thing, but if that's really all there was to it…

"…I could've had an answer for her more quickly," he whispered to himself as he walked through the doorway of his destination.

"Oh, Maouuu!"

He heard his name called, with a tempo and intention that seemed to at least imitate Chiho's, and looked up.

"Good morning, Kusuda."

Kusuda jogged up to him. Maou didn't recall her first name.

"Did you think of any place good for the meetup Nitta mentioned?"

"…Nah, not really. We'd all be coming from different places, so I know it's pretty obvious, but somewhere around Shinjuku's probably best."

"You're right. We don't have the contact info for all the trainees yet, either…"

This training session was populated by a motley crew of students from assorted fields, but between the shifts they all had to work at their respective MgRonalds, it wasn't like every student attended the same classes. Since the teachers hadn't said just how many students were in this session, this meetup was de facto limited to the people that Nitta, as organizer, had met enough times.

"If you ask me," Kusuda continued, "I think it's still kind of early to hold an after-hours meetup like this, huh?"

"Oh, maybe, but if the opportunity comes up, I don't think it's a bad thing, per se."

"Yeah, maybe you're right, but I think we'd get to know each other well enough while we work and train together, like we're doing now. I gotta admit, I feel like Nitta's treating this like a college frat welcome party, like *Let's get together and all be friends!* He's, like, all over me, you know?"

She sees right through you, Nitta, Maou said in silent prayer. He wasn't sure if Nitta was scheduled for today's session or not, though.

"Oh! By the way, Maou, while I've got you, I'd like you to have this."

"Huh?"

Maou looked at the thing Kusuda offered him and raised an eyebrow. It was a small box with cute wrapping paper and a ribbon on top.

"What's that?"

"Aww, can't you tell? It's some chocolate!"

"Huh? Chocolate? Oh, for Valentine's?"

Only then did Maou realize what Kusuda meant. Today was February 7—a bit early for Valentine's Day activities, but if you weren't sure whether you'd see your target on the big day or not, the timing wasn't too unnatural. Besides, in Japan, women often gave little Valentine's gifts like this to men in their lives out of politeness more than anything else. Nothing really deep was meant by it.

"Wow, are you sure?"

"Yeah! Go ahead! Oh, but I don't have any for Nitta, so don't tell anyone, okay?"

Maou began to honestly pity Nitta.

"Well, thank you. I'll be sure to enjoy it."

This sort of polite gift played much the same role as this upcoming meetup. They were both tools meant to smooth personal relationships.

Maou didn't take this to imply that Kusuda had any feelings for him at all, but if someone like his coworker Kawata found out about it, he was sure the man would be telling him to go die in a fire or get stabbed in a back alley. The tradition in Japan was for women to give men gifts on Valentine's, then for men to reciprocate on White Day a month later; he didn't know if they'd have training on March 14 or not, so he thought it best not to discuss that yet.

"If I see you in March, I'll be hoping for something back, okay?"

With that knowing sort of prompt, Maou gladly accepted the chocolate. The ritual was complete.

"What do you think we'll be doing today?" she asked.

"I dunno. It said something about a preplanning meeting."

Before long, they were bantering about today's schedule, Maou shaking the cobwebs from his conversation with Acieth and switching into business mode. But Maou had forgotten something—because he had avoided seeing her in person lately, as Shiba and Amane had been watching the girl. He forgot that when it came to the topic of food—especially certain sweets, such as chocolate—Acieth could be downright diabolical.

✳

The next day, Acieth was crouched down next to Suzuno, who was in the middle of weeding the vegetable garden Shiba let her build in Villa Rosa Sasazuka's backyard.

"Hey, Suzuno! When do I get chocolate from someone?"

"That is rather out of the blue."

"They have the thing, it is called Valentine's, yes?"

She had only just fallen asleep inside Maou's body, but then, her sensitive nose picked up the aroma of chocolate—chocolate that should've still been inside its wrapped box—and it promptly woke her up. Hoping to know why Kusuda was giving Maou sweets like that, she explained everything she saw to Suzuno, who was back on Earth to work on the garden.

"Oh, Valentine's Day?"

Suzuno had no idea what kind of sleeping beast she was prodding. The issue was twofold—Maou was working over at Hatagaya Station that day, and Suzuno didn't think to ask why Acieth would take such a sudden interest in Valentine's Day. She had been in Ente Isla until that morning, holding Mass for the knights of Saint Aile stationed near Devil's Castle, so it'd be asking too much of her to consider that.

"Well, my apologies, Acieth, but as a woman, you will not be receiving any of that."

"Wha—*whaaaaaaaaaaaaaaaaat*?!"

Suzuno's statement resulted in an apocalyptic scream.

"How—how can world be so much of the cruel...?"

"That is simply how it is. That is how Valentine's Day works." Suzuno, kneeling by the garden, looked up at the aghast girl and chuckled. "There are several theories behind how the tradition began, but the day was christened to commemorate a saint, and now, in many nations, it is a day where women give sweets to men. The exact kind of treat is up to the gift-giver, but in Japan, chocolate has been the historical favorite."

"Chocolate... My chocolate..."

Acieth still hadn't recovered from the shock. Exactly who she thought she was getting chocolate from remained a mystery.

"But why can't the woman receive it...? Can—can I become the man from now on?"

"You intend to change your gender just for the free chocolate?" Suzuno snickered further at the deadly serious girl. "Well, as I said, nothing can be done. The whole day is a way for women to express the love they have for the men in their lives."

"Huh?"

Acieth blinked.

"But there is no need to worry. Here in Japan, there is another custom known as White Day. On March 14, a month after Valentine's, men give women chocolate as a way to return the favor."

"Really?!!" Acieth, spirits fully recovered, clapped her hands, her mind made up. "Kusuda, she said she 'hope for something back' in March from Maou! She means that, yes?"

"Kusuda? Maou? Um, Acieth, where did you hear about Valentine's Day in the first place…?"

Hearing an unfamiliar name next to Maou's made Suzuno's heart freeze. But Acieth wasn't even paying attention, fist raised high in the air as flames danced in her eyes.

"So… Wait! Kusuda, is she *gunning for* Maou?!"

"Acieth? I hesitate to ask, but this Kusuda person…"

"Yes! Kusuda! The girl who give Maou chocolate at training! She makes it all seem, '*Oh*, this just my obligation,' but I think she means it for real! If no, then why care about March?"

"What?! A-Acieth?!" Suzuno, fearing she'd said something she could never take back, ratcheted up her voice a little. It scared her to see how Acieth went from knowing nothing about Valentine's Day to spouting off all the intricacies of the holiday and how it figured in Japanese life.

"Well! No time to waste! Maou is the poor man! I cannot have Kusuda take my chocolate from him on the White Day!"

"Calm down, Acieth! We need to talk this out! In the workplace, women give chocolate to men all the time on that day. It is just a harmless little social custom; there is nothing special about—"

"Oh, I must tell Chiho! Chiho, she can teach me how to make chocolate treat, and I give to Maou and get big brownie points! My big sis, she gets all attention lately, so now is the big chance!"

"Wait…!"

Her fears were realized. Suzuno had no idea what had transpired between Maou and this Kusuda person, but if it was Acieth telling the story, she'd no doubt take a packet of cheap candy and turn it into a triple-layer chocolate cake. And with Chiho so concerned lately about what distance to take with Maou, if she heard about him getting intimate with another woman on Valentine's Day, Suzuno could only imagine her sobbing, head in hands, all over again. But it was too late.

"Chiho! I smell her over there!"

"W…wait…"

By the time she sputtered it out, Acieth was already running, leaving a footprint as deep as a fence post in the ground as she set off. Suzuno, grasping at empty air, slowly lowered her hands.

"I will have," she said in a quivering voice, "to apologize to Chiho and the Devil King later." She took out the phone tucked behind her kimono belt and began sending a warning text to Maou, no doubt giving his all to work at the moment and blissfully unaware of anything.

"Umm... Acieth has learned some...mistaken facts about Valentine's Day... Ah."

She pecked away at the keys, wiping the dirt from her hands first, but then noticed the clock on the upper right-hand corner of the screen. The blood drained from her head.

"No!!"

It was a little past three in the afternoon. She flung off the cloth she used to tie her hair back and stood up.

"Wait, Acieth! Chiho is still at school!"

It was Suzuno against a Sephirah child in this short-distance sprint to Sasahata North High School, and she had already given her a minute's head start. But she ran off anyway, fervently hoping to keep Chiho safe...but before leaving the apartment grounds, she hit the brakes and ran up to Room 202.

"Ah, Alas Ramus! I cannot leave Alas Ramus behind! *Ugh*! Why did this have to happen?!"

Alas Ramus, left by Emi this morning and currently in dreamland for her afternoon nap, awoke to find herself on Suzuno's back. Now Acieth had *two* minutes on her. And with every fiber of her being, Suzuno knew just how fatal those two minutes would be.

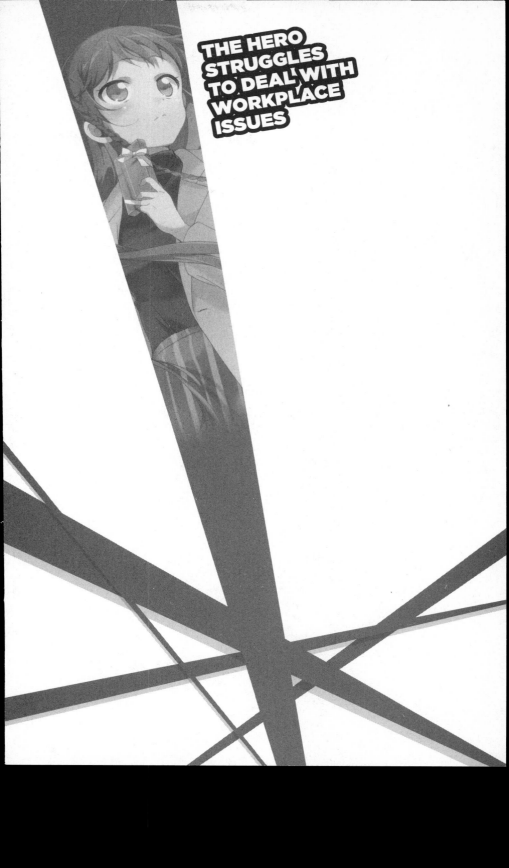

THE HERO
STRUGGLES
TO DEAL WITH
WORKPLACE
ISSUES

"Wait, you don't do it?"

"Why would we? It's a pain in the ass."

It was just past the lunch rush, and Emi was giving a smiling Akiko Ohki, coworker and veteran kitchen jockey, a surprised look. It was well into February by now, and as she compared the order forms for the seasonal Mini-Chocolate Pies with the inventory that came in, Emi thought to ask Akiko about how this MgRonald location's staff handled Valentine's Day. It turned out the female crewmembers didn't bother with chocolate or any other gifts for the guys.

"Did you do that at your last job, Emi-Yu?"

"Not *me*, so much as everyone at the office."

"Ahh, yeah," Akiko replied as she stocked the heater with Mini-Chocolate Pies. "Call centers usually run on pretty stable shifts, so that makes sense, but there's never been any obligation like that here in Hatagaya. I was expecting something like that when I came here last year, but it came and went with nothing to show for it, so I brought it up to Kisaki eventually."

It seemed that Mayumi Kisaki, manager at the MgRonald, had a less-than-rosy impression of the tradition. "I wouldn't recommend the custom between crewmembers," she had said, effectively prohibiting it. "You're free to give whatever you want to each other outside the property, but that's strictly between you and the other person."

"I think she'll probably tell you and the other guys who came in this year about it soon," Akiko added. (That would include Chiho as well.) "And besides, do you actually find giving out chocolate *fun* at all? I'm not expecting triple the amount back or whatever, but we got more guys than girls working here, so that's more to ask of them. Plus, if you don't have shifts around those times in February and March, it's like you get shut out of the whole thing. Neither side really gets much out of it. But anyway, no, we don't do it, for all those kinds of reasons."

"Oh. I didn't know that."

It wasn't called Valentine's Day, of course, but Ente Isla's Western Island did have a tradition of women baking sweets for men as a sign of their feelings for them. Back in the village of Sloane, where she grew up, this usually meant cookies and sweetened bread around harvest time, but Emi wound up being thrown into battle against the Devil King's Army before anyone taught her that custom, so she had never gotten to join in. Learning about Valentine's Day last year, while she worked at Dokodemo, therefore made her more than a little excited. She gave her obligatory chocolate to her boss and her boss's boss; they replied on White Day with little boxes of *rakugan*, a traditional Japanese treat, to all the women on staff.

"*Rakugan*?" Akiko remarked. "That's those hard sugar candies that get served with tea and stuff, right? Those are neat."

Emi recalled how enthralled she was by the intricate shapes and designs *rakugan* came in. She became a regular purchaser for some time afterward.

"So…"

"Hmm?"

"Talking about outside MgRonald…"

"Yeah?"

"Do you have, like, a reason to think about Valentine's Day this year, Emi-Yu?"

"……………Oh."

There was nothing very sudden about the question. It was Emi who brought the topic up. But still, for just a moment, her brain shut off on her. She groaned, and that groan kept her from answering immediately. Akiko, of course, picked up on that interval of silence.

"Whoa, no way."

"N-no! I don't!"

It was really remarkable. Subtle shifts in breathing rhythms and microscopic changes in your line of sight could sometimes be so much more eloquent than the words themselves.

"Wow, I'm surprised."

"I *said* I don't!"

"I didn't think you were into that kind of romantic stuff."

"Akiko!"

"But he doesn't work here, right? You're part of the team by now, but you haven't been here *that* long... Oh, but you knew Maou before now, didn't you?"

"W-Wait..."

This was tremendously frustrating to Emi. She wasn't trying to hide anything, but there was no way to phrase a response that implied the opposite. She could feel her cheeks redden—not out of shame, but out of simple panic. Akiko wasn't the type to take a topic and go hog wild with it, but given the air around them as of late, her and Maou being treated as an item was beyond inconvenient.

"Aw, there's no need to get so worked up about Valentine's chocolate. It's not like one or two boxes are going to dictate the rest of your love life."

"I'm not getting worked up!"

But Emi knew full well that it looked that way. Or maybe she really *was* worked up. Because when Akiko—who was now smiling warmly at Emi's reaction—first asked the question, she had, for a single instant, a thought. The time lag between having the thought, and realizing she was now capable of naturally thinking such thoughts, was what sealed her fate.

"By the way, there's a superawesome chocolatier near my school. You wanna know more about them?"

"No, thank you!"

"Aw, you're so *cute*, Emi-Yu."

Emi, realizing this line of talking would only drag her further into the swamp, ended it and tossed the final chocolate pie into the heater. But then, demonstrating perfectly terrible timing, Maou made his way downstairs from the café counter.

"What're you two chatting about? Kisaki would yell at you if she was here. Do you have a copy of the order form? There's something I need to check upstairs."

"Um, oh, uh, right. The order form... Oh, here it is."

Emi had been raising her voice. Realizing the cause of her delayed response to Akiko pitched it up even further. Akiko, whether she picked up on this or not, grinned to herself as she walked by Emi.

"Sorry, sorry. Emi-Yu just said she passed out chocolate on Valentine's Day at her last job, so I was telling her how we don't do that here, y'know?"

"R-Right," Emi stammered.

"Oh. Valentine's, huh? ...Ah, yeah, we got one extra pack here we didn't order."

Maou demonstrated little interest in the topic as he skimmed through the order form, eyebrows lowered. Seeing this annoyed Emi a bit, but Maou lifted his head before she could fire back.

"Hey, speaking of Valentine's, I got some thank-you chocolate just yesterday."

"Huh?"

"Oh, did you?"

Emi looked taken aback. Akiko, on the other hand, leaned forward to hear more.

"Yeah, but I don't know what to do about it. It's not like her and I have any relationship at all, so..."

"Maou, if Kawacchi heard that, he'd diagnose you with rich-kid disease and kill you."

"No, I mean, we haven't even seen each other all that often. What do people normally do with things like this?"

"Well," Akiko said, "a lot of people give out chocolate out of habit more than anything, instead of expecting anything back. I'm not saying you should ignore it, but there's no huge, pressing need to give her something, is there?"

"Mmm, maybe, but it came from a pretty fancy place. Have you two ever heard of..."

The French-sounding brand name Maou then uttered was unfamiliar to Emi's ears. Akiko, on the other hand, blinked a few times in response.

"That's...that's the chocolatier I was gonna tell you about, Emi-Yu."

"Oh..."

"Choco... What was that?"

"Chocolatier! A person who makes fancy chocolate for a living. There's this little one in a residential neighborhood near my college. It's not even all that well-known on the net or anything. Wait, are you sure this was just 'thank-you' chocolate? 'Cause that place doesn't go cheap at all."

"I...I'm pretty sure? She's one of the people training with me, but this was only the third time we've seen each other."

"Hmm... It's hard to tell from that, but that chocolate seems like more than a thank-you to me."

Akiko scrunched up her face a little, although there was still brazen curiosity peeking out from it.

"Well, what are you gonna do about it?"

"Huh?" Maou frowned at Emi's oddly blunt question, then at his own indecision. "...Well, I dunno what. Aren't you supposed to repay a gift with something half the value or whatever? Ashiya will yell at me if I just let it be, but I have no idea how much this cost her. I don't have a computer at home right now, and it's kind of a pain to search on the net with my old phone..."

"Half the value?" Akiko rolled her eyes. "This isn't a business negotiation."

"It doesn't matter whether it's expensive or not," sniffed Emi derisively, "or how rare it is. You think she gave it just to be polite, don't you? Then why don't you be polite to her in return?"

"Is that all there is to it?"

"What else is there to it?"

"Yeah, I guess so, huh?" Maou looked convinced enough at Emi's dry assessment. That, too, got on Emi's nerves. "Ah, well. Sorry to take up your time with that."

"Yeah, I bet Kisaki would yell at you if she heard this."

"I hear you. See ya for now."

Maou breezily returned upstairs, with Emi glaring at his back and Akiko watching her from the side before saying something that snapped Emi back to reality.

"...You think Chi knows about that?"

Emi turned toward Akiko. "I don't think so!" she blurted with the urgency of a war declaration.

"Yeah, probably not. You know how Maou can totally forget about stuff like that sometimes. I feel like Chi's intelligent enough to not let things like this faze her, but intelligence is different from feelings, so..."

The fact that Chiho had feelings for Maou was an open secret, clear enough to anyone close to the two of them. Those emotions were so clear and straightforward, everyone around them hesitated to mess with or poke fun at them about it. But this wouldn't be the first time mental lapses on Maou's part affected Chiho's public behavior—something Kisaki upbraided him about every time it happened.

"Yeah," reflected Akiko, "Maou may look nearly perfect, but that's the one bad habit he has, and it's a killer."

"You said it."

Emi could name quite a few more bad habits (or worse), but she held back on saying them out loud. If she did, she knew Akiko would ask how Emi knew all that stuff about him.

"How much you wanna bet that in a few days, he'll be all like *Oh no, I got chocolate from Chi, too,* now *what?*"

Judging from past behavior, that sounded incredibly likely to Emi. But if she ordered him to keep quiet about this other woman, she knew it could come out anyway and damage Chiho's pride. Letting

Chiho know in advance, meanwhile, would just mess her up even more. And considering all the warnings Ashiya and Suzuno had given him, not even Emi thought Maou was dumb enough to ask Chiho directly for advice.

"......"

But thinking that far, a bizarre supposition formed itself in Emi's mind: *What if he receives this chocolate but can't talk to Chiho about it, then gets guilty about hiding things from her, so he starts acting all weird in front of her and she figures out the truth anyway?*

As her friend, Emi never wanted to see Chiho's feelings get hurt. Turning her thoughts around, this was a situation Emi needed to keep an eye on for Maou's sake, lest Maou's thoughtlessness traumatize Chiho. But would "looking out for him" wind up making *her* the person acting weirdly, exposing it all?

Emi felt frozen in place. And while Akiko knew about Maou and Chiho, she didn't have all the facts. She didn't understand they were purposefully keeping some distance from each other. And given her personality, any lecturing she might give Maou about it would have little effect.

"...Why do I have to go out of my way to worry about the Devil King's personal life?"

The propellerlike motion of Emi's brain was frustrating her. Now she wasn't so sure why she hesitated to answer Akiko's question earlier. She, of all people, had no reason to consider this matter for even a moment:

What kind of chocolate would Maou like?

Thanks to that ridiculous thought crashing through her mind for a single instant, she had to deal with yet another wave of pointless anxiety. Neither she nor Maou had the wherewithal to address silly little events like that. She had a semiliteral *god* to defeat. Why did she have to get so worked up about some contrived Japanese custom like this? She had so many other things that required her attention.

Attempting to get her mind out of its current rut, Emi turned toward the restaurant entrance.

"""..."""

Akiko saw him at the same time she did. The sight made both of them visibly frown. Mitsuki Sarue, manager at the Hatagaya location of Sentucky Fried Chicken directly across the street, was passing by. His eyes, as he peered into the MgRonald dining room, were as pure as a child's, eyeing something he knew he could never attain. One look at them indicated to Emi and Akiko that his expectations for Valentine's Day were *way* off the charts.

He didn't venture inside, as he was busy with his own job at this time of day, but Emi and Akiko still exchanged glances with each other.

"...Akiko, did she tell you what to do if...something happened?"

"...All I know is, Kisaki won't be here on the fourteenth."

"...No? He's gonna pitch a fit, isn't he?"

"...He hasn't done anything before, but we're supposed to call the police if that kind of thing happens."

No matter how far-reaching and tragic their pasts were, Maou was currently the Devil King, and Sarue was an archangel. If Maou learned how preoccupied both he and Sarue were about something like Valentine's Day right now, the ancient Devil Overlord Satan would probably look for some shrub to weep behind—and Ignora, the "god" leading the angels, would probably call her whole mission off. It was a worthless thought, but it entertained Emi for a moment.

"You think he cares about this that much?"

"Hey, some people do."

Whether male or female, this land of Japan seemed to all but force you to keep Valentine's in mind. It puzzled Emi. And while she hadn't heard anything from Chiho yet, if Chiho was expecting to enjoy this Valentine's Day, Emi hoped whatever was going to happen would send her heart soaring into the heavens, rather than crashing down to earth.

However...

This fleeing hope was crushed before Maou or Emi could do anything about it.

"Maou received some chocolate?"

"Uh-huh! It was the very expensive-looking chocolate, too! And the giver, she was pretty beautiful woman! This is the big problem, Chiho! It calls for the swift action!"

And at almost the same time as a wide-eyed Acieth blurted out the news to Chiho at Sasahata North High School's front gate:

"I...I was too late..."

Chiho was surprised all over again by Suzuno crumpling to the ground, covered in sweat, a sleeping Alas Ramus on her back. And then:

"Sasachi, you...?"

Unfortunately for everyone involved, Chiho wasn't the only person to hear Acieth's report.

"You still haven't settled things with that guy?!"

Kaori Shoji, who was about to walk home with Chiho, heard it all. And as she put it later, Chiho could barely stand to watch the mask of despair that descended upon Suzuno's face.

✳

Even after she learned the truth about Ignora, Suzuno Kamazuki retained her faith in a benevolent god. She was currently begging this god she held inside her for forgiveness.

"What, so you finally gave up, Sasachi?"

"No, I haven't."

"But it is *the* Maou! You know, Chiho, he is the easily manipulated!"

"That's...well...not *un*true, but..."

For whatever reason, Suzuno had taken Chiho, Acieth, and Chiho's apparent classroom friend Kaori Shoji to the Sentucky Fried Chicken in Hatagaya.

"Didn't you tell me before, Sasachi, that he's got a lot more freedom in his life than you do? He's busy with this training right now, and if he gets hired on full-time, he's gonna start meeting all kinds of people, isn't he? You don't have any choice but to be a student for now—if you keep wasting time, you're gonna be left in the dust, you know?"

"But we were on the same page back at Christmas…"

"You are the too gullible, Chiho! Kaori, she is correct! And maybe not right now, but as long as Ashiya is there, Maou only has so much of the time to return favor! You must take the brisk action!"

"Yeah, but what kind of action?"

Suzuno was curled up next to Chiho, still holding Alas Ramus. Acieth and Kaori—remarkably kindred spirits, considering this was their first meeting—were busy interrogating the poor teen in front of them.

"Acieth is right! You can cook, Sasachi. Just attack him with some homemade chocolate and beat an answer out of him! Ambush him when he's done with his shift or whatever! It's okay if it's a few days before or after the fourteenth, besides!"

"Homemade, huh? I haven't really done any confectionary work before."

"Huh?! Chiho, you cannot make the sweets?! Me, I counting on you!"

"It's not that I can't… I mean, like, I haven't made anything too fancy yet…"

"Then go buy a candy bar or a bag of chips from the convenience store! I'm telling you, you've had all these near misses—it's time to put an end to it! You gotta start applying some pressure, lady!"

"Hmm…"

"Stand! Stand up, Chiho! Maou, we will wow him! Make him give you chocolate back for White Day!"

"I—I dunno if that's really what I want…"

"…zzz…"

In front of Kaori, who presumably didn't know what was going on with Ente Isla, and Acieth, who could never lie or deceive anyone, Suzuno sat straining, sweat pouring out from her body as Alas Ramus kept sleeping in her arms.

Emi had been put in a similar situation at this same exact fast food joint in the past once. Her friend Rika Suzuki didn't know anything at the time; she was just curious to uncover the truth about Maou and Emi's relationship.

Ashiya's sudden intervention saved the day then, but Suzuno was still an unknown to Emi at the time; she must have been on pins and needles trying to keep her secrets away from Rika. Now, Suzuno couldn't help but feel Rika was paying the price for it.

Kaori knew nothing about Ente Isla, but she seemed fairly intimate with Chiho. Judging from the way she seemed to easily accept Acieth, Alas Ramus, and Suzuno—all three rather uncommon sights around the city—Chiho must have told her about them, in a nonincriminating fashion. That was Chiho's decision to make, and Suzuno didn't resent that, but the problem was Acieth. She had none of Ashiya's quick-wittedness, and her being around the same age (?) as Kaori meant they instantly got along. There was no telling when a slip of her tongue might arouse Kaori's suspicions. Plus, the guy running this place was still, in the end, Sariel. Considering his usual behavior, holding a conversation about Valentine's Day in here ran the considerable risk of making life miserable for Chiho, Emi, Maou, and everyone else at Sentucky and MgRonald in very short order.

With all this in mind, Suzuno was honestly scared out of her wits. But even though she was in the exact same position, Chiho seemed perfectly natural as she fended off Acieth's and Kaori's barrage of questions. Suzuno had chased down Acieth out of concern that Maou's lack of forward thinking would hurt Chiho yet again; now, her mind was filled with the single desire to make this situation a thing of the past as soon as possible.

"By the way, Suzuno, what do you really think of him? Maou, I mean."

"Hwah?!"

Kaori suddenly tossing the subject her way almost made Suzuno leap out of her seat.

"What do I…think? Think how?"

"Is he the type of guy who'd appreciate some homemade chocolate?"

"Ah, um, I wonder… I think he would appreciate most things edible, but, um…" She realized midway that wasn't what Kaori asked. "I mean, he isn't the kind of person to fail to notice the feelings behind a gift...I think."

"But then," a dissatisfied-looking Kaori replied, "what about all the meals you've been preparing for him, Sasachi? Because I think you put a lot of feeling into those."

Suzuno couldn't help but feel like she was being assaulted. Maou never failed to thank Chiho for whatever she brought in, but nonetheless, Kaori wouldn't be satisfied. Chiho, for her part, seemed to know that.

"It's not really about that," she said, backing up Suzuno more than Maou at the moment. "I did it because I wanted to have dinner with the whole gang."

"But Maou being there wasn't exactly a minor part of that decision, right?"

"Um... When you put it that way, then no, but..."

In the end, it was Suzuno who induced Chiho into providing that support. She had been serving consecrated food to the demons, hoping to sap them of their powers, and Chiho had stepped up to counteract that with her own cooking. It made it hard to comment on this line of questioning, even though it led (after a long, winding road) to things like Suzuno teaching Chiho how to cook and learning about Japanese and Earth cuisine herself. It built a relationship between them, and that relationship taught Suzuno how to understand Chiho's thoughts on Maou. And now, despite the conflicts she felt about it, she had settled into a position of support for Chiho.

"I mean..."

"Hmm?"

"I think," Chiho said, "I've been a little too selfish lately."

"Huh?"

"I've been so reserved up until now, so I guess I didn't really know how I should break through that. And now I've caused all this trouble for you, Kao, and for Suzuno. Acieth, too, I guess."

"Huh? You mean, this is the payback for something?"

"Yeah."

Acieth wouldn't have known, but the night Rika tried and failed to make Ashiya her boyfriend, Chiho had taken a step forward thanks to the words Acieth had given a confused Chiho inside Sasa-zuka Station. *So say the thing when you can, before you cannot say it anymore.* Chiho had "said the thing" long ago, and she had shown, through her behavior, that she still meant it. All that remained was to trust in him, and wait.

"I'm just thinking I should stop pestering him until next July."

"Huh? Next July? That's so arbitrary."

"You—you will extend the Valentine's until July?!"

Acieth was in her own dimension as usual. But Suzuno, know-ing where the July deadline came from, turned her eyes down at the heavy child in her arms. The Obon Festival next July. The "birth-day" of Alas Ramus, and the deadline Maou set for their journey to destroy heaven. To Maou, of course, defeating Ignora was a side quest; the main goal was to give Alas Ramus the best birthday she'd ever had, and Chiho agreed with him.

"So I mean, I'm just not sure I should worry about Valentine's right now."

""*Whaaat?!*""

Kaori and Acieth both lunged at her.

"What do you mean, you're not sure?! Are you crazy, Sasachi?"

"Chiho, have you lost the mind?! You must give chocolate, or he no give you the chocolate back!"

They were criticizing her from two rather different vectors. Chiho raised both hands to calm them down.

"No, I mean, I'll probably do something. Probably. But…Suzuno?"

"Hmm?"

"Have you seen Maou at his apartment lately?"

"Yes, I saw him as he left for work this morning."

"I was just wondering, how's his place looking these days? I feel like the fatigue's getting to him lately."

"I am not sure. We have said little but hello to each other as of late."

Suzuno's schedule was structured more around Emi's than anyone else's, so she'd often not see anyone at all on the way back to Room 202.

At that point, Acieth spoke up. "Maou, he is the really, really tired. I know. He even said 'Oh, I'm sick of eating out anymore!'"

"He's sick of eating out?"

Chiho took a moment to ponder what this could mean. It didn't take long to glean something from it.

"Ah... Ohhh. Ashiya isn't there, so he has to deal with breakfast and dinner himself. I get it."

"Ch-Chiho?"

"And lunch is one thing, but I know he's been closing a lot of days lately. I don't know when he'll be home from training, so it's hard to drop in on him. I could leave something with Yusa, but it'd have to be on a day when they're both working."

"Um, Sasachi?"

"Hmm... Okay." Chiho's voice went flat. "Kao, Suzuno, Acieth... What do you think about me giving Maou a freeze-dried miso soup set for Valentine's Day?"

"""" ... """""

Suzuno's, Acieth's, and most of all, Kaori's faces told the whole story. Something was *wrong* with Chiho today.

"...Are you serious?"

"Huh? Kind of."

"This isn't a classroom party!!"

"Yeah, but if I want to bake him something homemade, I'll have to spend a lot of money buying good chocolate somewhere. If I'm gonna invest in that anyway, why don't I spend it on something he actually needs?"

"Um, Suzuno? From what I am discerning, Valentine's Day, it's that kind of thing, no?"

"I am impressed you are 'discerning' anything at the moment, but yes, I agree."

"You're right," Kaori said, "if this was for some normal day. But that's not any different from the food you brought over before, is it? You know what I mean? Valentine's Day is all about *chocolate*!

Even if you wanna get creative about it, it's *still* got to be something sweet!"

"I know. I know that..." Chiho sighed, shoulders drooping downward. "But I... I haven't said this before, but I actually *have* been pressing Maou for an answer, a little."

""Huh?!""

"Phew!"

Kaori and Suzuno opened their eyes wide. Acieth almost whistled her approval.

"Back when we all went to Nerima together..."

"Oh, back then?"

"So? So what did he say to you?!"

"Well... He *did* kind of give me an answer. He said he'll tell me once he gets everything in order."

"Huh?" Kaori gave her a stupefied tilt of the head. "That's the same as just stringing it out some more. There's nothing definite about it at all."

"No, I guess not..." Chiho gave the group a half smile, a tad embarrassed. "But it feels to me like we set a new deadline, kind of. I feel like, if I give him some fancy chocolate right now, that'll go beyond pressure and feel more like stress to him."

Suzuno, of course, knew the truth lurking behind Chiho's words. It kept her from saying *No, that's not true* right now. Certainly, here was a man who knew Chiho's feelings and was letting them float around aimlessly. Something needed to be done. But considering the enormous, complex issues Maou wrangled with, forcing him into a decision about Chiho felt like it'd bring nothing but bad repercussions.

"You...may be right."

"Of course, if Acieth is telling the truth, that's more stress for me, but..."

"Oh, it is no lie, I am the guaranteeing you of it! I saw Kusuda! She had the leer at him!"

"Acieth! You didn't say that before!"

"Hmm... Kusuda... Hmm..."

Chiho's face went blank for a moment. She shrugged, looking a little tired again.

"I didn't mean to let Valentine's Day go by without any comment. But looking at Maou right now, anything I do seems like pushing my emotions on him, or like it'd seem out of place right now. But I can't just sit by and pretend this day doesn't exist, so I thought over what I should do, and I didn't have any bright ideas, so here I am. I mean... like, Yusa or Suzuno or Amane, or their landlord even—that's one thing. But to get some chocolate from someone none of us even know?"

"Ahh... Um, well... True. Yes."

Acieth described it as "expensive-looking" chocolate. But it wasn't too long ago, Chiho felt, that Maou would've gone right to her for advice on what to do in social situations like these. It was exactly what Emi and Akiko thought, back at MgRonald, at almost the same time.

"I'm sure none of this would've happened if Alciel was around..."

Ashiya's absence from Room 201 had caused Maou to become fatigued, oblivious, and open to attack. It made Suzuno wonder how the Devil King's Army ever stayed together without him. No wonder Emi had plowed through them.

"Oh, right," Kaori said, face brightening as she sat up. "Kisaki is the manager at MgRonald, right? Why don't you have her mix it in with the rest of the chocolate getting passed around the staff? Just say it'd make things weird if you personally gave it to him."

Chiho scowled. "We're prohibited from giving out chocolate."

"Huh? Why?"

"She told me herself; the crew can't give chocolate to one another. Like, 'If you wanna do it, do it in private,' she said. I guess it causes problems."

"Ohhh, I see. Maybe that's what happens if you got a big staff like that. Hmm. What *should* you do? Are you really just gonna do nothing?"

"Honestly, part of me thinks that's the best solution right now."

"Mmmm... But... Mmmm." Kaori seemed to understand Chiho

but didn't seem willing to accept it. "But it's Valentine's and every-thing. You can't just... Oh!" She glanced at Suzuno, eyebrows raised. "You're friends with Maou, right, Suzuno?"

"Excuse me?" Suzuno froze. "Um, well, who can say? I suppose we are rather close fr...*neighbors*."

Suzuno had all but stopped bringing up the discord between humans and demons with Maou, unless she was deliberately trying to needle him. But being asked by an outside observer if they were "friends," she found it hard to give an instant reply. To someone like Kaori, they were friends and/or neighbors, but she just couldn't use that word, leading to an oddly ambivalent response.

"Well, if the workplace is a no-go, could we do a trade between close friends, and you can mix it in there?"

"W-Wait, Kaori, are—are you telling the rest of us to give Maou chocolate as well?"

"I'm pretty sure that's the only way to do it. Would you guys mind pitching in for Sasachi's sake?"

"H-Hold on, Kao! What are you even asking from Suzuno?! Sh-she's fine! This is all about my own stuff; I can't put that on her shoulders!"

There was something very "teenager" about Kaori's out-of-control suggestion. Chiho almost felt the need to apologize to Suzuno. Suzuno, meanwhile, was blushing ear to ear and staring at Kaori.

"M-Me? Give chocolate to him? Wh-what?"

"...Suzuno?"

"How could I look at him? What excuse could I give? And what would I give him? Matcha powder? *Wasanbon* sugar? *Kuromitsu* syrup?!" Her eyes darted from person to person as she mumbled. "I—I am not sure about any of that! Perhaps, if it was seen as the polite, social thing to do, it would not seem unnatural... Would it? I did give him those udon noodles at first... Oh, but things are so different now!"

"Suzuno? Suzuno, you are the seriously worried? Why?"

"Ah!"

Acieth's cold voice snapped her out of her stupor. Noticing the three pairs of eyes staring at her, Suzuno looked downward, face reddening again.

"I—I am sorry. I mean, something like Valentine's... I have never done anything of the sort before. So...the idea of giving sweets to a member of the opposite sex..."

""Huhhh?!""

This came as a surprise to Chiho and Kaori. To the latter, someone as young-looking but mature as Suzuno having no experience with this was an honest surprise; to the former (although she never worried about it before), the thought of her never giving any man a gift in Ente Isla was beyond her wildest dreams. Chiho and Kaori weren't so experienced that they had a right to look down on her, but Valentine's was something you learned in preschool, really, or within your own family.

Suzuno used the hand that wasn't supporting Alas Ramus to reach up and hide her watering eyes. "R-Regardless," she said, voice low as she tried to defend herself against the two teens, "if I gave him sweets as well, that would be all the more unnatural. To Maou, I am, er, not at all the sort of person to do that. I think the camouflage would be all too obvious."

"Then let me do it, too!" Acieth blurted out, whether she knew Suzuno's feelings or not. Acieth, of course, wasn't even hiding her desire to be showered in chocolate on White Day; it'd be much more natural for her to do the Valentine's deed.

"Hmm... Sorry, Acieth, but I think it'd still be a little tough."

Acieth's presence still wouldn't be enough to dull the impact of Chiho presenting chocolate to Maou. To serve as camouflage, their gifts would need to be presented to Maou at the same time—but if Maou was in Sasazuka right now, he likely wouldn't return until late at night, and he'd be right back at work in the morning. Chiho's high school schedule kept her from visiting his home that late, and workplace chocolate was already deemed verboten. It was hard to picture a situation where both she and Acieth could give him a gift at the same time.

"So what're we gonna do?! It's like there's no way out!"

"Umm, well, if I can pair up with someone, I can do that," Chiho stated, "but now's not the right time for it, and I can't really expect someone to join me on this. I don't think we can do anything."

There was no answer they could ever reach. Beyond anything else, Chiho just didn't have the drive to push through this apparent impasse. The conversation was starting to visibly fizzle before their eyes.

"Nh...*fwahhhh*..."

Then, in Suzuno's lap, the napping Alas Ramus lifted her heavy eyelids open.

"Aw, cute!"

Kaori, seeing her awake for the first time, fawned on the awkwardly squirming toddler.

"Oh, Alas Ramus, are you awake?"

"Hahh... Suzu-Sisss... Goo' morrrning... Uh?"

As she sleepily greeted Suzuno, she turned and realized she was no longer where she was before she began her nap.

"Magrobad... No? Where aww-we?"

"Good morning, Alas Ramus! No, this isn't MgRonald. This is Sentucky."

"Snntuh-key?"

"That's right, Big Sis! The place evil, annoying angel runs!!"

""Uh, wa—!!""

Chiho and Suzuno panicked, as Acieth treated Alas Ramus the way she always did. Fortunately, the novelty of a young child in front of her caused Kaori to pay it no mind.

"You're so *cute*! Wow, and she's so small, but she's got a big vocabulary, huh? You guys are pretty far apart in age to be sisters, huh, Acieth?"

"Oh," Acieth replied, "not as much as it looks."

"...Whozzat?" Alas Ramus asked, a little suspicious at the unfamiliar face.

"Oh! Um, uh, hi, my name's Kaori Shoji..."

Kaori found herself flustered, unsure how to deal with such a young child. Chiho deftly stepped in.

"Alas Ramus? This lady's my friend. You can call her your big sis Kaori!"

"…Kao-Sis?"

"Oh, man, that is soooo cute! I'm about to have a nosebleed! I would totally wanna take care of this little girl if I knew her! Especially if this little angel calls me something like that!"

"My big sis is not angel, Kaori!"

Acieth had such an aversion to the word *angel* that she once again made Chiho's and Suzuno's hearts skip a beat. Kaori still didn't notice.

"Aww, but Maou… I mean, I've only met him a few times, so I only kinda recall his face, but he's got black hair, right? If they're related, it must be a pretty distant relation, huh?"

"Y-yeah, I guess… Ha-ha-ha…"

"Distant? He is the dad of her, you can say."

"Y-yeah! They're so close, it's almost like father and daughter!"

Again, Chiho and Suzuno scrambled to rein in the fallout from Acieth's incessant bombshells.

"Father and daughter, huh…?"

Kaori, meanwhile, was too busy finding enlightenment about the joys of life to notice how unnatural all this talk was.

"K-Kao?"

"Sasachi, you know, I think I've found the most totally natural way to camouflage this ever…hee-hee-hee…"

"Kaori?"

"K-Kaori? What do you mean?"

"Okay, listen. Alas Ramus is related to Maou, but Yusa takes care of her, too. Acieth and Alas Ramus are sisters, and you and Suzuno are friends with all of them, Sasachi. Do I have all that right?"

"Y-yeah…"

"So far, yes…"

Chiho and Suzuno held their breath, dreading what could come next. Kaori grinned back at them.

"There's only one way you all can give Maou chocolate!"

Then, she began laying out the plan—a plan that, when she heard it all, made Chiho seriously wonder why it never occurred to her.

✳

"Alas Ramus making chocolates?!"

"Shhh! Please be a bit quieter, Emilia!"

Later, at seven that evening, Emi came to Room 202 to pick up Alas Ramus, only to find Suzuno looking notably more haggard than usual. The tale she had for her, of Acieth all but attacking Chiho at her high school, gave her a throbbing headache.

Thanks to that, not only had Chiho's friend, Kaori Shoji, made contact with Alas Ramus, but she had also suggested a way to use the child to help give Valentine's chocolate to Maou without applying undue pressure on him. As Kaori put it, making chocolate together with the little girl, who served as Maou's "daughter," would be acceptable enough to the guy without making it awkward. The whole story made Emi want to faint on the spot.

"Um, Bell?"

"Y-yes?"

"Looking back at everything…"

"Y-yes…"

Emi's low voice seemed to echo like a demon's.

"If we could've taken down Alciel, the whole Devil King's Army would've crumbled by itself, wouldn't it?"

"…Perhaps."

"What is with the Devil King? I mean, seriously! Why is he just so…so incorrigible the moment Alciel is gone?!"

"I suppose the real mastermind was in the Room 201 kitchen the whole time."

"Oh, this drives me up the wall! I was just telling Akiko at work a few hours ago that I hope Maou doesn't get all weird talking with Chiho about the chocolate he got!"

"I—I suppose I am responsible in part for that…"

"It's the Devil King's fault for acting like such a freak in front of Acieth when he accepted that gift!"

"There—there was nothing freakish about it. As Acieth put it, he immediately realized it was merely a token of politeness…"

"Then why couldn't he take care of it by himself instead of looking shocked and getting other people involved?!"

"That, um, well, yes..."

A valid point, Suzuno thought, even as she wondered why Emi was having such a mood-swingy day today.

"Suzu-Sis, Suzu-Sis!"

As her mother buried her head in her hands, Alas Ramus—playing around with a pile of books and magazines in one corner—tugged at Suzuno's kimono, pointing at an open page.

"I—I like this!"

Whether she had understood their conversation or not, she had it open to a Valentine's Day feature. It included a large picture of a "Tree of Love," complete with colorful hearts as the fruit, apparently on sale at a famous chocolatier in the trendy Harajuku district of Tokyo.

"Nh...!"

Suzuno tensed up and closed the magazine before Emi could glance at it.

"A-Alas Ramus, that, um, that can wait until you are older. It, er, it is quite expensive."

"Expensive?"

"Yes, expensive. All right? So be a good girl and do *not* show that to Mommy or Daddy, okay?"

"...Okeh!"

She didn't seem totally convinced, but Alas Ramus still relented. Suzuno wiped the mental sweat away from her mind. The sight of that colorful chocolate tree reminded her a little too much of the Tree of Sephirot, and that could put pressure of a much different sort on Emi and Maou.

"So... All right. I mean, pressure or not, I can see that making chocolates with Alas Ramus isn't a bad idea. But if we do that..." Emi balled her hands into fists, so hard that Suzuno worried her nails were breaking skin. "If we do that, it means I have to join them!!"

"I suppose so, yes," Suzuno replied, averting her eyes. She couldn't deny it. Even if Chiho wasn't in the picture, if she was making a present for Daddy, Alas Ramus would naturally want Mommy to pitch in. But no matter how much their animosity had lessened over time, there was no way Emi would volunteer to join a gender-specific event featuring a man like that as a recipient of favors. However, once she calmed down from that first onrush of emotion, Emi's voice took on a surprisingly calm demeanor.

"...And, you know, I was prepared to at least go through the motions with Valentine's."

"Oh?"

"Like, Christmas, New Year's... Once we're back in Ente Isla, Alas Ramus isn't gonna experience any of that. Compared with that, there is a tradition kind of like Valentine's Day over there. Plus, Alas Ramus even said she wanted to give Daddy some chocolate."

"She did?"

"I kind of explained the custom to her."

"You did?!"

This was a double surprise for Suzuno. The way this event worked, if Alas Ramus knew about it, Emi would naturally have to join in as well. But in terms of people both of them could logically give chocolate to, that was limited to Nord, Maou, Ashiya, and Urushi-hara. Suzuno watched wide-eyed as a grinning Alas Ramus flipped through the pages of another Valentine's Day chocolate catalog, before turning toward Emi.

"You were planning to give the Devil King a gift?"

"Well, Maou and everyone else in the Hatagaya location."

But Kisaki, as she now explained to Suzuno, had put the kibosh on the tradition Emi had learned at the Dokodemo office.

"I feel bad for Chiho. I know she's really serious about this. But if we could've just treated this as everyone having a little fun and trading a few goodies with one another, we could've done it without getting preoccupied with a bunch of crap. That's why I thought I wouldn't mind it too much."

"But you can no longer camouflage it in the workplace, so since you taught the custom to Alas Ramus, you are forced, in a way, to follow it and give the chocolate yourself?"

"Well…yeah." Emi's voice was more halting now. "…I know it's not my place to say it, but I'm in the same boat. I can't have the Devil King think about a bunch of extraneous junk, so I thought some camouflage would be a good idea. Now, after today, I feel like everything I worried about is coming true."

"Today, meaning the chocolate this Kusuda gave him in the training class?"

"Kusuda, huh? That was her name?"

Emi's eyes grew a shade colder as she repeated it.

"You know how serious-minded the Devil King is."

"Y-yes, I do."

"So like… We aren't at each other's throats any longer, but if I give him some chocolate on Valentine's, I thought he might start thinking a bunch of weird stuff again."

"A bunch of weird stuff?"

"Um, how can I explain it? I think our relationship right now is kind of mercenary in nature. I owe him for this, he owes me for that, kind of thing. He wound up helping me when we got attacked in the subway, so I have to repay the favor, and so on. And I don't mind that, but…"

Suzuno listened on silently as Emi attempted to summarize her feelings with a rapid barrage of words.

"But me personally giving him chocolate… It's not like that other stuff. And maybe it's just a polite custom, but I'm giving it to him as a way of expressing positive emotions, right? But I don't have the confidence to dare to feel 'positive' about him, and I think that's true for him, too. I can't kill him anymore, and he knows that, but still…"

"Ooh?"

Emi pulled Alas Ramus (and her catalog) toward her, placing her on her lap.

"If I gave him something *this* amazing, I think that relationship is going to change, somehow."

The child had the catalog open to a selection of offerings from Tokyo's department-store bakeries, from well-known, showstopping pieces to more budget-friendly options for gifts given out of duty more than love.

"…Do you think so?"

"Probably, yeah," nodded Emi, not looking too confident about it. "I don't hate the Devil King any longer, you know. But I haven't forgiven him. I know he understands that. So…"

Turning the page, she came upon a feature showcasing recipes for making chocolate treats at home.

"So I don't think I need to buy him something cheap from the store, just for the show of it. I'm sure Alas Ramus wants to give him something, though, and if she wants to, I'll be glad to let her. But… I'm sorry to Chiho, but I want Alas Ramus cooking for her daddy to be separate from *her* thing. I'm kind of hoping she can find another way to 'camouflage' it, if that's what she wants."

"Emilia…"

"And she went on about not wanting to put pressure on the Devil King, but she really *does* need to gradually step up that pressure. Like, you know him. He really isn't thinking about it at all, because he assumes she'll let him off the hook until this battle is over. And then, when *this* comes along, I'm sure he'll be writhing and wailing about it again."

It sounded extremely likely to Suzuno.

"So if Chiho wants to give the Devil King chocolate, I think she could throw her honest feelings at him, like she always has. Oh, but…"

Emi looked up, chuckling.

"What does Chiho herself think? Does she want to go with Kaori's plan?"

"That…is a rather delicate question."

Chiho had been pretty enthusiastic at first, going all "Wow, yeah, you're right!" toward her friend. But:

"Has she contacted you about it at all, Emilia?"

"No."

Emi took her phone out, checking for new messages. There was nothing at all from Chiho.

"You think maybe she agreed to it as a way to gloss things over with a friend who doesn't know about Ente Isla?"

If Chiho wanted Alas Ramus's help with this, she would naturally have to get Emi involved. But the way things stood, she'd likely hesitate to bring any Valentine's proposals to Emi's doorstep. The reason was simple: She didn't want her personal quest to make Maou clarify their relationship to trump the entire group's quest to storm the heavens and defeat Ignora.

"Devoting herself to the Devil King like this is such a waste of time."

"Indeed. I am with you on that."

"But it never runs on logic, does it? That kind of..."

...Love never does.

"...Hey, Bell?"

"Yes?"

"Have you ever been in love?"

"No." The reply came almost unnaturally fast.

Emi blinked in surprise. "No?"

"Well...not to sound lovelorn, but my family's position did not allow me my own choice when it came to partners, and there was never really a man who made me want to...push against them on that."

It made sense. Suzuno had led a hard life, in a way different from Emi. She didn't have any time to let herself get infatuated with some lofty ideal of love.

"What about you, Emilia?"

"Mm... Well, I... I think I may have."

"You think?"

"I'm just not sure you'd normally call it love. I'm talking about my father, after all."

"Oh." Suzuno laughed. "That would be different."

It was like a young child declaring to the family that she'd marry her father someday.

"I never had a mother, really, and whatever I did, I always had my father staying right behind me. So... I mean, someone who's strong,

who's worth relying on, and maybe who's got a screw loose sometimes, but who's always looking out for me..."

"...Wait. Emilia, do you mean..."

"No. No, not like that."

"Mommy?"

Emi buried her face behind Alas Ramus's head, hiding a smile
that nobody else could see.

"But maybe so, if I could forgive him in my heart."

That was the truth, the purest words to ever come from her.

"...There's no point thinking about it. If Chiho wants to go with
that plan, I'll consider it, then. I promised Eme and Al that I'd head
over to them today, so unless something comes up, I won't even see
Chiho until Valentine's Day itself."

"Ah, yes."

A little dumbfounded, Suzuno watched as Emi put down Alas
Ramus and got to her feet.

"Are you staying in Sasazuka today, Bell?"

"I think so. Acieth kept me from working on my vegetable garden
for long, so I would like to get it in decent shape first."

"All right. I need to return to Eifukucho and get my clothes and
stuff in order before I go, so I'll head out for now. We're going home,
Alas Ramus. Clean up your books, okay?"

"Okeh!"

At her order, Alas Ramus closed all the books she had strewn on
the floor and stacked them up at the corner—her personal approach
to cleanliness. Emi pulled her coat on, putting a wool cap on her
child before turning to Suzuno again.

"Hey, Bell?"

"Hmm?"

"You cooked a lot of food for the demons with Chiho and Alciel,
didn't you?"

"Yes."

"Did the Devil King ever tell you what he likes foodwise?"

"Well, when we were conversing once, Chiho mentioned that, for
all the scolding the Devil King gives Lucifer, their tastes are actually

rather alike. They enjoy dishes with bold flavors: meat, carbohydrates, and the like. A very childish palate, to put it in a bad way. But he hardly shuns vegetables or fish, either. I would not call him a particularly picky eater, I suppose."

"Hmm. What about sweet stuff?"

"I have not seen him have many, but when I had just arrived in Japan, Alciel mentioned using his rice cooker to bake a cake, and Chiho has delivered ice cream to their apartment before. He is familiar with the genre, at least."

"All right. Thanks. I'll see you later."

"Bye-bye, Suzu-Sis!"

"Of course. Take care. You too, Alas Ramus."

The two made sure their shoes were fully on before turning and waving. Suzuno heard their footsteps down the stairs outside as she stood up to lock the door.

"Hmm?"

Then, she stopped, gripped by the feeling that something was off.

"Hmmmm?"

Did Emi say something odd just before leaving? Something she'd normally never say at all? Suzuno brooded over it, her head tilted to one side, but soon turned the latch on the door, failing to pinpoint what exactly bothered her. She looked at the clock. It was a bit early still, but she decided to get her things and head to the public bath.

"Oh…"

Then, she realized what had bothered her, and it brightened up her face. That was right—it was usually Chiho who worried about the demons' food preferences. This was the first time Emi had demonstrated any interest at all, so it had thrown Suzuno a bit.

"Of course, of course. That's what it was."

But then, the clear skies in Suzuno's mind began to cloud up, turning into great, swirling, gray edifices that could start storming at any moment.

"Wait…"

Emi had wanted to know what Maou liked to eat.

"Waaaait…"

But what on earth for?

"Emilia?"

She called for her out loud, in the direction she'd walked off to, not really sure what to feel.

"Mommy, wait, wait! Too fast!"

Alas Ramus was pumping her legs at full speed to keep up with Emi, who was walking unusually briskly through the dark Sasazuka night. The pom-pom on her hat bounced around with each stride she took.

"Oh! I-I'm sorry."

Emi, apparently having no idea she was going so quickly, stopped and turned around. Alas Ramus, maintaining her momentum, wound up running right into her leg, wrapping her arms around it.

"Mommy, *boom*!"

"Ahh! Oh, Alas Ramus, that's dangerous!"

Emi laughed at the half-playing child. Then, the next question froze her.

"Mommy, you okeh? Your face's all red."

"…!"

She brought a hand to her face. It was a winter night. It'd be too cold to tell if it was "all red" just from touching it. Besides, she was under a streetlight. From Alas Ramus's position, the glare shouldn't have made it possible to see Emi's face. Maybe she was mistaken.

"Um, Alas Ramus?" she finally said, repeating those excuses in her mind.

"Yeh?"

"Alas Ramus, do you love Daddy?"

The young girl grinned, looking a little bashful.

"Hee-hee-hee-hee! I wuv 'im!"

"…Oh."

Emi nodded, lips pursed together…

"Ah! Mommy?"

…then she lowered Alas Ramus's hat over her face, before crouching down and embracing her.

"…Hey, Alas Ramus?"

"Waph!"

In a hug at such close range, the hat didn't keep the child from wrapping her arms around the smiling Emi's neck. Emi's face was blacked out by the glare from the lights.

"Daddy…"

Nobody would ever know what expression was on it.

"I wonder what kind of chocolate he'd like…?"

✳

It was half past ten, and Maou's shift ended a bit before closing tonight. The sight of a light on in Room 202 made him raise an eyebrow.

"Whoa, Suzuno's still here tonight?"

It wasn't like Suzuno was up late so she could bother Maou, but knowing he wasn't the only person in this whole building was still a bit reassuring. So he climbed the outdoor stairs, going over the routine he had ahead of him before bedtime.

"You're back?" she asked.

"Agh!"

Suzuno popped out of the Room 202 door right as he got there. It startled him majorly.

"Wh-what?! What is it?!" he screeched.

"…"

But despite the sudden ambush, all she seemed interested in doing was silently staring at him.

"Suzuno?"

"I have a few things I wish to ask you…"

"Huh?"

"But could you please show a little more resolve? Like a Devil King?"

"What the heck?"

This wasn't exactly the greatest way to be welcomed by your neighbor after a long evening shift.

"Silence. You are the one letting a little gift of chocolate rattle you to the core. The more you act like that, you realize, the more pain you put on others."

"Wait a sec! Why do you know about that? ...Was it Emi, or Acieth?"

If Suzuno found out today—right after coming back from Ente Isla—it was either Emi, whom he told, or Acieth, who was there.

"Both. Acieth, in particular, ran us through the wringer."

This was a double surprise to Maou.

"B-Both? Through the wringer? What did Acieth do...?"

"I no longer wish to talk about it. If you want to know, ask her yourself. Or Chiho."

"Ngah!"

That was more of a noise than a coherent response. Why was Chiho's name coming up?

"You..." Suzuno continued, uncorking everything she had bottled up upon a bewildered Maou. "What are you even doing? Because lately, I am having trouble surmising your motives. What are you thinking about, as you go on in life?"

"What am I *thinking* about? Why're you lecturing me like Urushihara?"

"You may want to conquer the world as the Devil King. You may want a full-time job as a human being. I care not. But what is your name? *Devil King* or *Full-Time Employee*? Because if the demon Satan, or the human Sadao Maou, is neither Devil King *nor* salaried worker, what will you live for, then?"

Suzuno was being much harsher than usual.

"...Did something happen?"

"Nothing!" she all but cried out. This was clearly a lie, but Maou didn't have it in him to pursue it. The buzzing of the nearly burned-out fluorescent light above them seemed like a roar to him.

"Look, Devil King."

"...Mm?"

"I have no idea what the demon realm is like. I have no idea how you came to be the Devil King. But you have Alciel, you have Lucifer, you have Camio and the Malebranche; you have these massive hordes of demons following you, and you unified them all under your rule."

"Yeah... Pretty much."

"You became a king because you were stronger, more charming, and more magnanimous than any other candidate. Am I right? So would you mind showing me some of that magnanimity? Because as a Great Demon General, I find it difficult to respect my leader at the moment."

"...You always bring that up only when it serves you, huh?"

"That is how you put it, but I only use a title when it needs using." Suzuno gave him a vexed look as she clutched at her kimono sleeves with her cold, trembling fingers. "When my leader, the Devil King, is lost in life, I may wish to help him. But would you even listen to a human? A member of the Reconciliation Panel? You would not, would you?"

"Well, no, I wouldn't..."

"So I have to be a Great Demon General, do I not? Because that is the only way I can serve you."

"Suzuno?"

Maou blinked. This was a lot of strange stuff she was saying. Suzuno, perhaps realizing this, brought her clenched hands up to her mouth.

"Re... Regardless."

"Yes?"

"I just wanted to tell you to get it together. That is all."

"Right. Um, thanks. I'll keep it in mind."

"...Good-bye, then."

Suzuno turned toward her room, in the dry air of the hallway.

"Uh, Suzuno?"

"What?" she said, stopping but not turning around.

"I know I'm in the doghouse already, but can I ask you something? Did Chi..."

"No."

"……Huh?"

"No, you can*not* ask me something. I do not want to hear it. I do not wish to say anything irresponsible, and there is nothing I could say to you anyway. I lack the……to do so. I do not wish to say anything careless."

"Wh-what? You lack the what?"

"If Chiho is an important person to you, then go find out for yourself. Farewell."

With that, she went back into Room 202 without awaiting a reply. Maou heard the latch locking, followed by empty silence, but he stayed in the hallway a while longer. She had mouthed off at him and left without letting him get a word in edgewise—but something must have happened today. Something that drove her to wait around for him and say all that.

"…Ahhh."

He scratched the side of his head, then slammed the Room 201 door behind him—attempting to calm his dispirited heart, but knowing full well that things had changed. That they couldn't go back to how vague everything was before.

"…………Ahh."

Suzuno crouched down on her side of the front door, unable to venture farther inside. Her light, hurried breaths, exhaled through her fingers, were turning white inside a room that had grown cold in the night.

"What a liar…"

Removing her hands from her face, she looked at her palms. Palms that were once stained in blood, in the name of her duties—but were now refined, pretty, bearing the smell of peaches from her hand soap. The kind of feminine hands you would see anywhere in Japan, or Earth, or Ente Isla.

"What a liar," she whispered to herself again. "Do I need a reason to take a detour like this?"

No matter how cheap and thin the walls were in Villa Rosa Sasa-zuka, the sound of her voice would never leave the room. Then, as if to shake off all the weakness, she rocketed back up to a standing position.

"...What is so wrong about it?"

Tossing her sandals off, she stepped onto her tatami-mat floor, eyeing the pot on top of her oven burner. It was full of *nikujaga*, a hearty stew with meat and potatoes, and there was clearly too much of it for a single woman's dinner.

"Who cares about beliefs? To hell with all of them."

She reached out to turn the dial for the burner, then quickly removed her hand.

"All these lies, this dishonesty, this total lack of drive to surpass anyone..."

Suzuno put the lid back on the pot, then laid out a futon before unraveling her belt, changing into her *nemaki* pajamas, and snuggling in.

"And the worst thing of all," she dryly whispered as she closed her eyes, "I have no right to criticize him. The Reconciliation Panel would have a field day with me."

Then:

"Hmm?"

The phone next to her pillow chirped out a message notification. She picked it up. The name on the screen read "Shirou Ashiya."

"Alciel?"

He was in Devil's Castle at the moment. This was an Idea Link-based text. Suzuno opened it, suspecting a potential emergency, only to find something even more surprising.

"We have located the Nothung and the Sorcery of the False Gold. Please contact me. I wish to discuss our search for the Astral Gem and recovery of the Spear of Adramelechinus."

In relatively short order, they now had two of the four parts needed to turn Ente Isla's Devil's Castle into an interstellar ark to drive them to heaven. If two of the three relics they assumed were in the demon realm were already discovered, the third would no doubt come along soon after. The problem, then, became the Spear of Adramelechinus, the sole relic in human hands, and how to procure it in a peaceful manner.

"Hard to say if this is perfect or awful timing," Suzuno said with a smile. "But this should amp things up a bit. For me, and for all of us."

She texted out a quick acknowledgment before setting her phone on mute and gently shutting her eyes.

THE DEVIL KING AND THE HERO DON'T HAVE VERY MUCH TO DO

"It was common knowledge in the demon realm that the Spear of Adramelechinus is a weapon passed down from generation to generation in the Bluehorn clan, one of the realm's most powerful families. As anyone who knows or has fought Adramelech knows, it was, like, huge. Incredibly long, even by demon standards."

"Yeah, the handle alone was as thick as a support pillar in a castle."

To any of the regulars at Room 201 in Villa Rosa Sasazuka, the conference of these two speakers would have been quite an unusual sight.

"The Bluehorns wield a lot of magic that works best with water and ice, and it's said that spear has something to do with it. I guess that was the reason Adramelech was the demon-horde commander in the Northern Island, as water-rich and close to arctic climes as it is."

"Makes sense to me. When Adramelech first took over the continent, we started seein' these trees of ice dotted here and there. We called 'em ice-tree towers, but when I learned they were magical plants born from the demonic force Adramelech ran through underground springs to watch over us, I was pretty shocked."

The scene was the general headquarters of the group known among its members as the United East-West Anti-Divinity Alliance, situated on Isla Centurum, the Central Continent—and when Suzuno returned there, upon hearing Ashiya's news that two of their targets had been secured, the sight of Urushihara and Albert leading a strategy conference was so novel, it made regular novelty seem trite by comparison.

The sight of Urushihara—the model jobless slacker—assuming a leadership position in the force was like the extra-special secret sauce liberally sprinkled over such a crazily novel sight. Neither Maou, nor Emi, nor Chiho were there. Ashiya was off on business in the Eastern Island, and Emeralda had returned to Saint Aile for keeping matters on the Central Continent safe. Suzuno rued the fact that she had nobody to commiserate with about how bizarre this setup looked.

"But…yeah. When our little questing group defeated Adramelech, we kinda left the Spear to our friends in the Northern Island as a memorial present."

"Right. Now, I'd like to make sure no one outside our group knows about our operation to invade heaven. We have Hazel Rumack conducting business for us in Saint Aile, but neither the emperor nor his administration are aware of this. If we have all those Northern Island dudes coming in to crash the party, it's gonna be such a pain in the ass that I'll want to throw in the towel right there."

"Yes. So the first order of business is to discuss how we can swipe Adramelech's relic from the Northern Island with as small a party as we can manage."

The meeting, led by Urushihara and Albert, was attended by Suzuno, Rumack, Farfarello, Laila, and Nord.

"You described it as a 'memorial present' for the Northern forces," Nord hesitantly said, being the most normal human being in the group. "So where is it right now?"

"I think this'll be the easiest way to explain it," Urushihara replied, taking out his familiar laptop. The screen showed a photograph of a town located in what looked like a range of high mountains. "I had Ciriatto from the Malebranche take these pics with Maou's digital camera, and y'know, considering how he's all claws and no, like, anything else, he's pretty handy with that thing. Anyway, this is a shot of Phiyenci, which is the capital shared by the clans in the Northern Island. It's nicknamed the 'Goat Pasture.'"

The shot depicted a wide plain that was filled to the horizon with uniquely low-roofed brick buildings. In one corner was a wide-open space that took up about a fifth of the landscape, like a sports ground too big for its own good. In its middle stood a high, towering structure, apparently some kind of monument. With a tap of the keys, he switched to a close-up photo of this edifice, revealing it to be some kind of giant metallic pillar.

"Look at that," Rumack sighed as she looked at the high-resolution image. "Such an incredibly detailed depiction... I want this."

"Don't abuse it," warned Albert, taking Rumack out of her reverie. She sat back up, straightening her posture.

"Dude, I'd be happy to show you a few models way faster than this pile of crap."

Urushihara never missed a moment to slam Maou's Luddite approach to electronic purchases.

"But anyway," he continued, "I think these pics give us everything we need. It's pretty clear, right? They put up the Spear of Adramelechinus in the middle of the Goat Pasture as a monument to symbolize the defeat of the Great Demon General of the North."

It seemed like a natural, preplanned part of the Pasture, staring down with all its glory at the largest city in the Northern Island. The butt end of the Spear was buried in the ground, secured with something resembling cement around the base, and visitors could go right up to it if they wanted. It almost looked like a gravestone memorializing Adramelech, and judging by the people lazily picnicking and meeting up around the site, it was clearly a bit of a tourist attraction.

"So I guess you can tell," concluded Urushihara, "that we can't just take the Spear or ask for it or whatever, right?"

Suzuno, Rumack, and Nord nodded back.

The fact that the Northern Island, a geographically punishing land filled with innumerable races, ethnic groups, and clans, was heralded as the most peaceful of Ente Isla's five continents was mainly thanks to Phiyenci, the Goat Pasture.

Every five years, the Island held a "zirga," a large, united gathering of representatives from all the major players native to the land. On this occasion, they'd hold the election for the chief herder, the head of state for the entire Northern Island. This election took a good two weeks to carry out, and it turned the Goat Pasture into a huge festival, filled with the produce, culture, and customs of people across the region.

The zirga was also an occasion for all the Mountain Corps, the elite fighters picked to defend the Northern Island, to assemble and (if necessary) hold combat games in order to solve deeper problems that no measure of discussion between clans could solve. This meant that the history of this land involved very few massive, blood-soaked wars; it also meant that the clans almost never dared to invade one another's territories. If the times called for it, all these clans could unite to form an astonishingly well-oiled machine of warfare, but in times of peace, it was much more of a "what's yours is yours, what's mine is mine" climate.

Thanks to this national character, the people's image of Adramelech fundamentally differed from the way other lands thought of their local Great Demon General.

"I mentioned this in passing to you a while ago, Bell, but seriously, Adramelech was *this* close to having the Northern Island welcome him with open arms," Urushihara volunteered.

"What? Why?" a surprised Rumack asked. When the Devil King's Army invaded the Western Island, she was vice-captain of the palace forces, only to have her land subjugated by the very slacker leading this meeting right now. Under Urushihara's, or Lucifer's, rule, the Western Island—while not as much of a mess as Malacoda's Southern Island—was not at all the well-oiled bureaucracy Alciel ran in the East, and the human casualties and chaos were at least as bad as anywhere else in the world. It was hard for Rumack to imagine that a Great Demon General nearly took over the North without a fight.

"Yeah, I guess you could say Adramelech's personality was a good fit for the Northern Island's people, hmm? In an understated way, he had a real human side to him."

"Hee-hee!"

Suzuno snickered a bit at this. She had heard it from him before.

"Once he disarmed the Mountain Corps and booted 'em from

the island, he made the chief herder hold a zirga, where he talked about the policy behind his invasion and let the opposing clans have their say. Anyone who didn't go along with the guy got slaughtered, of course, but he actually accepted some of their feedback, too. I dunno. Just the fact that he was open to talking at all, you know; that was enough for the folks up there."

It wasn't that anyone actively wanted the Devil King's Army to be there, but compared with elsewhere, the people were more willing to accept a negotiated defeat.

"Kinda weird to think, though," Urushihara went on. "Like, when I think of Adramelech, I picture this dude who couldn't think his way out of a paper bag. I can't believe he'd be crafty enough to try currying favor with humans."

"Lucifer, can you shut up a sec? Rumack's glaring at me."

"Ow!"

Albert, much larger than the twiggy fallen angel, gave Urushihara a sharp elbow.

Here at this meeting, Rumack was the only person who actively saw Urushihara as a foe. Albert had only joined Emi's quest after she had defeated Lucifer, but having him and Rumack—villain and victim—face-to-face made for a very delicate situation.

"Anyway," Albert continued, "the problem is that Phiyenci, along with all the clans in the Northern Island, have accepted Adramelech's occupation as part of their shared history. I'm from there, and since I helped Emilia beat 'im, that spear he left kinda symbolizes a turning point in that history, y'see? Defeat, followed by victory."

"So you're sayin' they need it? That sucks. It's kind of ours, dude."

"Shut up, Lucifer."

"Are you saying," Suzuno ventured, "that you would not intervene with them for us, Albert? You don't think they would give up the Spear?"

"It ain't gonna happen," came the point-blank reply from Albert. "Never in a million years. That's why I got you all together here, ain't it? Anything I'd try is gonna cause drama. If we really mess this up, we might wind up prodding the Southern Island, too."

"…True," Suzuno groaned.

Maou and Emi might have only been in this for Alas Ramus, but Rumack and the knights under her command had a clearer, more present reason—to defeat Ignora and avoid the potential destruction of Ente Isla's humanity in the nearish future. But doing this involved finding the Noah Gears and launching Devil's Castle into space, and the humans and the demons had to team up to achieve that. That was only possible thanks to Maou's deep links to Rumack and Emeralda from the holy empire of Saint Aile, as well as Ashiya's extremely personal relationship with Hu Shun-Ien, the Azure Emperor of Efzahan. Most other nations weren't even aware of this operation, and for that matter, it had never been formally announced to the world that the Hero Emilia and the Devil King were even alive.

If this effort got out to the public, whatever the truth was behind it, everyone knew people would hear it as *Saint Aile's Hazel Rumack and the Azure Emperor forged a secret pact with the demons* and run with that. It'd sow the seeds of suspicion all over the North and the South, as well as the smaller kingdoms in the West.

No one in this group had ever suggested that they should elicit support from other nations—this being a quest to save humanity, after all. The state of the Sephirah and Tree of Sephirot was something you really had to be close to Maou and Emi to fully grasp. In areas where Church influence was still weak, it'd take decades to even persuade people that Sephirot was connected to the holy force that ran the world. There was no way to convince everyone that teaming up with demons was the only thing to do, and no nation was about to sign off on a mission as daunting as "slaying a god."

Without any real, visible danger like the Devil King's Army coming their way, there wasn't going to be any teamwork—the power struggles taking place within the Federated Order that was formed to rebuild the Central Continent made that clear enough. And these power struggles were laying themselves out like capillaries, along the lines of every political and economic issue facing every nation in the post-Devil King world, making the players ever greedier as they laid their cards down.

That was why Rumack, Emeralda, and the Azure Emperor decided to hurry things along themselves instead. That would make everything go far, far smoother, and keeping it confidential would also put a lid on most of the ensuing power games. It meant a large, heavy burden for Saint Aile and Efzahan, but this burden was also an advantage—the ability to tackle this potential threat ahead of anyone else, a chance that far outclassed the potential losses that prodding the heavens and Sephirot might lead to. Saint Aile and Efzahan definitely had other motivations as well, but there was no doubting that this alliance was the smoothest way to handle this heavenly war.

And now, there was a thorny problem—or rather, a pointy one. Having the Spear of Adramelechinus inside Phiyenci, the shared capital of the Northern Island, presented numerous difficulties. It was physically and politically impossible to take the Spear without the common people knowing.

"Even if we negotiated with them," Suzuno mused, "the question becomes who *we* would send. We would need Albert to bear the full brunt of responsibility, but he could hardly handle it by himself."

"Yeah, that's the thing. Lemme make this clear: All right, my name's a bit known around there as a heroic companion, 'n' all that. But once I set foot back home, I'm my momma's boy all over again, you know what I mean? I ain't really got the clout to pull a bunch of clan chiefs my way. And this is Adramelech's final relic! We'd have to get the chief herder involved, and by that point, there's not much even Eme could do. In terms of overall balance, I'd say people like Rumack or Emilia are our best bets to contact them with."

A chief herder didn't have the absolute authority to (for example) give direct orders to all clans on the continent, but the leader's words truly did have force behind them. Everyone knew the extent of the powers they wielded; they wouldn't recommend someone apt to abuse them. Besides, however things worked inside the Island, if an outside visitor wanted to see the chief herder, they would still need an ambassador-level title if they expected an audience this lifetime.

"In that case," Urushihara said, "let's break out Emilia. If we explain things to her, I doubt she's gonna say no."

"No," Rumack flatly replied. "If you're considering her, go with me instead. This way will take longer, but it'll save us trouble later. With Emilia, things would get too big, too fast. Depending on how the chief herder responds, it could turn into a fight for control of her, like in Efzahan. With me, if anything happens, Saint Aile can step up to put it out."

"Hold on," protested Albert. "If you're not on the scene here, it's gonna be hard to balance out the human side. Even if it's me, Eme, and Bell, we can't deal with Efzahan and the emperor leading them *that* well."

Suzuno sighed. "No matter what we do, we keep running into these stupid power struggles…"

The literal end of the world didn't mean political and monetary issues simply disappeared. Very little of Saint Aile's government—not even the imperial court itself—knew about this operation. If word got out, Emeralda and Rumack would get hauled in front of their parliament and probably banned from further participation. It'd also mean the Northern Island would become broadly aware of foreign elements from Saint Aile and Efzahan attempting to influence political matters in their homeland. Rumack's public presence in the Northern Island was thus unwise.

"Besides," Albert continued, "what do you think would happen if we sent Emilia up there? The Northern Island would welcome 'er, yeah, but to the Southern Island, we'd be a bunch of outcasts. All that stuff at Heavensky's been kept on the down-low, except for a few rumors here and there. All the world has so far are these sketchy tales of Emilia with nothing solid to back them up. If the Northern clans accept that she's alive, Emilia's never gonna have a calm day for the rest of her life. The fallout might even extend all the way to Japan, that other land."

"You humans are so meddlesome," noted Farfarello. "It is just as Lord Lucifer says. The Spear belongs to Lord Adramelech. If all you humans have to offer us are petty excuses, we demons can simply seize it any time we please, can we not? There is no need to burden your human nations any further beyond that."

"Right!" Urushihara gave the demon a sarcastic round of applause. "I was waiting to hear that, Farfarello."

Albert, on the other hand, gave him a rap on the head. "Hold it, you fool of a Malebranche! Did you forget how you lost several generals out of your Efzahan volunteer army with that logic? If a cadre of demons attacks the Goat Pasture now, at a time of peace, you could wind up baiting the Federated Order into wiping out any demons left on this planet. If this castle here gets attacked, getting up to the moon's gonna be the least of our worries, let me tell you."

"Pfft. What is your bright idea, then? If we left matters to you humans, judging by this conversation, it sounds impossible to retrieve the Spear without any difficulty or loss of life."

Albert and Rumack winced. The demon was hitting them where it hurt.

"Yes, the demon realm has been racked with strife and disorder as of late, but now, we have banded under the banner of the Devil King, ready to follow his orders. You humans, meanwhile, are too obsessed over honor and greed to even care about the future of your descendants. I can hardly see how we'll kill any gods like this."

"Enough, Farfarello," Suzuno interjected. "If anything, this whole effort is a huge step forward for us."

"…Pfft."

The demon held his tongue. Suzuno was a Great Demon General, more or less, and he had some respect for that.

"Then how about this, Albert? I could work through the Reconciliation Panel and request that we borrow the Spear in order to investigate the remains of the Devil King's Army. We can return it once our battle is over, and I think if we give a bare minimum of explanation, the reaction should be rather more measured…"

"That could work, yeah. It'd get it in our hands, at least. But I guarantee ya someone from the North's gonna be with it the whole time. And how're we gonna explain it when it's people from the Central Continent hauling it off—not Sankt Ignoreido, headquarters of the Church? We can't casually say *Oh, we'll explain everything later once we give it back*."

"…Yes. Good point. We *are* taking one of the island's most valuable assets."

"Yeah, and don't forget the other problem, Suzuno: Even if we manage to make off with the Spear scot-free, someone from the North's gonna be looking over it. If they're good people, then great, but if they start carryin' on about what the Island or the clans get out of this, it's gonna blow up on us before we can launch the castle. The North and the West could wind up at war by the time we get back from the moon."

"Man, what a pain, dude," Urushihara grumbled. "So what can we even do, then?"

Albert was proving to have a knack for shooting down every suggestion from his companions. Everyone was starting to feel weary.

"Besides," Urushihara went on, "why do you have, like, so little influence in the Northern Island, Albert Ende? I mean, Emeralda Etuva's one thing, but a word or two from Emilia was all it took to get the head of Saint Aile's palace guard here on our side."

"Quit remindin' me," Albert groused resentfully. "Yeah, maybe I helped the Hero, but before then, remember how you whipped my ass and the asses of my whole Mountain Corps? Folks have long memories up there! And between all the stuff I've been doing for the West with Eme and the fight I had with ya, I ain't exactly on great terms with the clan chieftains at the moment, no. Plus, the current chief herder—Dhin Dhem Wurs is her name—she's the one who banded all the clans together when Adramelech took over and the one who slapped the demon's spear up as a monument. I just haven't helped out the North enough to ask her to borrow the Spear for—"

"Whoa. Albert?!"

"...Mm? What?"

It was Laila, who had taken a step back from the group and listened silently, who sent up the whoop of protest.

"Who did you say the chief herder was?"

"Huh?"

"You said it was Dhin Dhem Wurs?"

"Yeah..."

"The Dhin Dhem Wurs who was born from a side family of the Wurs clan? The youngest of eleven boys and girls, but so talented with a bow and arrow that the legends say she was born 'with enough bows for the whole family'? The Dhin Dhem I know from the Wurs clan is small, pushy, and never one to humor fools..."

Albert opened his eyes wide. "What, you know the lady?"

Given the chief herder's position as head of state, it wasn't too unusual for someone to know her name and history. Laila went far beyond that.

"Dhin Dhem was the last person I gave a Yesod fragment to outside my husband and Emilia."

"What?!"

"Huh?!"

"Whaaa?!"

Suzuno, Urushihara, and Albert understood the portent of that.

"This was a good sixty years ago! She still went by her childhood name of Lidem Wurs at the time." Laila blinked a bit, not expecting all this attention. "Before my husband and Emilia, Dhin Dhem was the last of...what I suppose you could call *candidates* to be a Hero."

She held her right hand out, palm down.

"Is that...a Yesod fragment? The cores for Emilia's holy sword and the Cloth of the Dispeller?"

Rumack couldn't help but nearly shout at the small, mesmerizing stone she had in her hand. Laila focused on it for a moment, and it began to faintly shine, then silently emit a purple light that extended out in a line pointing northward. She turned toward the ray of light, eyes closed, for a moment, then raised her face up as the beam disappeared.

"Albert... Rumack... Do you think things would be less complicated if I could speak with Dhin Dhem Wurs real quick?"

"Ah, ah, that..."

"Less complicated ain't the half of it."

Albert and Rumack exchanged looks with each other.

"Let's go, then."

"Go?"

"Yes," declared the purple-haired angel. "To the chief herder. And don't worry. She'd remember me. She is a kind person, more sensitive to the flow of earth and air than anyone in the Wurs clan. I'm sure she will hear us out."

✳

Suzuno was still anxious.

Back on Earth, Laila had the troubling habit of manipulating everyone around her and failing to wrap things up neatly at the end. It meant her claim of Chief Herder Dhin Dhem Wurs carrying a Yesod fragment seemed implausible at best—and even if it was true, Suzuno wasn't sure the head of state would remember Laila after six decades.

But the moment they all stepped out from the Gate in the main Church cathedral in Phiyenci, she discovered a group of large, muscular men in the Northern Island's colorful garb waiting to greet them. Or Laila, really. It surprised her a little.

"Which one of you is Lady Laila?"

Four of them had taken the trip to Phiyenci—Laila, Albert, Rumack, and Suzuno. Before any of them could speak, one of the men was asking for Laila by name, eyeing the three women in the group.

"I am."

Laila took a step forward. The man looked at her, confused.

"I understood that Lady Laila had silver hair with a twinge of blue to it."

"Well, after sixty years, a woman will want to change her hair color sometimes."

"…!"

After the fracas on the Fukutoshin subway line, Maou's magical force had healed Laila, giving her hair the purple tint it still had today. She claimed she could reverse the dye job if she wanted, but it was a pain, and she didn't like her original color that much anyway, so she kept it.

The excessively casual nature of their exchange made Suzuno internally sweat a little, but the man looked only a tad let down. "I see," he said. "I suppose you *are* the woman I heard about."

"How did Dhin Dhem Wurs describe me?"

"She described you," the envoy immediately replied, "as 'a handful.'"

"I see the years haven't dulled her tongue at all," Laila said with a smile. It was not met by the envoy, who spun around and motioned for the quartet to follow him.

"Come this way, please. The chief herder is waiting for you."

The other three in the group meekly followed the order, all of them unsure what Laila and the man's banter meant for them.

Phiyenci, it turned out, was wholly deserving of its nickname.

The Goat Pasture was filled with countless examples of the animal, in all shapes and sizes. Many were on sale in the market streets for their fur, milk, or meat, while others, large enough to give an adult horse or cow a run for its money, were pulling carts and transport wagons. Young girls, clad in the traditionally colorful, natural-dyed wear that was a trademark of most mountain people, even had baby goats tagging along with them like dogs or cats, which was the most darling thing ever.

This city was around three thousand feet above sea level, resulting in thinner air and lower temperatures. Given the lack of flat land to build on, Phiyenci was relatively crammed with people; as Albert explained, the port town on the continent's southern tip was much larger and more commercially active. Still, the zirga had never moved from here in all its years. Every road and back alley was well paved, and the current Mountain Corps kept the order in every corner of the city. Diplomatic missions from nations in other continents were dotted around town, affirming its position as the nerve center of the Northern Island.

Suzuno, Laila, and Rumack had all come prepared with heavier outfits to deal with the cold, but Albert was in his same old leather jacket. Phiyenci was where people from every clan in the island gathered, and they could see a vast variety of ethnic groups running up and down the streets. One would expect a lot of people who looked like Albert, dark-skinned with white hair, but some from the northern reaches boasted lily-white skin and golden hair instead, while others looked little different from the average Efzahanian—perhaps some Eastern blood had mixed in at one point.

The one thing that united them—and made them all eye-catching— was the flashy, colorful clothing. Only a very small handful took Albert's approach and went with all black. Some used almost every color in the rainbow, while others dressed in nothing but red or orange (the color of their clan, perhaps?). Every clan seemed to have their own style, color selection, and materials; it almost seemed like too much of a jumble for a city meant to be the capital of the continent, but it certainly offered insights into the character of the Northern Island—a gigantic federation with hundreds of clans that somehow found a way to all get along.

Suzuno and Rumack paid it no special mind, both having been to Phiyenci on official business several times. But considering how their envoy was taking Laila to the chief herder, it seemed strange how he was sticking to the city's busiest business streets.

Their destination, in the end, was even more confusing. "Um, is this it?" Albert asked, unable to contain his curiosity. They had walked for less than twenty minutes from the cathedral, only to stop at a place not at all grand or lofty. In short, it was a cheap restaurant selling goat meat cooked on an iron plate, the kind of place you'd see everywhere in town.

"Sir Albert Ende Ranga," the man said, turning toward him.

"Ranga" was Albert's clan name, one he was forced to abandon after Adramelech defeated his Mountain Corps force.

He continued, "The chief wishes to treat you to a grand meal."

"…!"

Albert froze for a moment, not expecting this.

"My lady wishes for our visitors from the West to enjoy this as well. She has been a fan of this establishment since a young age. She has reserved the entire dining room for the afternoon, so please, make yourselves at home."

And with that, the man walked away and into the crowds, not even bothering to open the door for them.

The four of them gave one another quizzical looks, before Laila decided to take the lead. "Let's go in," she said, pulling the door open. Inside, they found your typical restaurant space—a few chair-lined tables, all in the traditional Northern Island style. A more formal room lay beyond, its floors lined with woven mats; in the middle of it was a sunken fireplace that guests were meant to sit around.

"Come in already! It's too damned cold outside!"

The voice came from the other side of the hearth, as far away from the entrance as possible.

"?!"

Suzuno was the only one to pick up on who it was.

"I'm getting on in years, y'understand! This weather is killer on my knees! Get yourselves in here!"

The nasal griping reeled them all inside, Laila taking the lead as they walked toward the rear. There, they found a small, elderly woman using a wooden spatula to mix some meat and vegetables on the iron plate above the sunken hearth, adding in sauce of a shade Suzuno had never seen before.

"It's been a while, eh? I was surprised to hear you'd become chief herder."

Laila casually greeted the stern-looking woman. It made the spatula stop in place over the vegetables.

"I certainly can't call you 'Lidem' any longer."

"Anyone who called me *that* has been feedin' the grass and plants from six feet under for years! They're probably all mountain-deer droppings by now!"

The small head, covered in a multihued wool cap, was thrown upward, a pair of eyes looking up at the transfixed pair.

"!"

Suzuno gasped at the power behind those eyes. Was *this* Dhin Dhem Wurs—this old woman with a jeweled monocle, small and bent over even when seated?

"What, didn't you know that Dhin Dhem Wurs was this old lady with one foot in the grave?"

The woman who Laila had called Lidem, seeing through Suzuno's trepidation, half lunged at her.

"Who're you, then? Some young up-and-comer in the Church, if I had to guess. Now how are you gonna climb through the ranks if one glare from an old lady like me makes you ruin your garments?"

"Ah, n-no, I…"

"Laila! How could you be so impolite, so careless, so silent for so long?! I'm sure you got reasons for showing up in my life right when I'm old and decrepit, don't you?! And yet, you're just as much a young fashion maven as ever! You could at least look like a forgotten retiree like me!"

"I'm trying to look as plain as I can. Your hat's a lot prettier than anything I'm wearing, Lidem."

"Of course it is! The youngest daughter of my third son knitted it for me, back when she was little. It's the best you'll ever find!"

The old woman began mixing up the food on the plate again, suddenly remembering why she was here.

"So! Hazel!"

"Y-yes?!"

The woman's eyes were on Rumack now. "You're still single, aren'tcha? Maybe you think you'll be young forever, but lemme tell *you*! Between how you are and how *I* am, it's all in the blink of an eye, my friend! We don't have all the time in the world, you know, unlike that debauched, color-blind angel over there! Get yourself a man and settle down already!"

It was like Wurs was the head of the Federated Order of the Five Continents' nagging grandmother. The two of them knowing each other was no great surprise, but this wasn't the kind of conversation two political figures like this would ever normally have.

"Ah, but keep your hands off that fool, the crown prince of Saint Aile! He'd be such a waste for a smart cookie like you! I tell you, that brat hasn't gotten any more brains since he was a baby!"

"Um..."

She certainly wasn't pulling any punches. It was an almost treasonous way to describe the next emperor of Saint Aile.

"Mark my words, you'll never find any decent men in the West. I can see *that* much over in Sankt Ignoreido. They act sooo high-and-mighty, like *oh, I have nothing but a chair, a desk, and my scriptures at home*, but once they get old, all they do is compete to see which of 'em can pile up more gold and jewels in their vaults! I tell you, women like you gotta kick their no-good behinds outta there before it gets even worse! You hear me?!"

"Y-yes…?"

The target of her ire had switched back to Suzuno midway. Suzuno could do little but squawk awkwardly.

"And *you*, Ranga!"

But she saved Albert for the end. Wurs picked up an earthenware plate and a pair of chopsticks, using the spatula to shovel the meat onto the dish, then shoved it in Albert's face.

"Here."

"Uhh…"

"Here! Try it for me!"

"Um, okay…"

Albert, completely floored by the presence exuded by a woman less than half his height, reached out to take it.

"Did your mother teach you to eat standing up? Get in here and sit down!!"

"Y-yes, Chief!"

Cowed by the nasal voice, Albert quickly sat by the hearth. Suzuno could barely keep up with this torrent of events, but Albert did his best, gingerly taking the meat-laden plate and the wood-hewn chopsticks. Wurs jerked her head forward, motioning at him to eat up. Unable to say no to the lord of every clan in the Northern Island, he took in a mouthful of the steaming meat.

"How is it? You're trying it for me, so you gotta say what you think of it."

"…Um."

Albert was just as confused as everyone else. This was the chief herder, the head of state in the Northern Island. And although he led the Mountain Corps at one point, Albert had exchanged only a few words with Dhin Dhem Wurs in his life. The Wurs and Ranga clans were far removed from each other on the social ladder, and in terms of their standings within their respective families—one way people up north judged each other—the pair couldn't be further apart. But she wanted his opinion, and he needed to give it.

"It's good. Really takes me back. It's a lot like what my grandma cooked for me as a kid."

"It is?" Albert's whisper didn't move Wurs an inch. Then, as flatly as ever:

"I've put you through a lot, haven't I."

Albert took a moment to chew over the observation before quickly replying:

"...Well, it's resulted in a lot of good memories."

"No, no, go ahead. Badmouth me a little."

"Hey, I'm a grown man. If my friends here saw me crying into the shoulder of someone old enough to be my grandma, I'd never live it down."

"Hmph. That's not very nice... And by the way, how long are you bums gonna be standing there? Sit the heck down!"

"Y-yes, Chief!"

"Er, do please excuse me."

"I would be glad to."

At the old lady's orders, Suzuno sat politely on her knees by the fireplace; Rumack attempted to but gave up and crossed her legs; and Laila casually flopped on the floor.

"Hohh! So you're the Scythe of Death, eh? I figured you'd be some sly, stealthy old lady, but you're still a young lass!"

"A young... Ah, um, Chief Wurs, I am..."

The preparation might be a bit different, but the results were pretty similar to what you'd get visiting a Mongolian barbecue place and going heavy on the spice. Suzuno was the only unfamiliar face to the chief herder, and it was only when she introduced herself that Dhin Dhem Wurs realized she carried out "holy work" for the Council of Inquisitors.

"Listen, you eatin' okay, young lady? I bet you ain't. That's why you're all stumpy like that! You're too busy doing a bunch of fuddy-duddy Church work to eat right!"

"St-stumpy...?!"

Suzuno took harsh criticism of the Church in stride at this point, but being called "stumpy" to her face made it hard to hide her shock.

"Lidem," Laila said, "Bell here is a very talented cook. I've enjoyed her food several times."

"Hah! Look at you! You couldn't even drain the blood from a goat carcass without almost fainting! Some angel you are! Now, come on! If you stay all thin like that, you'll turn into an ugly old Grim Reaper! Eat up! The meat, too, the meat!"

"Ah, ahhhh, um, I have more than enough here…!"

Suzuno could only stammer as a small mountain of goat meat ("the best part!") rose up from her plate.

"What're you talking about? You've eaten the least out of all of us! You still look like a little girl because you're skimping on the meat and fish, I tell you! Look at that midget of a court sorcerer on Saint Aile's payroll! She's living the high noble life and eating sweets all day, so she's gonna be shrimpy her whole life! Just you watch! In a few years, she's gonna plump up like a balloon!"

Suzuno winced at the pile of meat, more than enough to give anyone heartburn. Wurs was too busy berating the eating habits of Emeralda, a woman she couldn't have possibly had a connection to, to care. Suzuno was at the end of her rope.

"And Hazel!"

"Y-yes!"

"You, on the other hand; you're not a young lass any longer! You need to pick a drink and stick to it! The booze out west is all too sticky-sweet for me! Listen, lemme get some fresh fermented goat's-milk liquor sent to you soon! If you wanna drink, that'll be a lifelong friend to you, stick to that!"

"I… I can't say I like the fermented milk beverages of the North very much…"

"Well, if you keep drinking what you got now, you'll wind up with a big ol' wine-barrel belly like your emperor! You better lay off the grape and mead and spirits before they stick you up on a shelf in the cellar!"

"Hee-hee-hee! But Lidem, I remember your clan chief being livid with you after you stole some of that fermented milk and got cross-eyed drunk off it."

"Of course I did! When you're a young Wurs, you gotta learn

the difference between good and bad drink, or you'll never be a grown-up. But look at you, Laila! It's been sixty years! Have you learned how to keep your place clean yet? Don't forget, the only reason they found out I stole that drink was because you lost the bottle I used to sneak it out!"

"Whoa, whoa, Lidem…!"

"Hmph! Judging by the body language from Stumpy Scythe over there, I'm assuming you're as slobby as ever, huh?"

"St… St-Stumpy Scythe?! *Stumpy* Scythe… That, really, that is just…"

Suzuno knew that Wurs was only making fun of her *nom de guerre*, but her Japanese sensibilities told her that "Stumpy Scythe" sounded suspiciously like some cutesy character with its own cartoon and merchandising line. She cursed her body as she began stress-eating the meat on her plate.

Dhin Dhem Wurs's meddling and wheedling continued on for a considerable time to come, draining the energy from Suzuno and Rumack by the time all the food and veggies were cleaned from the griddle.

"Oh, and *also*, I had some ground-meat sandwiches made for you, so take them home with you, all right? You need to eat healthy, you hear me, Stumpy Scythe? You too, Hazel!"

""Yes, Chief…""

An afternoon spent slamming the younger generation made Dhin Dhem Wurs extremely self-satisfied. Adjusting her monocle, she turned to Laila.

"So what did you need? Lighting that up out of nowhere…"

"Oh, now you ask?"

Albert barely had enough breath in him to snap back, his stomach full to the point of bursting.

"Because you know, you gave that thing to me, then made me keep it on hand for the next sixty years without explanation."

The eye—or, that is, the monocle—she had pointed straight at Albert was festooned with a litany of fancy-looking jewels. It seemed like just the kind of garish fashion choice a woman like Wurs would enjoy. But it was only at this point that Suzuno and Albert spotted the light from one of the purplish jewels on the frame.

"You've been taking good care of it, I see."

"Well, of course I have. It's thanks to this thing that I've stayed chief herder all these years. It's the only thing I have you to thank for over the past sixty years, let me tell you. But you know…"

The eye on the other side of the lens glared at Laila.

"Here we are, this 'world-class danger' you told me about, and now I'm too damned old to do anything about it, aren't I? I can barely lift up a bow any longer. I had to force Adramelech's army on that kid Ranga instead."

"That… Well, yes. I suppose I can't blame you for seeing it that way. But Lidem, the real danger wasn't the Devil King's Army. It's coming for us right now."

"Oh?"

Wurs kept her eye on Laila, long enough for Suzuno to realize it was a Yesod fragment that was glowing on the monocle.

"I suppose you aren't lying, are you?"

"Of course not."

"But perhaps it's not true, and you just believe it is, is all."

"Oh, I assure you, it is. I was one of its causes, besides."

"Ohhh? And that isn't a lie, either. So you came over here for the first time in sixty years to tell me that? I can't wait to see what you're gonna order me to do next."

It seemed easy for Wurs to sense whether Laila was telling the truth. She didn't even bother to consult Albert about it.

"In that case, let me cut to the chase. We need to borrow the magical spear the Great Demon General Adramelech left behind. I'd like to have it taken to the Central Continent, and if possible, I don't want anyone besides you to know what we'll use it for."

For the first time this afternoon, Suzuno noticed Wurs change her expression.

"You're serious?"

First, it was surprise. Then, exasperation.

"Don't give me that nonsense. You know I could never do that."

"If you don't, the human race is going to die out."

"Oh, so it's war? And if Hazel and Stumpy Scythe are here, the

West must be involved, eh? If you want it, pry it out of our hands. Otherwise, you can't have it."

"Please, Lidem! Stop acting like a warlord! This is crucial!"

"Shut up, you slope-headed angel! If I gave you that spear without hearing the reason for it just because I knew you as a kid, I'd have every clan beating the crap out of me! They'd strip my title on the spot! So get out of here before I grind you all up and turn you into stuffing for smoked goat's intestines!"

"Lidem! Please! It's important!"

"Ugh, this is ridiculous! You never did think anything through, and you still don't! Look, whether the world's ending tomorrow or not, there're some lines you can't cross! Now get out of my sight! Ranga! Take this bum back to the West for me, now!"

"Lidemmmm! At least hear me out!"

Laila pleaded like a little girl begging for candy. There was no one else in the restaurant, but it still looked absolutely pathetic.

"You don't have a single thought in your mind, do you?" admonished Rumack.

Suzuno nodded. "And here I thought we could rely on Laila at least a little bit. I see my eyes have deceived me."

"Now I can see why people don't want to believe in gods and angels, huh, Stum—er, Crestia...?"

"General Rumack! You were about to call me 'Stumpy Scythe' just now! You were this close!"

"I—I was not! I didn't say it! I stopped midway!"

"Yes, you stopped because you *were* saying it! I am filing a formal complaint with the Devil King's Army!"

"What, not the Church?! What's happened to you?!"

Suzuno teared up a bit, cheeks reddened, as she whined at Rumack, a woman a good head taller than her and more fully developed in pretty much every other way. Rumack did everything she could to defend herself. And Albert, the only man in the room, watched this fruitless argument between two of the highest-ranked women in the world and sighed.

"...Can I go home yet?"

✳

"All right. I think I get the picture. You're gonna go shoot a fire-cracker at the moon, huh?"

The concept was massive enough to make any Ente Islan's head swim, but Dhin Dhem Wurs didn't bat an eye as she took it in.

"Laila," she said, turning toward her, "I think I *do* need to compliment you about just one thing here."

The chief herder supported her head with one hand. They had spent the ensuing hour keeping warm around the fireplace, the iron griddle trundled away now.

"What's that?"

"The way you brought Ranga, Hazel, and Stumpy over. If you had come by yourself, I would've taken this as the West wanting the Spear for itself. By the next evening, I would've warned every clan about those spear thieves, it would've killed relations between the North and the West, and Hazel probably would've lost her post."

""…""

Laila and Rumack went pale, each for different reasons.

"Still, this is a thorny problem…" Her eyebrows bunched downward as she looked at Albert. "The amount of holy force contained in Sankt Ignoreido's holy water has gone down by half in five years? You sure the groundwater hasn't changed routes due to a cave-in or something?"

"Yes. They worked in tandem with the Holy Magic Administrative Institute in Saint Aile to get those results. There's virtually no mistaking it."

"Huh. So the Church worked with the Institute after trying their boss for apostasy or whatever? That little broccoli-haired girl? I suppose I can trust in that, yes."

""*Bphht!*""

Albert and Rumack laughed at the same time. The nickname wasn't new to them.

"Wasn't there infighting between the Institute and Stumpy's group, too?"

"…No," Suzuno replied, wrinkling her nose at her own nickname.

"I was out on completely different business. I have simply built a close personal relationship with Emeralda."

It was a surprise to her, seeing how Wurs seemed to have her finger on everything going on in the world from this restaurant in the North Island. It would not be wise to defy her, Suzuno thought, just because she gave people offensive nicknames.

"Hohh. So a Church inquisitor and the head of Saint Aile's Holy Magic Administrative Institute? Strange bedfellows, I'd call that. I didn't think they'd work as closely as the Church's diplomatic mission and Saint Aile's administration would—on the surface, at least."

"Call it strange," Suzuno replied, "call it what you will."

"…I see." Wurs gave her a wry grin as her gaze shifted to Albert and Rumack. "I should have known the moment I saw Death Scythe walking around with Hazel Rumack. I'm going senile, I suppose. Hey! Ranga!"

She took a pipe and a box of tobacco out of her pocket, crushing some leaves in her hand as she pushed them into some charcoal. She put this mixture into her pipe, quickly smoking in peace.

"Is Emilia well?"

"…"

Albert didn't answer. But Dhin Dhem Wurs laughed anyway, the light glinting off her monocle.

"I see! I heard she died fighting the Devil King Satan, but… Well, well! I suppose the rumors of her being around when old man Hu from the East got his palace wrecked were true, then. Phew…"

She took two or three puffs, rather rudely using the edge of the fireplace to tap her pipe. The rapping brought Laila back to attention as Wurs stared at her.

"What's she to you?"

"What…?"

"Ranga fought alongside Emilia. That I know. Hazel was probably her legal guardian or something. And Stumpy Scythe, since she works under Olba, I can get. But what connects *you* to Emilia? And more than that, Laila—I don't think Emilia's anything like the girl you hope she is."

"…What do you mean?"

There was a touch of resentment to Laila's voice.

"Exactly what I said. Certainly, she must be a good fighter—good enough to beat Lucifer and Adramelech. But she's this sheltered little girl. She's got guts, yeah, but without Ranga, Olba, and Li'l Broccoli, she couldn't succeed on this adventure. She may be the Hero of the Holy Sword or whatever, but I don't see why you'd give her something like this."

She fussed around with her monocle a bit.

"If I could ask," Suzuno interjected, "what do you use your fragment for, Chief?"

It struck Suzuno just now that the powers of the fragments she had seen didn't follow any discernible pattern. Emi's sword and armor seemed to pop right out of her fragment, but the one Alas Ramus had in her forehead didn't demonstrate anything like that. She saw how fragments could cast beams of light between one another, but with Wurs, it seemed like Laila was using it to communicate with her in some way, too. That was the only way she could send an envoy to the cathedral to greet them, despite receiving no advance notice.

But Wurs simply glared at her. "You think this chief's going to reveal her hand to the West so easily?" She turned back to Laila. "I don't know how many people you've been tossing these fragments around to, but if all you guys are covering for Emilia, then what are you doing here, Laila?"

"There's nothing strange about it," Laila replied, head held up high. "Emilia's my daughter."

"………Your what?"

For once in her life, Wurs's jaw actually dropped.

"What's so strange about a mother working for her daughter's future?"

"Your daughter? Emilia?"

"Yes."

"This… Hoo. *That* is something. I can't even remember the last time I was this shocked. I can hardly believe my ears. Well! Hmm. You're the mother, eh? My, my, my…"

She opened her eyes wide, as wide as her wrinkled body would allow, and looked around the fireplace.

"You must be a real handful for your husband, eh?!"

"Lidem! What's that supposed to mean?"

"Exactly what it sounds like, ka-ha-ha-ha-ha!"

The chief knew exactly how Laila would respond to this.

"But... Hmm. Now I understand. I think I'll trust in all of you, then. But as you probably realize, whether I give you that spear or not's a whole other question. And I guess I see why it's bad if the world knows Emilia is alive, but wouldn't all this be a *lot* easier if she got involved?"

"We can't have that happen. For Emilia's sake."

"Yes, Hazel, I can see how you feel. But that's just a small sacrifice for the greater good. Emilia's not the type to go around calling herself a hero on a whim. It's not right to be so protective of her that other people's lives and honor play second fiddle."

This argument was perfectly valid, of course. But it made Rumack visibly dour.

"I don't see," she muttered, "how Northerners who pushed everything on Albert Ende and curled up in their shells can tell us what's right or not."

"Rumack..."

"Silence, Albert. This is the kind of 'pain' she was talking about with you, huh?" Rumack sternly gazed at Wurs. "That's like if we went into Saint Aile and the Church made Emilia into a 'Hero' icon, caring more about her glory than whether she was alive or not. You think I don't know what the clan chiefs who tarred you as a loser did when you came back with Emilia in tow?"

"...That's a fine point to jab at me with, Hazel," Wurs shot back. "You see, Stumpy Scythe? This is how you use intelligence. Remember that."

"What...happened?" Suzuno wondered.

Albert bristled. "Bell, please, don't get into—"

"Oh, come on, Ranga, it's true. Listen, Stumpy Scythe," the Northern Clans leader began sharply. "This kid here's the only Mountain

Corps captain who ever lost to an outside enemy. But it would have been the same no matter which warlord in our history was leading that army. Nobody could have defeated Adramelech. Nothing to be done about it. But what happened after that…wasn't great. This kid came back with Emilia, and he was gathering up the other clans he had been communicating with in secret…but then, there was this shameless leader who spat in his face, berating him for what happened in the past. All, you know, 'how dare you slither back here after losing so big,' and the like."

Even Suzuno could tell the "spat in his face" part was a metaphor. Judging from where Rumack was assigning the blame, this wasn't some impudent young man acting out of order, but the work of someone who let cowardice get the best of them, out of a need to separate the past from the present.

"But despite that," Suzuno reflected, "Albert beat Adramelech, he stamped out the Devil King's Army, and he is still working for people's futures—including people in the Northern Island. If you say you put pain upon him, Chief, would it be about time to repay him for that?"

"You want me to cover for being stingy with my pawns, eh? Hoo boy. Hard to mount a defense against that. I have a promise with Adramelech, too. What to do, what to do…?"

"You have a promise with Adramelech? What kind?"

Seeing the chief herder hard-pressed to respond to Rumack's ill-mannered accusations surprised Albert. Her bringing up a new name surprised him even further.

"Yes. He said, 'When that young, brave general returns to this land, you must reward him for his efforts.' That was just before he fought Emilia."

"Wha…?"

This shocked Albert enough that he forgot to breathe for a moment. All words left his tongue.

"I'm sure he saw the writing on the wall once you invaded Phiyenci. He wasn't there to fight a losing battle, of course, but Adramelech knew there was no such thing as absolutes in life."

Albert had faced off against Adramelech three times—the first when the Devil King's Army invaded, the second when Albert was ejected from the Northern Island, and the third when the demons were defeated for good. Losing the right to die as a Mountain Corps captain, and being denied the right to a final duel with him, must have filled him with shame somewhere in his mind, as if Adramelech never truly recognized him as a warrior. But no. The Great Demon General had recognized him as a true leader, through and through. And through his actions, he was admonishing Albert against an ill-advised death or duel, in order to show him he was a warrior with the hopes and dreams of his soldiers on his back.

"That...bastard... Why now?"

Wurs watched Albert as he struggled to deal with the swirling eddy of emotions in his heart, then pointed her pipe at Laila.

"Well, that's the long and short of it, so I guess I'll do what I can for you, eh? And in exchange for that, promise me you won't mess this up, all right? Because if you save the world and trigger a huge war afterward, I won't know why I bothered to listen to you!"

Laila spotted the glint in her eye. That advice was something everyone on Ente Isla should have taken to heart after Satan disappeared from the planet.

"Of course."

"I hate people who say 'of course' and don't actually do anything," Wurs spat out, missing no opportunity to gripe at her audience. "Now, kid, you know we're in the zirga season. If you're going to take the Spear, best to do it in broad daylight, with all the clans watching you."

"In broad daylight? What d'you mean?"

"Well, you've got Emilia, you've got Emeralda, you've got Ranga... Got any other pawns we can use?"

This sounded incredibly bold. The zirga was the biggest event Phiyenci hosted, attended by clans from across the continent, and she wanted them to settle things right in the middle of it.

"Because I'm gonna push the pawn of your choice toward the next chief herder election. With my backing, nobody's gonna protest you all joining the field. It'll be up to you to find a way to take the Spear without anyone minding. Don't use my influence to get the thing—participate in the zirga and make the clans want to have you haul it off. You got someone who can do that?"

✳

Upon leaving the restaurant, their hands laden with souvenirs and their clothes reeking of smoke, the thoroughly puzzled group returned to Devil's Castle.

"She wants us to pick someone to run for chief herder?" Albert scratched his head, pausing only to bite into the sandwich of ground goat meat, vegetables, and that singularly pungent sauce he took with him. "Who could we count on for that?"

"I can understand her logic," Suzuno remarked. "Dhin Dhem Wurs is just ensuring we set the stage correctly, so we can more easily access the Spear. The problem is..."

"Yeah," interjected Rumack, "she doesn't want it to look like some outsider borrowing the chief's influence, in the eyes of the other clans."

"So not even Albert's a possibility," said Laila, arms crossed and looking a tad lost. "He's too involved with Emilia and Emeralda. In fact, his name's still in the Saint Aile records as a substitute for Emeralda. Could anyone even match the conditions we need at all?"

If they wanted to get as much support from Wurs as possible, their candidate couldn't have even a whiff of political involvement with other countries. That was off the table, but within the group preparing to invade heaven, nobody could meet that condition while still being well versed enough in matters to hold the job.

"Being recommended for the position is a big deal, but the conditions are just too harsh..."

The chief herder, by the nature of the post, needed to be someone charismatic enough to enjoy islandwide popularity. It required different skills from the leader of the Mountain Corps, but battle prowess still wasn't optional. Chief herders had later become corps leaders several times in the past. One didn't need to be head and shoulders above the pack in every field, but they couldn't blow it in every field, either.

Rumack pored over the notes that Wurs gave her about the training a chief would be graded on at the zirga. "Personality, popularity, a superior education, archery skills in a hunting setting, familiarity with magic and horsemanship, no Eastern or Western influence, and aware of the heaven-invasion plan... It's silly. There's no one."

"What about Laila? Or maybe Gabriel? He ain't connected to the West or the East, is he? And he could beat just about anyone in combat or magic."

"I thought about that for a moment, Albert, but we had best avoid him," Rumack said.

"Why is that?" he asked back.

"He's simply not fit for the job. I doubt Lady Wurs would endorse him for us."

"What d'you mean by that?"

"Well, no offense, but it didn't seem like Lady Wurs trusted you a great amount. Besides, I fear his lips are too loose for his own good. I'd be on pins and needles the whole time."

She sounded reluctant to say it, but it was the unvarnished truth. Even Laila couldn't contest it.

"Besides, Gabriel's already been tasked with guarding Devil's Castle."

"Ah, yes, he was, wasn't he? Given how low the enemy's layin', I totally forgot."

No matter how rough they thought the chances were, the heavens could have picked this exact moment to storm the planet. The team had to put a sentry up around Devil's Castle, at least, given its crucial role in capturing the heavens. But since Maou and Emi couldn't be on call all the time, the job had to go to the second tier—Ashiya, Urushihara, or Gabriel. And since the first two were busy fixing the castle or carrying out other needed business, Gabriel needed to serve as the on-site security system, or else the safety of the whole operation was under question.

"We have to think about the human world, the enemies, and the demons, too. Maou and Lucifer look human, but their demonic force rules 'em right out." Albert sighed. "There's no way we can make that old bag happy. We're screwed! Hey, Bell, you got any bright—"

"There is one person."

"—ideas... Huh?"

"There is only one person."

The other three gasped.

"Personality, popularity, education, magical sense, and excellent archery skills. Horsemanship, no—but she is well versed in our plans, she has worked hand in hand with us, and there are no Eastern or Western influences in her background. Plus, she knows the truth about Emilia, the Devil King, and how we are all related to each other. She is the only one."

"Magic and archery?" Albert raised an eyebrow. "Since when did we have someone that useful?"

Laila, on the other hand, turned pale. "W-Wait! Wait! Bell, are you joking with us?! You don't mean..."

"Who else could we call upon?"

"But—but if we— If we go with that, you know Emilia and Satan won't take it sitting down!"

"Why inform them?"

"Bell?!" Laila was shouting now.

"There is no need to."

"But...!"

"The chief will understand why, too, once we explain matters."

"This is crazy! It's just so incredibly hazardous!"

"Nothing hazardous about it. The zirga is not a battlefield; nothing the heavens would pay close attention to. Once Chief Wurs endorses her, we can keep her under your and Albert's guard, and all is well. If we talk to the Malebranche about it, perhaps they would even volunteer to bodyguard her. Farfarello and Libicocco, at least, would almost certainly seize upon the offer."

"That—that *would* be enough protection...but..."

Laila started to stammer. Suzuno shook her head, her voice cold.

"We will need to check with her first, but—at this point in time—I think she will accept the offer."

"Wh-who are you talking about?"

Suzuno smiled a little at Albert.

"Someone you know quite well, Albert."

THE HIGH-
SCHOOL
TEEN
CHANGES
THE WORLD
A TAD

"Emi-Yu, are you doing okay? You don't look too good."

"I don't?"

"No. You getting enough sleep?"

Emi quelled the panic in her mind at having this casually lobbed at her by Akiko first thing in the morning shift.

"Oh, uh, I had too many drama series on my DVR, so I played them, and I couldn't stop watching."

"I've totally been there! Sometimes, I record a whole series and delete it before I ever watch it, but when I do start watching, I get the whole series queued up, and I wanna know what happens next, soooo..."

"R-right, yeah. So that kept me up late."

"Yeah, I need to start paring down my list, too. My whole family uses my DVR, so we're constantly running out of space!"

"Oh, yeah, that creeps up on you, huh? Ha-ha-ha..."

Emi *was* sleep-deprived, but she didn't want Akiko to know the real reason why, so she dodged the subject long enough to point her attention elsewhere. What a relief.

"Ahh, but I'm gonna get busy with school and work before long. I don't think I can just plop in front of the TV and start watching anytime soon."

"Oh, like tests and reports and stuff?"

"Pretty much. College might look like it's play, play, play all the time, but if you actually wanna study, it can keep you pretty busy!"

"Right," Emi said, "but work's gonna get busy, too, you know?"

"Well, I mean, there's a lot of churn at the start of spring. People leave to go find full-time jobs for the April hiring rush. We got people to cover for that, you included, but you know, we'll lose some high schoolers soon."

"Oh. I guess Chiho may not be here for long, huh?"

Emi, still not terribly familiar with the Japanese high school curriculum, thought a bit about what kinds of assignments and tests someone Chiho's age might have. But Akiko had other things on her mind.

"No! That's right! Losing Chi's gonna be huge!"

"Huh?!" Emi found herself almost shouting. "What do you mean?"

"Well, this is just my guess, so don't tell anyone yet, but Chiho actually called me about four days ago."

"Four days ago...?"

Emi looked at the calendar hanging on the other side of the counter. She didn't have a shift that day.

"I thought *Hey, that was weird*, and when I picked up, it really *was* weird. She asked me if I could cover a few shifts for her."

"What?"

This surprised Emi. At the Hatagaya location, if you couldn't make a prescheduled shift for whatever reason, you were supposed to talk it over with Kisaki first. If she agreed to it, it was her job as manager to find someone to cover the shift for you. Crewmembers weren't allowed to swap shifts among themselves.

"Yeah, pretty crazy, huh? I mean, just the idea of Chiho missing shifts blew my mind, so I asked her why, and her voice went all low, and she was like 'it involves my future, and there's this place I gotta go to help figure it out.'"

"Her future...?"

"Yeah. She's gonna have college exams in the next school year, and that's coming up soon, right? So I said yes, 'cause I figured it must've been something serious. I mean, Chi would never say something like that casually, right? And I got the okay for it from Kisaki later, but… I'm thinking, you know, maybe Chi won't be around here much longer."

The thought seemed to perturb Akiko.

"Like, it took me a year before I got into college, so I'm not one to talk, but right now's about when teens really start prepping, you know? Some kids figure they're okay waiting until their final year of high school begins, but if you consider the standardized public-school tests that took place back in January, there's really less than one year until college exams for girls like Chiho."

"So maybe she'll start going to a test-prep center or something?"

"I didn't get that nosy about it, but that sounds right to me. Kisaki looked like she knew something."

She probably would, given how she had likely seen off dozens, if not hundreds, of teenage part-timers like that over the years. She could see the signs, the general trends, that dictated how much staff she had to work with, and she knew that February, just before the new fiscal year began in Japan, was a pretty frenetic time. It was common all across the country for high school workers to come back from spring break, then quit soon after to devote time to test prep.

"Wow… Chiho, though, huh?"

It was weird. Emi understood that Chiho was in the late stages of high school, but it was still hard to imagine her sitting in a class-room, getting test-prep advice from a tutor somewhere. The Hero didn't know any other high school students, but based on what she had seen, she knew Chiho was way ahead of her contemporaries in talent. Maybe she figured she wouldn't take such a…normal route in her life.

But that was the thing. Chiho was just a normal, Japan-born, Japan-raised girl. Since becoming involved with Ente Isla, she had navigated her way through innumerable crises, developing her mental and emotional fortitude. That was how Emi and Suzuno thought of her, and they would know, having both gone through far more than she had. And something in Emi told her that something as normal as college exams, at this point, wouldn't be formidable enough to alter Chiho's regular schedule. She had thought, selfishly enough, that Chiho would always be there for her.

"That *was* selfish, I know."

Quitting MgRonald to prepare for college didn't mean Chiho would be cut off from Emi and the rest of the staff. But it did mean a little more distance—and now the demons, Emi, and Suzuno had let the battle against Ente Isla's heaven pull them further away from Sasazuka. Emi couldn't guess what things would be like by July, Maou's ordained deadline for the whole thing, but July meant summer break for Chiho's last high school year. A time when she'd have to focus the most on her exams. Even if everyone was back in Room 201 by then, they wouldn't be eating together as frequently as they used to.

"Thank you for calling MgRonald at Hatagaya Station. This is Yusa speaking. Did you want to make a delivery order?"

Nodding at Akiko, Emi turned toward the delivery computer as she answered the call on her headset.

"…All right, and barbecue sauce. Will that complete your order today? …Thank you. Let me repeat your order, just to be sure…"

Chiho was drifting away from Emi's regular life. It seemed bizarre to consider. But thinking about Emi, sitting here in front of Hatagaya Station, wearing a MgRonald uniform and taking phone orders, it showed that "regular life" had a way of changing all too easily on a person. Emi, for one, changed jobs due to personal reasons (albeit rather unique ones), and since then, she hadn't been able to see her old work friends, Rika Suzuki and Maki Shimizu, as much. Little changes in life could make people seem that little bit more distant.

"Okay, we should have your order there in approximately twenty minutes… All right, thank you very much! Bye-bye! …Phew. Delivery up. You're heading for southern Sasazuka, Maou."

Even with those gloomy thoughts in her mind, Emi kept up the pace, switching her headset to in-store mode and sending orders to Maou, who was on standby upstairs.

"Roger that. I'll head out. Aki, you take the upstairs counter for a bit."

Akiko went up the stairs to replace him. She wasn't a certified barista, but *MgRonald Barista* was more an honorary title than anything. An experienced staffer like Akiko or Kawata could man the MgCafé space just fine, as long as they knew how.

Heading down the stairs, Maou looked at the address on the receipt and studied the delivery map hanging next to the scooter keys for a few moments.

"Oh, okay, over here. There's a lot of twisty back alleys down there, so it's kinda hard to figure out. The apartment buildings all look the same, and stuff."

Emi absentmindedly watched Maou as he squinted at the map, working out the route to take. She wondered if he knew Akiko was swapping shifts with Chiho, but she resisted asking him—not when he was about to leave. Instead, she silently prepared the pieces of the delivery order she could handle behind the counter.

What would he think if he grew more distant from Chiho? In Emi's mind, they were closer than ever now that Chiho was going to Ente Isla. If she quit her job to study for exams, it wasn't like there'd suddenly be this chasm between them.

Emi herself had no plans for her life after the Ignora battle. If she wanted to, she could continue with life in Japan, following in Chiho's footsteps and preparing for a higher education of her own. But Maou couldn't. As Devil King, once he was done in heaven, he'd be responsible for commanding his demons. And if he got accepted for a full-time position at MgRonald and decided to try juggling a job in Japan with a job in the demon realm, there's no way he'd continue the lazy, poor, yet generally contented life he'd led in Villa Rosa Sasazuka up to now.

If it came to that, the question became how he'd want things to be with Chiho...

"...Well."

Emi shook her head, brushing away the bizarre thoughts taking over her mind. Maybe things were temporarily calmer between humans and demons, but there was still no real détente between the entire human race and the entire demon realm. Maou still hadn't taken any responsibility for invading Ente Isla in the first place. But whatever happened with him and Chiho in the future, why was it so easy for her to imagine a future where Maou remained Devil King?

"…I wish he'd get hired on full-time, or do something that'd compel him to stay here for good."

"Hmm? Did you say something?"

Maou must have heard part of her muttering, because he lifted his eyes from the map and turned her way.

"No, nothing. The order's all set to go."

Making sure the burgers and fries were done, Emi placed the cold drinks into the delivery bag and handed it to Maou.

"Thanks."

He took out his outdoor windbreaker and helmet.

"Oh, and Emi?"

"Yes?"

"You look kinda pale today. Are you sleeping all right?"

"It's nothing! Get going!"

"Uh, sure. The place is yours."

The tone of her voice all but pushed Maou out of the store.

Listening to the sound of the engine fade away, Emi let out a little sigh. Maou was just as right as Akiko about the lack of sleep. But she could never reveal to anyone that Maou himself was the cause.

Ever since that night when Suzuno gave her that strange news, Emi had been pressured by Alas Ramus into thinking about what kind of chocolate to give to Maou almost every evening. But perhaps that was shifting the blame. It was Emi, after all, who had planted the thought in Alas Ramus's mind in the first place.

"…My brain's coughing up errors again, maybe."

Why did he have to ask Alas Ramus *that*?

As explained by Chiho's friend, if Chiho could give her chocolate alongside Alas Ramus's own homemade creation, that would take any awkward burden off Maou's mind. As Emi immediately saw it, this meant she'd have to get involved with the child's baking. That, in itself, was fine. It was her job to help this tiny child with this messy job, so anything Alas Ramus gave Maou would inherently be a collaboration with Emi. It was a perfectly natural thing for a mother and child to do, and even if Maou accepted it knowing full well Emi was involved, she doubted he would think anything special about it.

But if she did that, *she would have to think*: What kind of chocolate would make Maou happy? And also: Why did she consider the question at all? Was it simply because she thought Alas Ramus should make something Maou would enjoy? Or was it because she wanted the results to be on par with Chiho's no-doubt masterpiece, to make the camouflage complete?

Or...

"Ugh... This is so stupid. Stupid."

Or is because she wanted to do something for Maou's sake?

"This isn't funny."

Her brain was just one big error message. What would thinking any of this accomplish for her?

"What does it matter? If I say Alas Ramus made it, he'll love it. That's good enough."

Saying it out loud—as if that made it more convincing, somehow—Emi switched mental gears and went back to work. A little box on the side of the cash register's touch panel showed the date as February 13, but she paid it no mind. She didn't care at all that the following day was Valentine's Day. Or so she thought.

"Hello! ...Oh?"

She thought this new customer would be the perfect way to distract herself. It turned out to be someone she knew well.

"Hey! How's it hangin'?"

"Hello, Rika. You eating here today?"

"Well, I guess so, in the end."

Rika Suzuki—Emi's best friend, and one of the few people on Earth who knew everything about Ente Isla—looked a tad ill at ease. Her caramel-colored long coat and white pants were normal enough, but she also brought in a small, wheeled suitcase, as if embarking on a weekend trip. Emi gave her a look.

"Hey, I don't see Maou, but he's here today, right?"

Emi gave her another look. "Huh? Um, he's out on a delivery right now…but did you need him?"

"Yeah. Well, him and you both. You and Maou work 'til six, right?"

Rika checked her watch. It was four in the afternoon—a bit early for dinner—but why was she aware of Maou's and Emi's work schedules in the first place?

"Once you're both off, there's some place I want to take you guys to."

"Me and Maou?"

"Yeah. Oh, um, and I'll just chill out and have dinner in the meantime, so no need to hurry on my account. Uh, I'll have a fried-pork burger combo with fries and hot tea, please. I got a coupon for it."

"Uh, uhhh, oh, thank you. One moment…"

Leaving Emi in the dust, Rika barked out her order, then gave way for the customer behind her. By the time Emi was done handling the line, Rika was already seated at a faraway table.

Maou came back to the restaurant about fifteen minutes after Rika showed up, delivery bag and helmet under his arms. He spotted her right off.

"Rika's here?"

"Yeah, she came just now. It sounds like she wanted to see us both."

"Me, too? Really?"

"I guess so, yeah."

Maou seemed exactly as clueless as her about what it could be.

"Ah, well. We got a bit over an hour until we're off. Anything else happen?"

"Not in here, no. Nobody went up to the café while you were gone."

"Ah."

Maou nodded as he put the keys, helmet, and windbreaker back in place, washing his hands thoroughly before running back upstairs.

"Rika?"

Then, Emi noticed Rika following Maou the whole way with her eyes. When he was gone, she hung her head low, as if exhausted. She had come to visit many times before, but this Rika was like none she had ever known.

Akiko breathed a sigh of relief as she came back down. "Whew! I was worried there'd be some complicated coffee order before Maou came back." Then, she ran into the restaurant space, looking for work to do.

"...Something's going on."

Before Emi's eyes, Rika was engaged in some truly bizarre behavior. Chiho, meanwhile, hadn't been acting like herself, either. She pondered this, growing increasingly uncomfortable.

"Ah...*nnh*."

She stifled a yawn shortly before it escaped her mouth. Right then, another customer had come in, headed her way, and there was no way could she greet a customer with a full, cheek-stretching yawn. Of course, the cause of that nervous yawn, when you got down to it, was the fact that she had to deliver chocolate to Maou sooner or later. Was she really acting any less strange than Rika or Chiho? Maybe she was the weirdest of all.

"Hello! Feel free to order at the counter when you're ready."

It took a mental reset to drum up the energy to deliver that peppy greeting.

"Sorry to bother you guys out of nowhere."

"No, it's fine, but where are we going?"

Emi and Maou were following Rika as the three of them took his usual commuter route.

"Um, it's right nearby. You mind walking a little bit?"

"Sure, but..."

"Uh, wherever we're going, I'd like to stop by my apartment first..."

Rika turned her head toward Maou, who was already busy griping as he walked his bike along, and nodded. "Sure thing. It's right by your place anyway."

"It is? *What* is?"

"You'll see, you'll see. Hey, Emi, is Alas Ramus with you?"

"Huh? Yes…"

Neither Suzuno nor Urushihara were available today, and since she only worked until six anyway, she decided to just give Alas Ramus a bit more time in "fusion" mode than usual.

"Good. Because I'm sorry, um, the person we're meeting with said not to tell you anything until we all arrived, so…"

""Huh?""

This was making less and less sense to Maou and Emi. If they were headed near Villa Rosa Sasazuka, neither of them could think of any place Rika would know about. Maybe Shiba's home next to the apartment building? If so, then why all this secrecy? And what was in that suitcase of hers, making a huge racket as she rolled it down the asphalt? She looked like she was about to board a train for a quick overnighter—there was no reason at all for her to stay at Maou's deserted apartment building.

So the procession continued, Rika leading the way for the thoroughly perplexed pair, until they reached Villa Rosa Sasazuka.

"Okay," Maou said as he parked his bike, "so seriously, where are we going?"

"It's no place bad, I promise. Oh, and we'll get dinner over there, too, so don't worry about that."

"Dinner?" Emi reflexively asked. "Is it a restaurant or something?" Rika was sounding extremely weird to her. If they were going someplace that offered dinner, she would have mentioned that first thing, not right now.

"Not…exactly, no. But I guess they got a lot of stuff you wouldn't normally get to eat, so…"

Rika put her hands together.

"But save the questions for later and just get ready for me, okay? If you don't like it, you can leave anytime. I can make up for it."

"…All right. Whatever!"

Maou looked as confused as ever; however, he was getting a bit sick of all the local restaurants he knew. If he could try some uncommon cuisine tonight, that was as good an excuse to go out as any. Plus, it was Rika inviting them, and he knew Rika wouldn't hang out any-where *too* weird. It wasn't exactly normal, no, but so be it.

So Maou asked the other two to wait a moment as he climbed the stairs—but the moment Maou disappeared down the upstairs hall, Rika lifted her suitcase and ran up herself.

"Whoa, Rika?"

Emi, in a panic, followed her. But Rika was so far ahead, she even had the time to see if she was being pursued. And before Emi could make it up, Rika was in the hallway and plunging right into Room 201.

"Whoa! Wh-what're you doing? I told you to wait!"

Maou, about to take a puffy winter jacket off a hanger in his room (a little extra layer for the cold night), gave Rika a shocked look. Emi, following close behind, was astounded to find Rika standing on his tatami-mat floor, not even bothering to take her shoes off.

"Okay, sorry, just one sec..."

Rika walked around the side of the futon freshly laid out on the floor.

"What're you doing?!"

"Hang on, this'll take just one moment."

"What are you...?"

"Aghh?!"

Maou froze, hearing the hysterical scream from Emi out in the hallway. But before he could ask what happened, Acieth was upon her, picking her up in her arms.

"Oooh, good timing, Acieth!"

"Whoo-hoo!"

Rika gave her a thumbs-up. Acieth replied with a wink.

"Acieth, what are you *doing*?! You too, Rika! What's going on?!"

"Hey! What the hell, guys? What are you up to?!"

"Okay, I don't wanna bother flipping this over, so sorry, guys..."

Ignoring Emi's and Maou's shouts, Rika took something unbe-lievable out from her jacket.

"Here we are!"

With a little grunt of effort, she plunged it into a space between the tatami mats.

"Rika?!"

Emi's surprise was understandable. Rika had an angel's feather pen, allowing anyone to create a Gate to another world.

A well of light bubbled up from where the pen stood as they watched. The mat in the very center of the cramped room burst into radiant light, as bright as the sun, enveloping a bit of the comforter on one side of the futon.

"Whoa, I did that?! Wow! I'm some kind of sorceress. This is so exciting! Oh, right, your shoes, Maou..."

As if forgetting about them until now, she picked Maou's shoes up from the front door...and, with them and her suitcase, plunged into the Gate.

"Ah! Hey?!"

Maou and Emi stood motionless for a moment, dumbfounded at Rika's brazen behavior.

"Wh...what're we gonna do?!"

"What are...? I dunno! Acieth, put me down a sec! We gotta go after Rika...!"

"Don't worry, Emi! We will certainly chase her, no questions!"

"Huh? What? W-Wait, Acieth, are... Ahhhh?!"

Incapable of putting up any resistance, Emi found herself dragged into the Gate by Acieth. Maou froze again, this time for a few seconds, as he took this in.

"Wh-what—what the hell? Uh, uh, the door, I gotta lock the door... Hey, hang on!"

Snapping out of it, he latched the front door, then darted around the room for a little bit, making sure he had his wallet and phone even though he knew the Gate was connected to Ente Isla. Then, with a nervous nod, he jumped in.

"Guys, wait up!"

He swam across the dimensional trail, trying to catch the three small figures far ahead of him.

"Goddammit! Why can't I use one of those?!"

The Gate that Rika opened up with her feather pen tried to allow Maou in, but as a demon, he was forced to overlap the path with his own magic in order to navigate. It was vastly different from the Gate he personally used to travel between planets. There was no way Rika, who boasted zero holy force, could build a Gate this stable by herself.

"...Hmm?"

But then, an odd thought crossed his mind. A question that struck at the core, one that seemed even stranger than Rika's odd activity. A feather pen like that was made from an archangel's wing, making it impossible for demons to use. Laila taught a young Maou that herself, and when other demons tried sticking the pen into the ground, nothing ever happened.

Rika had now proven that any Earthling could use the thing, as long as they weren't demonic. If the sorcerers on Ente Isla—messing around with the Stairs to Heaven and other fiddly Gate spells, as they had to have been doing—heard about this, they'd probably be livid.

But they would need to wait, because another question just entered Maou's mind. If it was this easy to open a Gate connecting planets to planets...

"...Why didn't the people back on those guys' home world open any Gates?"

✳

"Oof...nnnnngh."

"And down!"

"Ahh!"

"Ow!"

After an interdimensional journey of some forty minutes, Rika, Acieth, Emi, and Maou landed in order...

"...Where are we?"

...in a spot that definitely wasn't Devil's Castle on the Central Continent.

"What the hell?"

Neither Emi nor Maou recognized the spot at all. But they could tell what kind of place it was.

"A church… Wait, a full Church cathedral?!"

"What?!"

Maou opened his eyes wide at Emi's exclamation. Then, he stared at Rika, the woman who brought them here. The decor did resemble the Church cathedrals he had seen in the cities of the Central Continent, back when he was sacking them.

"A-Acieth! Rika Suzuki! What the hell are you…?"

But before Rika could answer, another voice came up from below.

"Oh, you're here?"

"…Um, who's that with you?"

It was Albert, along with a large, muscular man whom Maou and Emi didn't recognize and who was a measure larger than Albert himself. His eyes looked weirdly sinister, but his hair was waxed up and combed into a straight split down the middle.

"We did it!"

"Sorry we're late!"

With Maou and Emi too flummoxed by this cavalcade of events to respond, Acieth and Rika gave the pair a hearty hello.

"Hey," Albert replied. "I'm glad it worked. Bell 'n' I spent hours debating over whether you'd pull it off."

"Oh, I was so nervous! I didn't know whether this feather pen would work for me or not, so my heart was racing the whole time!"

"No, you did a real good job, lady. You even nailed the landing out of the Gate."

"Ohh, man, I need a rest…"

"Ahh, Rika! I love you! Big drive to do this! Me, I cannot believe it is first time for you!"

"Wha, who, why, what, wait…"

"What?! Who?! Why?! What?! Wait!!"

Both Maou and Emi had generally the same reaction.

The unknown man stepped up to them, solemnly taking a knee.

"I must apologize, Your Demonic Highness."

""Huh?""

The man, who resembled a football or rugby player, was now bowing his head toward Maou. He was a demon.

"Y-you…"

"This is the form I have taken, but you are speaking to Libicocco."

"L-Libicocco?!"

Maou was floored at being greeted by a Malebranche chieftain in a cathedral. But looking back, Farfarello had taken a human form on Earth as well. Libicocco was enormous by Malebranche standards; maybe this was the shape he'd naturally take as a regular guy.

"My liege, the Great Demon General of the East and Lady Bell have granted me the honorable role of accompanying you."

"Ashiya and Suzuno?!"

"Alciel and Bell?!"

Albert, Libicocco, Rika, and Acieth certainly made for a ragtag bunch, but if it was Ashiya and Suzuno planning all this, it made even less sense than before. Albert, perhaps realizing this, grinned at them.

"You two are lookin' great, guys! First off, I guess I oughta tell you, you're in the Northern Island. This is the Church cathedral in the Goat Pasture, better known as Phiyenci."

"The—the Northern Island?!"

"Phiyenci… That's the united capital, isn't it?! Why would Rika Suzuki take us someplace like this?!"

"Ah, well, we figured you'd be livid if me or Eme or Bell took ya. I wanted someone who'd never spill the beans to you if asked, and Bell said this lady Rika ought to fill the bill. So she introduced her to me."

"Well, I'm just glad I had Acieth to help me out! Man, I thought I was gonna have a heart attack those whole forty minutes. Not as bad as when I first heard about all this stuff, but still. Man, it's cold!"

Rika opened up her wheeled suitcase. It contained a toiletry bag and a few outfits geared for cold weather, the perfect overnight-stay package.

"Stop lying there in the heap forever, Maou and Emi! We have the free time for now, but the food stalls, they not open forever! And Laila, she save the good seats for us, so let's be quick!"

"W-Wait! Wait a second! Laila did what?! Please, guys, stop having fun confusing me like this! What's going on? What is all this? What are you bastards scheming?!"

With nobody coming forward with a coherent explanation, things grew more confusing by the minute for Maou and Emi. But what Rika had for them next made everything else seem trivial.

"So they're having this archery exhibition today, right? It's, like, the biggest event in the whole zirga, and Chiho's entered into it, so we're all gonna go cheer her on!"

"Uh............"

"Wha............"

This was exactly what being at a loss for words meant.

Chiho was entered in the archery exhibition? One of the events in the zirga, a large conference convened to pick the next chief herder? Maou had no clue why any of this was happening.

"But hey," Albert told the stunned pair, "seeing is believing, right? She's been shootin' up a storm."

"Oh! Hey, over here, you two!"

Lost in a vast crowd, Maou and Emi heard a voice calling them.

They were in the central square of Phiyenci, and right in the middle of it, the Spear of Adramelechinus loomed higher than any watchtower, basking in the afternoon sun and casting a vast shadow over the peaceful world it lorded over. Truly, a weapon worthy of Adramelech himself, head of the Bluehorn clan. A sort of ad hoc arena had been built nearby, allowing you to look straight up at the Spear, and inside it was a gaudily decorated wooden stage, where the archery exhibition took place.

The grandstand, built parallel along the paths the arrows took from the stage to their targets, were packed almost to the brim—but one section was built like box seats, allowing you to sit any way you wanted inside them. Laila was waving at them from one such box, so Emi pressed on through the crowd, Maou following behind.

The archery exhibition had already started. Many young people filled the stage, showing off their shooting skills with the hunting bows unique to the Northern Island. Bets were apparently being taken in one corner of the stands, judging by the large board full of names and inscrutable numbers that changed with every arrow unfurled, and how the crowd was filled with calls of joy or despair in turns. Considering this event would help decide the next head of state, it felt more like a raucous town festival.

Emi and Maou picked their way through the stands, rubbing their shoulders against the crowd. "I'm glad you made it in time," Laila said with a smile as they approached the box. "Chiho's group should be up in about half an hour, so *ngh...?!*"

Emi marched straight into the box, shoes and all, and immediately grabbed Laila by the collar.

"Could you tell me what's going on?"

"Um, ah, the *mmph*?"

Maou, arriving a beat later, then grabbed Laila by the head.

"You've gone over the line one time too many."

"Ah, w-wait, guys! You're scaring me! People are watching! They're gonna see us!"

"I don't care."

"So what?"

"W-Wait! Wait, I know this sounds like an excuse, but I was against it at first, too, I said it was just too crazy to work, I did, I stopped them, I said we can't get Chiho involved in this, but Bell suggested it, and when she brought it up with Chiho, she was all for it, raring to go, and she said we needed to keep it secret from you both until today, so I couldn't say anything, and honestly, I didn't think Chiho would remain such a zirga contender all the way to today, so if we got this far, you know, she said if she made it to the end of the exhibition, she wanted you to see it, so I really didn't do anything this time, in fact, I tried to put a stop to it, believe me, please, *ow, ow, ow,* you're hurting me, everyone else agreed to it, but I was against it until the end, I heard you were angry when she did the same thing at Tokyo Tower before, so I was the only one to say no until the very end, and it was Chiho herself who convinced Alciel to do it, so please, let me go, I can't breathe, I can't *breeeeathe!*"

Being lifted into the air by Emi, Laila thought it prudent to use what could potentially be her last breath to fully outline her defense. Her head grew visibly paler with every syllable, so the two of them finally felt it prudent to let her down. They were still less than convinced.

"What do you mean, Bell suggested it?"

Not even Maou had heard Emi's voice go this murderously low very often. It made Laila go even paler before she could catch her breath.

"Haaah, haaah, that—that, you know... Huff... If we just asked them to hand over the Spear, haaah, the Northern Island wouldn't go for that, mmph..."

It was Emi and her band, after all, who left the Spear here. They didn't leave any instructions on what to do with it, and given that this was the only relic of the Devil Overlord everyone knew the exact location of, Emi knew the wrong approach could lead to head-aches later on. That was why, once Emi and Maou had learned about the relics, they had informed everyone that they'd be ready to do anything asked of them in order to retrieve it. Emi, in particular, intended to make a personal plea to the chief herder to borrow the Spear, if all other options were exhausted. She had decided as much long before they had any concrete plan for the relic, because she knew their group likely wouldn't stumble upon any other bright ideas.

Thus, she had been thinking this whole time about how to pro-ceed on this topic with Chief Herder Dhin Dhem Wurs and the other clan chieftains, without letting word about the true nature of their expedition to heaven get out, and without causing any political strife afterward. So how did this wind up with Chiho down there on the zirga stage?

"The Devil King and I didn't want to expose Chiho to any more danger. What do all you people think you're even doing…?"

"Of all the mean things to say about Chiho! You can see how aware she is of what's going on. Why not let her do what she wants a little?"

"Huh?"

"Wh-who're you?"

Just when Emi was gritting her teeth hard enough to require dental work, a voice interrupted her. It belonged to an old woman who had appeared in a nearby box seat at some point, intently watching the exhibition.

"Hmm, what a surprise…"

The woman, monocle covering one eye, looked up at Maou.

"So you're Satan, the Devil King?"

"""!"""

Maou and Emi gasped.

"This'll be our first direct encounter, won't it? I was surprised enough about Stumpy Scythe, but you're pretty young, too, eh? You don't cut too impressive a figure for someone goin' around callin' himself a king. You getting three square meals a day?"

The compact old woman's weirdly overwhelming presence was too much for Maou to bear at first. But Emi, having met her once, couldn't hide the shock of seeing someone she never expected here.

"…Are you Chief Dhin Dhem Wurs?"

"Been a while, hasn't it? And hopefully, you won't mind if I don't call you by name. Never know who might be listening in on us!"

Dhin Dhem Wurs, chief herder and leader of the Northern Island, kept her back turned to the Hero Emilia. She didn't hesitate to bandy the "Satan" name around, oddly enough, but their seats were a fair distance away, and her voice was all but drowned in the clamor and excitement as the next archery contestant approached. Any attention generated by Emi assaulting Laila was now squarely focused on the festival.

Taking another look around, Emi found Albert, Libicocco, Acieth, and Rika seated in the box to the left. The one on their right was empty.

"Dhin Dhem Wurs? Hey, isn't that the chief herder's name?!"

Maou, taking a moment to come to that conclusion, was sent reeling by it. The woman herself gave him a peeved sneer.

"Well, look at that high-pitched voice you got! Why don't you quit your whining and sit down? This is the archery exhibition, the biggest event of the zirga! We have wannabe stars from every clan in the land, and people islandwide betting on them. I pulled a few strings to get the best seats in the house for you; the least you could do is watch!"

Emi confronted the woman just a tad more politely than how she usually treated Laila: "Chief Wurs, what is going on here?!"

"What's going on? It's you all who want the Spear, is it not? And the North can't exactly give it away for free, can we? But now we're on the cusp of a war that could determine the fate of the human race, right? So I've arranged things so you can get your hands on it about as quick as you're ever gonna."

"A-Arranged things...?"

"I have a vague idea of what you've been up to over the past two years. You and the Devil King were goofing around on another planet, and now you're going to try fighting a god so you can reunite that daughter you two made and her friends?"

That was a little less than "vague," and "making" a daughter sounded kind of suspect, but it was clear Wurs was aware of Maou's and Emi's lives in Japan.

"So you know, normally, I'd take anyone asking for the Spear and throw them out on their ear, but this was my childhood friend asking, so I said 'all right, I guess I'll pitch in a little.' I'm sure you guys don't appreciate being left out of the loop, but not even the Hero can play the, um, hero all the time. So deal with it!"

Wurs took a moment to survey the entire arena, from one end to the other.

"Zirgas like this attract a scary number of candidates, and the funniest thing is, they're all volunteering to actually do something as annoying as be chief herder. We even get rubberneckers from other continents. That's why we've kept security tighter than usual, and my youngest granddaughter's one of the entrants in the archery exhibition, so this whole joint is on lockdown. So if you don't wanna be ashamed of your fancy title, lady, then sit down and cheer on my granddaughter, won't you?"

"Whoa, ma'am, please don't act like our talk is over," Maou interjected. "You haven't told us anything we asked about. Who the hell proceeded with this whole thing without telling either of us?"

"Yes! I refuse to accept this if you don't tell me anything!"

"Mmm?"

Wurs gave another annoyed look to the bitterly protesting pair.

"Laila, why are your daughter and son-in-law a couple of sticks in the mud, huh? Or did they get more of a conservative upbringing because you're such a piece of work?"

"I'm not her son-in-law!"

"He's not her son-in-law! And Laila, what's going on here? You *know* Chief Dhin Dhem Wurs?!"

"Um, she's a friend from the past."

"Some friend you are, you ditz. Y'see, I'm like this with her. Just like you two are."

As she spoke, one of the stones on her monocle began to glow.

"Oh?"

As it did, the mark on Acieth's forehead emitted the same glow, several seats away, and then:

"Pheww! Mommy, where are we?"

"A-Alas Ramus?!"

The other Yesod fragment separated herself from Emi.

Discovering another fragment bearer gave her and Maou the umpteen-millionth surprise of the day. Laila mentioned she had passed out several fragments around the world, but how did one of them wind up in Dhin Dhem Wurs's hands? It was left to Emi and Maou to fantasize over what could have happened between them sixty years ago.

"Ooh, and here's the fabled daughter of the Hero and the Devil

King, eh? Laila, you better not get involved with raising her, y'hear? Anyone influenced by you is bound to be rotten to the core when they grow up!"

"Lidem! You're seriously starting to make me angry!"

Despite the unfamiliar surroundings, Alas Ramus didn't seem too disturbed. Instead, she looked up at Wurs from her perch on Emi's knee.

"Who's dat lady?"

"Mmm? Well, little girl, I used to be friends with your granny."

"Um, Lidem? I'm not really her grandmother…"

"Huhh?! Wait, are you the type of gal who resents being called 'granny' in public? See here, you can look and act as young as you want, but to your grandkids, you're always gonna be good ol' Granny! So if you don't want her to get bullied in school, then just let her call you that! What was your name? Alas Ramus? Come here, girl. You should watch this with old Dhin Dhem. It's fun!"

"H-hey!"

Alas Ramus obediently crawled over to Wurs's lap, leaving Maou and Emi to blankly stare at her. Ignoring the pair, the chief pointed at one of the figures on the stage.

"See? Here she comes! Give her a big cheer! That's my precious granddaughter down there!"

"Oh, come on."

At that moment, the once chaotic crowd fell into a glassy silence. CHIHO SASAKI WURS, read the name on the board. On stage, with all the competitors dressed in their best archery gear, she had chosen a bright-white martial-arts uniform, a black chest guard, and a black pair of *hakama* pants, her hair tied back to avoid getting in her face. It was the classic uniform for *kyudo*, archery as practiced in Japan, and now she was in the *toriyumi* pose, standing boldly and quietly as she sized up her target.

From her left side, she held her *namiyumi*, a medium-sized bow by *kyudo* standards but still over seven feet tall. The *uchihazu*, the upper tip of the bow, dipped down to a spot just a few inches above the floor in front of her, and in her right hand were a *haya* and an

otoya, the two types of arrows used in the sport. It was the classical *toriyumi* stance, and once it was taken, Chiho took a deep breath and gave the audience a steep, polite forward bow, the top *uchihazu* edge not moving an inch in height.

Upon rising again, she took a large step forward with her left foot, then a smaller one with her right, both pairs of toes lining up.

"What a lovely stance!"

The chief herder's words summed up the feelings of everyone in the arena. Even to someone like Maou, who knew nothing about *kyudo*, the sight turned the churning waters in his mind into a perfectly still pond. That was the power of Chiho's presence.

✳

Four days beforehand, Suzuno's suggestion to have Chiho participate in the zirga received a chilly reception from nearly everyone involved—Laila, of course, but also Albert and Rumack, as well as Ashiya and Urushihara. The last two, in particular, emphasized that not only was the plan crazy, there was no way in hell Maou and Emi would sign off on it. Suzuno, for her part, agreed—but no one could think of anyone else who could join the zirga festivities, or any other way to bring the Spear off the island without a big ruckus.

"Of course," reasoned Suzuno, "I do not suggest we force Chiho into this. We need to explain to her why she is being nominated, how it has come to this, and what we expect to happen, and if she says she cannot do it, we will think of another way. But I believe that Chiho best matches the type of person Chief Wurs has described to us."

"But you seriously think we should say nothing to my liege and Emilia?" Ashiya asked. "The mere thought of their anger after all is revealed frightens me beyond imagination."

Anyone who knew the pair's relationship with Chiho could picture the same thing.

"I imagine so, yes. The Devil King and Emilia will be dead set against it. The former, in particular, was less than enthusiastic about Chiho visiting Ente Isla in the first place."

"Precisely. Thus..."

"So let us keep it a secret from them."

"How did we reach that conclusion?!"

Suzuno gauged the protesting Ashiya with a pair of cold eyes. "Telling them will not improve matters for us."

"Perhaps not, but..."

"Alciel, you have not forgotten why the Devil King and Emilia are spending an outsized amount of their time in Sasazuka right now, have you?"

She eyed the people around her.

"Let us be honest. In these preparatory stages, neither of them are capable of contributing very much. We will need their strength for the battle looming before us, but for the moment, there is nothing we can assign to them, even if we wished to keep them busy. So what will telling them accomplish, when we already know they will be against it? I am not asking Chiho to join us on the battlefield, amid intense combat. I would merely ask her to join in an Ente Islan festival. What need is there to be nervous? What basis does anyone have to be against Chiho taking this vital role?"

"Th-that..."

"After all the danger we have already exposed her to; after all the aid she has provided to our daily lives—after basking in all that, you wish to expel her from the group?"

"No way, dude," Urushihara said. "Look, whether it's Chiho Sasaki out there or not, assuming we can put on a good show or whatever at the zirga, how's that gonna convince everyone to let us take the Spear? The chief doesn't have the power to order anyone to fork it over. Whether one of our allies becomes chief or not, it doesn't change things too much."

He had a point. Wurs's indirect support was what made this plan possible, but exactly what this support involved was unclear. Zero details were nailed down.

"That," countered Suzuno, "we can tackle in the future, with the way we move things forward. Regardless of our approach, however, I guarantee to you all that Chiho is our best choice."

"Huhh?"

"...We cannot deliberate any further unless we know whether Chiho will accept. If she does, I would like to discuss the details at that point."

"Wh-whoa..."

"There is nothing to worry about. If she refuses, you may feel free to report my behavior to the Devil King or Emilia. That, and regardless of her response, feel free to debate over any other possible solutions we may think of. Now... Laila?"

"Huh? Um, yes?"

Laila, the first person to pick up on (and vehemently oppose) Suzuno's intentions, sat up in her seat.

"Come with me. If Chiho agrees, then whether we can actually take the Spear or not will be up to you."

Laila blinked at her, confused.

"...What?"

"Suzuno? Laila? Why are you here all of a sudden?"

It was a rare combination to see at the front door of her house. Chiho let them in and offered some tea and crackers in her room— Laila acting oddly antsy, Suzuno looking like she had the weight of the world on her shoulders.

"Yes, well, there have been some movements on the other side. We wanted to tell you about them, and we also had a favor to ask. Thus, the two of us came here, since our schedules were relatively free."

"Oh, I see! Ashiya texted me that you guys found a few of the Devil Overlord relics. That's good news, huh?"

It would be easy to imagine that the Devil Overlord Satan, were he alive today, might be flummoxed to hear that news of his relics was being texted to a human teenager's phone, as if those relics were a dropped wallet recovered at the local lost-and-found.

"Ah, yes, the Nothung and the Sorcery of the False Gold. They are in the custody of Camio in the demon realm at the moment, but Alciel will come fetch them before long. Out of the remaining two, we are still searching for the Astral Gem, but as for the Spear of Adramelechinus, well, we already know its location."

"Right, up in the Northern Island... Are you all right, Laila?"

Beads of sweat had formed on Laila's forehead as Suzuno spoke. Her eyes darted between Suzuno and Chiho, unable to stay in one place for long.

"Ah, um, yes. It, uhh, it's just a little warm."

"Oh, is it? Let me turn down the heat a bit."

Chiho meekly nodded and pushed the Down button on the wall unit a couple of times. It didn't change Laila's behavior much.

"So this spear was left behind by Mister Adramelech, the Great Demon General, right?"

The *mister* appellation had never before in history been applied to Adramelech's name by a human, as far as Suzuno knew. But come to think of it, Chiho had quite a few friends among the Great Demon General ranks by now. Suzuno herself had never seen Adramelech, but he was a member of the Bluehorn clan, gigantically large—more so than the rest of his species—and proud of it. She wondered what he would've looked like as a human, had he ever come to Earth. But that wasn't the issue right now.

"Right. That Spear."

Suzuno was leaning forward in her seat. Even her palms were a little sweaty.

Despite what she had told Ashiya, she now realized that this was the first time she had ever encouraged Chiho to become actively involved in Ente Isla events. She pondered whether this was a line she shouldn't cross. Could she really ask this of Chiho? Would discussing it with Emi or Maou first be better? Hesitation and regret welled in her mind...but just for a moment, a side of her she hadn't realized was there violently pushed away all the indecision.

"To retrieve the Spear, I am in need of your assistance."

"Pardon?"

Chiho didn't seem to understand what she meant.

"The other day, Laila, Albert, General Rumack, and I went to the Northern Island on an observation mission. There, we met a woman named Dhin Dhem Wurs, the leader of the island, and as a result of our talks, we've determined that you are our best choice for retrieving the Spear."

"Uhhmm..."

Chiho, not quite able to parse this, reflexively looked at Laila.

"That is apparently the case, yes," Laila replied in a barely audible voice, face turned to the side as she waved her hand at Suzuno to keep going.

"What would I be doing?" Chiho vaguely asked.

"We will debate over the exact nature of it from here forward. I can tell you, though, that your skills with the bow and arrow will come into play."

"Bow and arrow?" Chiho paused for a moment. Her bow and arrows were still in storage at her high school's *kyudo* club.

"And not to pry too much, but do you happen to have any equestrian experience?"

"E-*quest*-rian?"

The word didn't pop up in Chiho's vocabulary very often. It took a few seconds to figure out what Suzuno wanted.

"Um, I've never been on a horse in my life. I'm not sure what that has to do with anything, but..."

Of course not, Laila thought. Here they were, asking for her help out of nowhere, quizzing her on her archery and horse skills. She assumed Suzuno was about to go into detail on the Spear of Adramelechinus and their discussions with Wurs, but based on that reaction alone, she assumed Chiho wasn't aching to join in. It just didn't seem that way to her.

Until the next moment, that is.

"But are you... I mean, are you sure I'm who you want?"

"Chiho?!"

"You are. In fact, you are who we need. There is no other."

Chiho's cheeks reddened, her lips stretching out into a smile. This was what people did when they were brimming with happiness.

"But Ente Isla is so huge, and there's lots of superstrong people on it, and I'm sure there are tons of people better at archery than I am. So why me?"

"What we want from you," Suzuno pressed, "is not your skill in battle, of course. In fact, it is nothing that involves fighting and defeating an opponent. I am asking for your archery skills, but it involves more than that, and as you surmised, you will be accompanied by people far more talented than you. But despite all that, I feel your strengths are an absolute must if we want the Spear."

"Suzuno..."

"And let me add that while there is no threat upon your life and we will provide all the support we can, this is a task that involves a heavy physical and mental burden. If you hear me out until the end and feel it is impossible for you to accept, then please, say so to us. You turning us down does not immediately result in a crisis, and we have other measures we can take. It should also be said that this is an offer that everyone except for me has dismissed as too reckless."

"But," Chiho said, interrupting the impassioned plea, "but you nominated me, huh, Suzuno?"

"I did."

"Can you tell me why?"

"I will, after I explain to you everything that has happened and everything that could happen in the future."

"...A-all right."

Chiho felt a little steamrolled at the moment, but she still sat up in her seat and listened on as Suzuno described their visit to Dhin Dhem Wurs and her favorite restaurant.

Carefully omitting the dishonorable nickname Wurs gave her, Suzuno went over their entire visit to Phiyenci, emphasizing how Chiho was the only candidate to fulfill the chief's conditions.

"All right. I understand."

Chiho made a heavy sigh, letting the tension flow out of her body.

Taking a sip from a cup of tea that had long since gone cold, she let out another sigh.

"It sounds like this might take a little while. Do you mind if I make a phone call?"

"Of course not."

"Ah, wait, um… Chiho?"

Before Laila could stop her, Chiho already had her phone out.

"Hello? Hi! Sorry I'm calling out of nowhere, but do you have a moment to chat? Yeah, I needed to ask you a favor; do you think you can cover a few shifts at work? …Sure, I'll run it by Kisaki later, so… Yeah, it's really crucial that I get this time off. It involves my future, kind of, and there's this place I've got to go to. To figure it out, you know… Oh, good! Thank you so much! I'll pay back the favor later, okay? Again, sorry this is so sudden. Thanks again! Bye! …Whew."

The call was over virtually before it began. Chiho turned back toward Suzuno and Laila.

"All right. I'm free for the next week after school now. What would you like me to do?"

Even before Suzuno explained what was to be done, Chiho had changed her work shifts for them. And what's more:

"Oh, right. I didn't call Maou or Yusa just now, so don't worry about that. That was this college student named Ohki who works there."

"Chiho?"

"Maou and Yusa aren't aware of this, right?"

"!"

Laila was taken aback.

"I mean," Chiho continued before Laila could ask how she knew, "if they knew, at least one of them would be in this room right now. They're still spending most of their time in Japan, after all. And Maou, you know, I'm sure he'd slam his foot down the moment I said yes."

"I wholly agree with you. I was about to tell you earlier, but I want to keep the Devil King and Emilia out of the loop until there is no turning back on it."

"I hear you loud and clear!"

"Whoa, Ch-Chiho, why are you so...revved up by this? Are you sure?!"

"Sure I'm sure!" Chiho said sharply, smiling the whole way. "Thank you so much, Suzuno. You aren't still hung up about earlier, are you?"

"Oh, it wasn't the first time, if I may say so. That was something I felt needed addressing sooner or later. To be honest, regardless of what happened in Nerima, I can't help but feel like it hardly affected him very much."

"Kao always yells at me about how I'm too lenient, too loose with him... But thanks. And apart from that, I'll do my best on whatever you want from me."

"Wonderful. Thank you. And we will provide our full support."

"Great!"

"N-no! Oh, once they find out about this..."

"You think Maou will be mad? I'm not doing anything to get angry about here, I don't think. Ashiya and Urushihara are repairing Devil's Castle and working with people on Ente Isla without consulting Maou very much. I'm the same way. I want to help out 'my liege,' so I'm doing what I feel we need to do."

This wasn't what Laila was concerned about, something Chiho knew full well, but she continued on anyway.

"The title of Great Demon General is given only to those who stand at the very peak of demondom in strength and skill. It's up to me to carry out my duty as a General, and as a MgRonald Barista, to answer the expectations of His Demonic Highness."

Laila, unaware that Chiho had been named to the post, lost all ability to speak.

"But after being protected by everyone else for so long, now that Ente Isla needs me for the first time ever... That means I can help out Maou, too. So please, Laila, let me go to the Northern Island."

Chiho bowed her head toward her.

"...All right. All right."

With things having culminated to this point, Laila could no longer fight back.

"Thinking about it, I have no right to go against your will, do I? Not after I sent you out to battle myself. But all right. I'll have to be our contact with Chief Wurs either way. Now, we'll need to convince Alciel and the others, get you into the zirga, lecture you about the correct way to handle fragments... Talk about a rush project."

"Okay. I'll go to school real quick and retrieve my bow and stuff. I'd like to practice and fine-tune my moves for whatever's coming tomorrow."

"Good," Suzuno said. "Once that is done, I would like you to travel to Ente Isla at once. We need to introduce you to Dhin Dhem Wurs."

"Whoa! I'm gonna get to meet the most powerful person in the Northern Island? Wow, I'm getting nervous! I'm sorry, can you wait here one moment? I'll be right back!"

With that, she all but skipped out of her room.

"Do you think this is all right?" Laila asked.

"Nothing to fear. Apart from the constant griping the Devil King will give us later, it is smooth sailing ahead."

"That's what I'm afraid of the most. Plus, really, no matter how composed Chiho seems, she's just a normal teenage girl. The zirga isn't war, but it *is* a major political event."

"I think you need to learn a little more about Chiho, Laila." Suzuno stood up, looking out the window at the street running by the Sasaki residence. "She connected the Devil King and the Hero together, she is beloved by a Sephirah child, she is protected by the Hero's companions, she was promoted to the rank of Great Demon General, she had hordes of demons bowing down to her, and she uses holy magic to travel across worlds. How many teenage girls do *you* know who can do that?"

Suzuno smiled as she spotted Chiho jogging off to school.

"She is our friend. And she is the strongest person this world knows."

That evening, after enjoying an audience with Dhin Dhem Wurs, Suzuno, Albert, and Laila, Chiho was formally admitted into the zirga.

*

With a whistling tear that seemed to echo across the arena, Chiho's first arrow landed in the center of the target.

"She got it!" Maou shouted, despite himself. But he was drowned out by the rest of the crowd, far more enthusiastic about this round of archers than the previous ones.

"I don't know much about *kyudo*," Rika said to Albert, who was using holy magic to pick up the girl's Japanese, due to her lack of Idea Link skills. "Did Chiho just do something really great?"

"That girl's archery skills are beyond anything I've seen before," he exclaimed from the adjacent box, smiling and unable to contain his excitement. "As you can see, that girl's bow is twice the length of what's normally found 'round the Northern Island. The emphasis around here is less on the accuracy of a single bolt and more on mobility and the stopping power against an enemy force. The Southern Island is the same way, although you'll see a few differences between the Southern plains and the Northern mountains. I guess you can say it's not so elegant as all that, y'know? And here you have that huge bow, that unique stance…"

Chiho was still in her postfiring stance, her first shot landing right in the middle of the target, one a little bit larger than the standard used in *kyudo*. This was an exhibition, but zirga participants were still scored based on their bow skills, with points awarded based on how close to the center your arrow landed. Each round featured five volleys of arrows, and a shot on the star in the target's center was worth ten points, going down to eight, five, three, then one point as you ventured farther away. These zones were marked in concentric circles on the target, much like in typical archery.

In her first two rounds, Chiho had performed perfectly, an almost unheard-of feat, letting her finish over twenty points ahead of the runner-up. But due to her unique ("strange" by local standards) stance, she had been pegged as a dark-horse candidate by the bookmakers, meaning she was handicapped at pretty high odds.

"For someone like us, landin' it in the center of the target is a rush of excitement. But not her."

As Albert spoke, Chiho lowered her bow, then went back into her *monomi* stance, quietly sitting down and mentally preparing for her next shot.

"She's so...*refined*, you know? Mature."

The crowd was enrapt, watching on as she sat in silence for her next turn. The man firing after her was a muscle-bound giant, twice her size. He gave the seated Chiho a leer, then flexed his muscles to what seemed like three or four times their original size as he fired. The arrow certainly had the range to hit the target, but unlike Chiho's straight, calculated shot, it whizzed over in an arc and landed a fair bit below the center.

"Normally, that would elicit cheers, y'see? It sure won't today."

"Oh... Wow, Chiho's really good!"

"Maybe so. But I mean, her whole approach to archery couldn't be any more different from ours."

In a world like Ente Isla, where great advancements in holy magic had been made over the years, bow-and-arrow combat had undergone much less development. Unlike antiquity up to the Middle Ages on Earth, magic had always been the driver of long-range attacks on Ente Isla, along with things like one-shot surprise ambushes. The traditional approach in ancient Ente Isla was to start by lobbing long-range magic at each other, then charge forward with infantry or cavalry. Archers were, thus, only effective for a limited amount of time, and no nation dedicated themselves particularly to developing them. They were seen as mid-range threats, and tactics like firing rains of arrows from long distances were only seen in tomes and legends from the distant past, before magic made itself known. The accuracy of these descriptions, however, was an ongoing question. Apart from cross-bows and other bows meant for siege or defensive warfare, almost all archery used in Ente Islan combat was seen as an emergency mid-to-long-range backup when casting magic wasn't possible.

It might be expected to see it used in areas like sniping, assassination, and other long-range purposes, if it weren't for the simple fact that magic advanced more quickly. It was a given that any figure famous or notorious enough to be targeted for murder would always wear clothing or equipment enchanted to dull long-range attacks. And compared with the uncontrollable ranges of magic spells in ancient to medieval times, recent years had seen the rise of limited-range, self-repeating magic, focused more on pinning an enemy down than killing them—in essence, an upgraded version of the humble bow and arrow. Besides, a skilled sorcerer and a skilled archer took about the same amount of time and training to master their craft—but unlike archers, who needed high-quality tools and a ready supply of arrows to fight, a sorcerer could do their job as long as the holy force in the atmosphere was dense enough.

On the Northern Island, with its many jagged peaks and valleys forcing battle to remain small-scale most of the time, archery had been developed for hunting in mountains and forests, for guerrilla warfare, and for covert operations. The third use had proven somewhat effective in coping with the Devil King's Army in recent years, but a bow was still conventionally seen as a weapon that worked best in ranges of about 5 to 11 yards, so little development was done to expand on that.

The targets in this exhibition were normally positioned around 22 yards from the stage.

"Twenty-two yards?" Rika looked down as Albert explained all this. "It looks like more than that."

"Well, that's why this girl is so amazing to us. In our test runs, she landed every single shot dead center, so they moved 'em back another eleven yards to make it a fairer match."

A pity, then, that nobody knew *this* was close to the exact range Chiho worked with the most in her *kyudo* club. To be exact, most high school *kyudo* teams fired in the *kinteki* range, which was about 31 yards. The different measuring systems between the two planets meant they didn't add up exactly, of course, but to Chiho, the challenge involved was totally familiar.

In archery, being able to hit a 32-yard target didn't necessarily mean that closer targets were proportionally easier. But all fields of shooting sports featured separate techniques for short- and long-range targets, and *kyudo* was no exception. To a fan of the sport, it wouldn't be unnatural at all to expect Chiho to have no problem with the 22-yard distance.

But one other difference had quickly made itself clear. In the Northern Island, archery had evolved as a hunting tool, one whose practitioners did away with fancy logic and took an "if I hit it, I'm good" approach. In *kyudo*, with its origins in Bushido, a samurai code, and its emphasis on stances and mannerisms, that was not the case.

"And that," Wurs remarked as she tapped at her monocle, "is another reason why Chiho's out there. That fragment she has."

Then, as if waiting for that cue, Chiho looked straight at them.

"...That's right," Wurs said, as if Chiho was right next to her. "Calm down. You're more steely-eyed than anybody else on stage. Keep up the good work."

Chiho, despite being far too away to hear her, nodded deeply. Even Maou and Emi were floored. Chiho probably saw them in the audience just now. Their voices wouldn't carry, but the box seats were close enough, and empty enough, that they'd be visible. But she didn't acknowledge them, instead turning her face ahead and closing her eyes to focus her spirit. That face, right now, wasn't the face of the high schooler who smiled at them all the time, who warmly accepted them.

"Chi-Sis is tough!"

"Huh?

Alas Ramus, seated on Wurs's lap, must have seen her face, too. Maou assumed she was talking about how resolute she looked, but Acieth saw it differently.

"Not a single thread of the fear. She has the strong heart right now, she means! Her heart, it is settled."

Looking toward them, Maou realized both Acieth's and Alas Ramus's foreheads were still faintly glowing, ever since Wurs's monocle emitted that first flash of light. Startled, Maou looked more closely. Then, he saw it.

"Whoa, Laila, is Chi...?"

"That's right."

Laila nodded as she revealed a faintly glowing Yesod fragment in the palm of her hand.

"But in the end, this is the result of Chiho's internal strength and training. If she didn't have the fundamentals down, any further power I could send to her would be worthless. I tell you, any normal teen wouldn't be able to handle it."

She seemed to almost enjoy this.

As they carried on, Chiho's turn came up again. The crowd let up a mighty cheer as Maou strained his eyes, trying to peek at her right arm. The angle blocked it from his view most of the time—but the moment she launched her second arrow, he spotted a glint on her ring finger, sticking out from the archer's glove she had on. It was the ring with the Yesod fragment in it.

"...Mm?"

Proceeding with her follow-through, Chiho saw her second shot had landed true and put her bow down.

She had wanted this to go like any other *kyudo* session, so she only had her *haya* and *otoya* arrows in hand, but there were three more rounds to this exhibition. So far, the shots had been routine for her.

"Well done. Nobody can stop you now."

Retreating to the waiting area, she found Nord Justina, serving as her assistant, greeting her with a smile.

"I was pretty nervous with that one. Emilia and Maou are here. Seeing them made my hands shake."

"Your performance looked exactly the same to my eyes," Nord replied, gently smiling like he hadn't a care in the world. "Simply being here would make any of us nervous, but when your turn is up, it's like your entire spirit is unified. That's not something just anyone can do. You should be more confident."

"...Right. Oh, the feathers are a little messed up on that arrow. Can you replace it with the one over there?"

"Got it."

Following her instructions, Nord replaced the arrow.

"...Three to go."

Leaving Nord to care for her arrows, Chiho sat down, gathering herself. Nord was here because he all but fell over himself volunteering for it. He was no powerful sorcerer or fighter, but he was the least public figure among the group, so his assistance would not be seen as political or unjustified. His past tribulations had given him nerves of steel, he had hunted with a bow enough to know how to handle them, and he looked like a tall, muscular, bearded man, which let him play a bodyguard role for the small, young Chiho in this zirga full of huge, lumbering behemoths.

He had just given some encouragement to Chiho, and in Chiho's eyes, Nord wasn't at all drowned out by the event. The presence of his wife, Laila, in the audience was one factor behind that—but like Chiho, he was thrust in the middle of this battle against heaven, fully aware of everything going on, but ashamed that he couldn't help out Emi or Laila in any real way. That's why he had told Chiho beforehand that being able to help in this world-saving quest behind the scenes came as a sheer joy to him.

In turn, Chiho said to him in her mind,

I'm counting on you.

She was competing in this archery exhibition right now, but her position meant she was a part of all kinds of other ceremonies and conferences, and it was Nord who guided her through them. Having experienced life in the Western Island under Lucifer's occupation, he knew exactly what refugees returning to their homelands would need—information that proved helpful to Chiho during tortuously long policy discussions. He wasn't much help with horses, but if she navigated this exhibition the way they had planned it, Chiho wouldn't have to wing it in the equestrian events anyway.

"Three left."

Chiho brought her eyes down to the ring on her finger for just a moment, then focused on the star mark on the target far ahead of her. She scowled.

"...Chief Wurs? Laila? I have a favor to ask."

* * *

"Hmm?"

The wrinkles on Dhin Dhem Wurs's face suddenly deepened.

"Hey. Devil kid."

"Huhh?!"

The great demon who once had the world wrapped around his finger was now demoted to "devil kid." Maou might have lived for much longer than Wurs ever would, but the sudden outburst made him all but gasp in response, not that Wurs cared.

"So from what I'm hearing, you know that brave, gutsy girl over there's fallen in love with you, but you're just toying with her emotions, huh?"

"Who said that crap to you? Was it you?!"

"Hey! Why're you blaming me?!"

Laila immediately protested, but she had no right to blame him. She had a rep, and she knew it.

"'Toying with her emotions'... You might be toeing the line toward that lately, yeah."

"Emi!!"

Satan, the Devil King, didn't want to give these baseless accusations the time of day, but then, Wurs looked at him again, tapping her monocle.

"She says she wants to go without this from now on. She wants you two to see what she's capable of."

"Huh?"

It wasn't Maou or Emi, but Laila who voiced her surprise.

"...Hmm?"

Chiho was still standing there, in her follow-through pose, but the arena was erupting. For the first time, her arrow was just to the right of the star. They were practically neighbors, there on the target, but the first taste of vulnerability she had given the audience today completely changed the atmosphere. The other competitors smiled, looking forward to chasing her down on points, but Chiho remained quiet, returning to her standby position.

"I guess I really am nervous," she told Nord, before he could speak up. "My stance wasn't right there."

"What was wrong with it?"

"I pulled my face up. That's why it went right."

In *kyudo*, any issue or bad habit that affected one's shooting was called *fusei*. In this third shot, the first one fired without the support of her Yesod fragment, Chiho grew so anxious about her arrow going straight that she lifted her face toward the back—a classic *fusei*. This caused her whole body to lean ever-so-slightly to the right, and that was what pulled the arrow away from the star.

"All right. Well, let's fix that next time. If your muscles are getting sore, I think we'll get a longer break between the third and fourth rounds, so try to stretch yourself out a little."

"Oh, do we...? All right. I'll do that."

She didn't know the time schedule for this event. It came as a relief to her. So she released her focus and stretched out her body, working all the soreness and anxiety out.

"...I'm sorry. That's not actually the only reason."

"No? What is it?"

Chiho showed Nord her right hand as she gave him her equipment to hold. It had no ring on it.

"I wanted to compete with my own abilities. I kind of got carried away."

"Oh..."

Nord looked a little nonplussed, but then, he turned toward the targets and shook his head.

"Maybe, but you had it almost in the middle. A lot of the competitors here aren't getting nearly that close. It's nothing to be depressed about."

"...Right."

She knew Nord was trying to make her feel better, but Chiho was starting to feel deeply anxious. She might have missed the star, but given Chiho's inherent abilities, it was rare for her to score a hit that close to the center at all. In terms of force and stature, she was completely average for girls her age, which meant she hadn't developed the muscle strength to fully support her stances.

When it came to archery, there were often large performance differences between high school and college, and between college and adulthood. Growing in size was one cause of this, but another big one was whether or not your body was up for the sport. If it was, that connected to confidence, which, in turn, created internal strength.

Chiho, meanwhile, lacked the physical strength to overpower anyone else. An outside instructor once told her she had good focus, but focus didn't matter much in sports if it didn't connect to results. Plus, this habit of turning her face back before firing was one *fusei* habit Chiho had a difficult time shaking. It often put her in the hole during interschool competitions.

In short, no matter how much adulation Laila had for her, that was really the long and short of her latent abilities. Ninety-five percent of why she was setting this zirga meet on fire came down to the Yesod fragment—but unlike Emi's sword, the fragment in Chiho's ring didn't work directly on her. The superhuman exploits she showed off in Tokyo Tower against Gabriel and Raguel were the result of Laila's magic coursing through the fragment, basically making her a puppet.

Here, though, at this archery competition posing as an exhibition, it was difficult for Laila to control Chiho without at least someone in the Northern Island noticing. If people picked up on the holy force Laila used for the job, Chiho would be instantly booted out of the zirga and deemed unworthy of serving as chief. Instead, Laila had given Chiho a crash course in how to use the fragment, instructing her to use her own holy force to draw power from it and support her archery skills. Simply activating the fragment, however, would drain Chiho's holy magic by the second half of the event, so instead, Laila activated her own and Chiho's launched off that.

In other words, Chiho's current *kyudo* performance would never have happened without Laila's power.

To someone like Chiho, who had never systematically learned

magic and wasn't even from Ente Isla, being placed on this planet didn't make her any better a magician. She had only the barest minimum of natural recovery skills. As Nord put it, borrowing the fragment's force to boost her stamina and skills put a major toll on Chiho's body. She had very little holy force left to work with. It was common knowledge in Ente Isla that all fighters had a store of holy force inside them, large or small; using that force to improve your archery skills wasn't seen as cheating or otherwise improper. Tapping on some external force, however, was more akin to doping, so she needed to save up as much holy force as possible for today's events.

"...No, that's not it."

But even that was only one of many reasons Chiho thought about.

If all she wanted to do was carry out Suzuno's mission, she wouldn't have bothered with all the pomp and circumstance of *kyudo*. She could just fire away, instead of going through the whole power-draining *kai* procession with each shot, and nail every target. But to her, that option was never on the table.

So she softly said the name of someone important to her.

"Maou..."

She wanted to show a part of herself that Maou had never seen before. She wanted to show that her friends were looking to her for help, that she was standing here under her own power. She wanted to show that she had the strength to help him out. That's why she didn't want to cheat.

"Looks like you're still first up. Come on."

After a while, the notice for the fourth round was announced. She took up her bow, like she always did. She wasn't using the Yesod fragment. Or any holy force.

"......"

Her steps were good.

Her chest positioning was good.

Her string pulling was good.

Her hands were stable.

Her sighting was a little tense, but she felt like she wasn't pulling back too much this time.

From the draw to the extension, she felt her right shoulder going up a bit, but she calmly returned to the correct stance. The time had come to engage.

In her head, she recalled a moment just after she got into high school, gauging which clubs to join. She recalled the beautiful stance of one of the upperclassmen, drawing a white, bamboo bow on the stage in front of her. Now, she was facing a target, like a full moon, straight in front of the *yasurido* band above her grip.

"!"

The arrow, fired away from the bow, made what was probably the most comforting sound she had ever experienced in her short *kyudo* career before hitting the target.

"...Mm?"

Ahead of her lowered bow, she saw the arrow was a tad left of dead center, but still within the star.

Returning to standby for her final shot, she breathed a heavy sigh for the first time all evening.

"Well shot. You must be feeling better."

Chiho's face softened a little at Nord's applause. She smiled at him. "Normally, I'd be jumping for joy right now." She looked at the targets, face filled with emotion. "I hit the star for the first time in competition...with my own ability."

Right here, at the biggest stage of her life, she had done something she never accomplished before.

"Too bad this wasn't the final shot..."

There was one more to go. And after she had just fired the best arrow of her life, she could easily let her guard down for the last one. She took a deep breath, trying to dispel the tension and self-satisfaction. Then, another roar came from the crowd. She looked up from the stage, wondering what it was about.

"What...?"

Nord, picking up on things before she could, looked up and down the scoreboard, which, featured the competitors' names and points, on the stage.

"Oh my goodness, Chiho!"

"Yes?"

Nord stroked his beard hard enough to practically scrape it off, more excited than he normally ever was.

"You won!"

"Huh?" she yelped, any focus she had instantly vanishing.

"The second-place archer missed the target!"

Shock filled her mind.

The large man from before, the only competitor at all close to her in points, was apparently from the Welland clan in the southern flatlands. He had just whiffed his fourth shot. Thanks to that, even if Chiho missed the target on the fifth and everyone else hit dead-center with the rest of their turns, nobody could catch up to her in points.

"Wh-what happened?"

"I don't know. I don't know, but... Hmm? Look at that...!"

The Welland archer's bow sat limply in his hand, the string broken and hanging limply below. He stared at it dumbfoundedly for a moment, then shrugged, waved broadly to the crowd, and went to the back of the stage.

Then, he came right up to Chiho.

"Uh, umm..."

"..."

The man, who stood a good head above Nord, unnerved Chiho at first. But:

"Your bow skills are excellent."

He looked on, admiring her.

"If I fought you in battle and lost, I would ask for nothing more. I tried to follow in your footsteps, but I pushed myself too hard. I am simply not worthy."

He chuckled at his broken bowstring, then took a knee in front of Chiho.

"Scion of the great Wurs clan, I ask a favor of you."

Given his participation in this zirga, the man naturally knew Chiho's name.

"Y-yes?"

"Would you allow me to touch your bow?"

"My bow?"

Chiho looked at it. It was glass fiber with a bamboo core, purchased by her father when she began *kyudo*; maybe a bit high-end for high school sports.

"I know it is unbecoming of me. Asking a fellow warrior, the descendant of Chief Wurs, to reveal the—"

"Sure."

"—very tools that keep her alive in... Really?!"

The man, not expecting Chiho to give it up so easily, shivered across the entire mass of his body.

"Go ahead. It's no big deal."

"Th-thank you."

He bowed at Nord, likely mistaking him for a Wurs clansman, and accepted the bow from Chiho.

"So light! And this smooth feel, on the surface... It looks like bamboo, but there is something else, as well..."

Saying it was glass fiber was unlikely to mean anything to him, and Chiho didn't really know what "glass fiber" was anyway. So she decided to repeat what the guy at the store said when she went to buy the equipment with her dad.

"It's a combination of bamboo and this special core material. It allows beginners like me to fire fast-moving arrows with relatively little recoil."

This was the bow the shop recommended after she said she'd like to have a bamboo bow in the future. It felt close to bamboo, bending softly on the draw, but still packing a punch on the release. At the same time, the recoil was on the lighter side (a trademark of the series), which made it feel stiffer and stronger than its specifications showed. Thanks to that, the clerk had said, she'd need to get some muscle on her to take full advantage of it.

Whenever she fired a good shot from it, it tended to make this higher-pitched sound, as if informing her whenever she got her stance right. It was said the average glass fiber or carbon fiber bow didn't last as long as pure bamboo, but she intended to stick with this one as long as she could.

"Beginner? You?"

The man couldn't hide his shock. Chiho had landed all but one shot perfectly today, and she called herself a beginner?

"Yes, I've only been at this for around two years. Honestly, all I can say is I felt really good and had a lot of luck today."

"Unbelievable..."

There was also the Yesod fragment, but no need to complicate matters.

"I am sure all the clans are reconsidering their opinions of you Wurses, now that this wunderkind has made herself known. You may be selected as Chief Dhin Dhem's successor, you know."

"Oh, I doubt that. I may be all right with a bow, but I'm terrible on a horse, and I don't know nearly enough about politics, and economics, and the other clans, and stuff. But that lady—um, I mean, Chief Dhin Dhem—she insisted I take my place up here, so..."

She was really here to retrieve the Spear, and she was also the one who insisted on doing this, but she felt at least a few pangs of guilt over butting into one of the most venerated events in the Northern Island. Never in her life did she think she was chief herder material.

"Oh, no need for modesty. The fact that you didn't even let the other clans finish their rounds will certainly earn *yours* respect today. Tell Chief Dhin Dhem I wished her hello. And also..."

The man cheerfully smiled, handed the bow back to Chiho, and clapped her on the shoulder.

"I cannot wait to see what you'll do in the Bowman's Offering."

"...I'll try my best."

The Bowman's Offering was the final event of the day, where the stage was taken away and the exhibition's winner would demonstrate his or her best trick shot, dedicating it to their clan, the powers of nature, or the assorted gods worshipped in the Northern Island. This could involve, for example, expressing one's appreciation for the vast earth by hitting a succession of targets on horseback, or shooting down flying targets (representing the birds that contribute to nature, vegetation, fruits, and meat supplies) like in clay pigeon shooting. Once, a stout archer loaded his bow with three arrows and hit three separate targets at the same time—which, while a bit lacking in religious (or practical) significance, was certainly a shot to remember.

By this point, however, most of the ways one could fire an arrow in a flashy fashion had been exhausted, so the more talented competitors were usually asked what they'd bring to the Bowman's Offering in advance should they win. Chiho had submitted hers, then discussed and worked it out with Suzuno in advance.

Once the Welland archer left, Nord went up to her.

"Now for the real excitement, huh?"

"Yep."

"The championship finished early, so we'll have more time to prepare for it. It doesn't sound like they'll move the Bowman's Offering up in the schedule, so go ahead and rest up 'til then."

Chiho nodded, stood up from her kneeling position, bowed to the stage and the targets, and finally felt the tension flow out of her.

"Oh, it's over?"

Maou sounded a little disappointed as workers began to dismantle the stage and people began to shuffle around them.

"Huh?" Wurs whirled around at him. "Weren't you complaining about it this whole time?"

"N-no, um..."

"Oh, but I get what Maou's talking about," said Rika, still clapping at the stage from her box seat. "Chiho got so far ahead that they called the game, huh?"

Over to the side, the oddsmaker's booth was a scene of alternating joy and chaos, the dark-horse Chiho's stunning victory wrecking the entire script of the evening.

"But man, Chiho is sooo talented! I've never heard about that part of her before. I bet she's doing pretty great in her high school team, too. This was so exciting! Maybe I should get back into swimming myself!"

Rika basked in the excitement, nearly driven to tears by the scene, before looking around, distracted.

"Huh? Emi, what's with your mom?"

"...Oh?"

Emi, who had watched the exhibition at rapt attention and was already swept up in the flurry of emotions leading up to the Bowman's Offering, only now realized that the seat next to her no longer had Laila in it.

"Mm? Whoa, and what happened to Libicocco over there?"

Maou, for his part, then spotted a distinct lack of the enormous Libicocco in Rika's box.

"The two of them," Wurs said, "need to prepare for the Bowman's Offering."

"Laila and Libicocco? Prepare how?"

Maou knew that the Offering was a memorial event, a way to honor the winner of the archery contest, but why did they need three people for it?

"Guys, we've gone over this. Are you deliberately acting dumb, or what? Is Japan peaceful enough that the Devil King's and the Hero's brains have shrunk to a worm's size? You know what they left to pick up."

She motioned with her chin up at the Spear, even now towering over the arena.

"So Chiho's gonna team up with Laila to perform an Offering that I guarantee you've never seen before. Meanwhile, the Malebranche is going to attract people's attention with a little trick of his. While all eyes are on him, Stumpy Scythe's gonna open a Gate and ram the Spear through it."

"She—she can do that?"

Maou and Emi had no idea how they were going to retrieve this huge spear during the evening, or how Laila and Libicocco were involved.

"Hey, lady, I've been meaning to ask you something..."

Maou took this opportunity to ask Wurs about a term she had been bandying around all day.

"By 'Stumpy Scythe,' you don't mean..."

"A nickname as fancy-pants as 'Death Scythe' goes to waste on her," she bluntly replied. "'Stumpy Scythe' is good enough."

"'Bpph!!'"

Maou and Emi had suspected an answer like that. They weren't disappointed. It made both of them crack up at once.

"What's with you Westerners anyway? Giving a nickname as scary as that to such a cute little lady? Just go with Stumpy Scythe! It's perfect!"

Every time Wurs used the name, Maou and Emi shuddered a bit, trying their hardest not to burst out in massive, sidesplitting laughter. It was so rude to Suzuno, in so many ways, but Maou had already decided: This was how he'd get back at her for leaving him out of the loop.

"From this point forward, she's Stumpy Scythe until I get bored of it."

Just then, a gong sounded to signify that the Bowman's Offering was ready to start. Maou and the rest of the crowd turned their attention to the arena—then, another clamor rose. In the arena was...nothing particularly special. Chiho assumed a firing pose, and there was a simple archery target and the shadow of the Spear cast over the grounds.

"Uh... Is this gonna work?"

Maou, despite knowing little about the archery scene on two different planets, couldn't help but be concerned. The distance between Chiho and the target seemed impossibly long. By Maou's estimation, if the range during the competition was about thirty-three yards, this was a good three times that or so. The sight of Chiho focusing, sizing up this target over a football field's length away, would've stupefied anyone.

In Japan's feudal days, it was said that even the greatest of archers could not capture a target beyond 30 *ken* (about 60 yards) in length.

The official rules of *kyudo* offer an *enteki* (far-target) version where they could be placed up to about 66 yards away from the shooter. The *Toshi-ya* archery competition, held in Kyoto's Sanjusangen-do Temple for over two centuries in old times, once featured a samurai who fired an arrow about 131 yards—but that was strictly a length competition, not aimed at a target. These days, Sanjusangen-do held a yearly competition called *O-mato Taikai*, or "Festival of the Great Target," modeled after *Toshi-ya*, but that ran under the 66-yard *enteki* rules. In other words, attempting to hit a target that was about 109 yards away with a regular bow and arrow, both on Earth and in Ente Isla, was unthinkable.

Before the commotion could die down, the event continued with the announcement of the contender's name, what she was devoting the offering to, and what was about to be attempted. The crowd roared once again. As it was proclaimed, Chiho Sasaki Wurs, winner of the archery exhibition, wished to express her respects for the spear Adramelech left behind by executing a *tsugiya* to imitate its shape.

A *tsugiya*, in *kyudo* parlance, referred to an arrow lodging inside the nock (the notch at the back end of an arrow, for engaging the bowstring) of a previously fired arrow on the target. This was a rarity, but not unheard of in the world of high school archery, and pulling it off earned you the previous arrow's score added onto the current one. But this occurred almost exclusively in close-range contests, and even then, through sheer coincidence; it was nothing you could really aim for. It was a bit more common for an arrow to bounce off one lodged in the target and fall away; this was called *hazu-uchi*, and the arrow was deemed off target for no points. (If a person ever did pull off a *tsugiya*, it was prudent to temper the celebrating—after all, the contestant just damaged one of their opponent's arrows beyond repair, which could hit the amateur archer's wallet hard.)

So the boast of Chiho performing this move on a 109-yard target was shocking enough. But:

"Are those three arrows in Chiho's hand?"

Emi noticed it first. Short- and long-range arrows differed in structure and shaft diameter; long-range ones had more narrowly sculpted shafts, which made a *tsugiya* even more difficult to pull off.

"Yes," Wurs effused, "Chiho said that if we're dedicating this to the Spear, two arrows alone wouldn't have enough impact. She really wants to help you guys, you know? It looks to me that you were too busy looking down on her to notice her feelings...or her strengths."

They looked down on her.

The words stabbed into Maou's and Emi's hearts. Had they only assumed that Chiho, unable to fend for herself in battle, was this thing that required constant protection? Had they decided, somewhere in their minds, that Chiho was, at best, a supporting actor in this effort to invade the heavens? After Chiho made it no secret that she wanted to help Maou and Emi, never wavering from that position for months, did they brush it off as her just being polite?

"If you really intend to kill off our god, then this arrow will serve as the signal flare for the next hundred years of Ente Islan history."

Chiho gave the crowd a graceful nod of the head, then took an arrow in her right hand, lifted her bow, and assumed the stance. Not a single shred of hesitation was in her eyes, the arrow loaded into her taut bow making her look like the subject of a fine Japanese artwork painted on a folding screen.

"Chi-Sis! You kin do it!"

"Chiho! You've got this!!"

"I like those eyes. Those are fighter's eyes."

The fragments held by Alas Ramus and Dhin Dhem Wurs lit up. Chiho's right hand exhibited a faint light of its own to match.

"...!"

With a clear, high-pitched *zing*, the arrow went aloft—and the next moment, it was lodged right in the middle of the target. The roaring of the crowd dominated the scene. A perfect shot, from 109 yards away.

That alone was hard enough to believe, but even more astounding was the way Chiho immediately began loading her next arrow.

When she extended her bow, the crowd fell into nervous silence once more, Alas Ramus and Acieth watching Chiho with bated breath. Maou could almost hear his own heart beating.

"!"

Again, a high-pitched whine heralded the arrow's trajectory—and then, a lower sound, duller than the thud of hitting the target.

"......Whoa."

"Wow, Chiho..."

Maou and Emi couldn't help but mutter it to themselves. The second arrow was lodged halfway down the shaft of the first. It almost looked like Chiho had simply fired one extremely long arrow into the target.

But the cheers didn't come. There were three arrows. Everyone was waiting for a three-arrow *tsugiya* from long range, a feat like none before in history.

Taking up the final arrow, Chiho once again took her firing stance, the entire audience focused upon her.

"!"

Her eyes met Maou's. Her back was turned to the box seats, but just as she was loading the arrow on her bowstring, she turned her head enough to catch a glimpse at Maou. The single eye looking over her shoulder felt to Maou like it was sucking him in; it made him forget to breathe. He thought she was smiling—but the next moment, Chiho was staring down the target.

Maou wasn't sure if that was really Chiho he saw there at all.

Chiho could feel the holy force bubbling up all across her body. With this final shot, her role would be complete.

This had begun by tricking the rest of the zirga participants into letting her in. She was so happy Suzuno had sought out her help, so happy to help Maou for a change, that she gladly became a part of the Spear-snatching operation. But all those confusing feelings were gone now—and the only thing ahead of her was that tiny, tiny star, barely visible on the left side of her grip...

...or, to be exact, a point even beyond that.

And with that, Chiho called for the great demon who had fought against Maou, trained Maou, fought alongside Maou, and become friends with Maou, a demon whom no one would ever see again.

"May you wield the ancestral spear of the Bluehorns once more, for the sake of Satan, the Devil King."

The moment the holy force within her activated, the bow and arrow in her hands began to shine a silvery color.

"Wha...?"

Maou had seen that light only once before. It was the light Chiho exuded up on Tokyo Tower. Back there, with Laila and the Yesod fragment backing her up, she had gathered up the demonic force in the area and melted it into the air, as if purifying the barrier around the area. There was no demonic force here. Pulling off the same act wouldn't accomplish anything. But this could only be interpreted as Chiho exerting her full force to its limits, and not only she, but everyone else involved in the plan—Suzuno, Laila, Wurs, Libicocco, Albert—all expected that much from her.

But what happened next was something that nobody could explain later.

Around Chiho's feet, narrow spikes of thornlike ice sprouted up from the ground, slowly swirling around her body like a protective force field before merging with the silvery, shining arrow.

"What...the...?"

Now Maou's breathing stopped. He never thought he would see that magic spell again. Albert and Wurs also sat to attention, not expecting any of this, but Chiho didn't move an eyebrow, her spirit focused solely on the target.

"Thank you, Adramelech."

Then, she fired.

The arrow, spewing off silver light that trailed behind it like powdery snow, made a beautiful sound that seemed to make the earth itself tremble as it reached its target. When it hit home, the three arrows, along with the target itself, were encompassed by a blast of ice from the ground. It spiraled upward to the heavens, shaking off more snow as it did, and, in short order, took on the exact shape of the Spear of Adramelechinus, encasing that miraculous three-arrow shot inside its transparent ice.

"..."

The crowd barely stirred, their eyes darting between the girl and the pair of spears. Chiho, the light surrounding her gone, lowered her bow like nothing was amiss, bowing to the spear of ice that just encased her masterpiece.

"Wh-what is that?!"

The shout from someone in the crowd turned everyone's attention upward.

"Wha...!"

"What on...?"

Maou and Emi followed their neighbors' gazes, gasping in surprise. Chiho was the last to turn toward it—the original Spear, the one that was there before. Now, on one side of it, was the feared and venerated Great Demon General that once ruled the Northern Island.

"Adramelech..."

As if amplifying Maou's whisper, the name Adramelech began to ripple across the grandstand. Adramelech, the great founder who created the Bluehorn clan, had made his fabled return. All his attention was focused on a single point. When the crowd got over their shock enough to follow his eyes, they found the small girl who pulled off that miraculous offering.

"You supported me, didn't you?"

Chiho smiled at the demon before her, with the great, blue head of a bull and a body several times larger than her own.

"Thank you very much."

She then lowered her equipment and bowed at her superior officer in the Devil King's Army.

"Ahh?!"

Then, Adramelech vanished into thin air once more, as a blue light began to descend upon his Spear, forming a shimmering column that began altering the weapon, seemingly melting it into nothingness. Chiho stood back upright, watching the light do its work.

And when the blue light finally faded, its blinding sparks no longer illuminating the night, both Adramelech and his Spear were gone, revealing the clear, uncluttered skies of Phiyenci.

All that remained were the befuddled people of the Northern Island and the new spear of ice, forever commemorating the greatest arrow shot ever made. That, and the girl who triggered the entire miracle.

＊

On a set of tatami mats built in the middle of Devil's Castle on the Central Continent, Maou, Ashiya, and Urushihara were enjoying lunch around their low *kotatsu* table.

"I swear, man, if you guys all knew, why didn't you tell me?"

"I told you, because we all knew you'd say no. What's the big deal? It worked, dude."

"My sincerest apologies, Your Demonic Highness. By the time I was aware of everything, Bell and Dhin Dhem Wurs were already well into their planning. I was unable to put a stop to it."

"Well, yeah, I'm glad it worked out in the end, but..."

Maou put his bowl down, swallowing the remaining rice in his mouth, then looked at the giant object lying by the wall of his cavernous throne room. It was the Spear of Adramelechinus, just as it was before disappearing into that pillar of blue light.

"Do you have any idea how many years of my life that whole experience in Phiyenci took from me?"

"So what? It was cool, huh? That cranky-ass old lady was falling over herself praising you all, and Bell and Laila and Albert Ende were all 'Oh wow, oh wow...'"

"Well, if I was in on the script, maybe I could've appreciated it a little more!"

"Oh, shut up, dude! Since when were you such a timid man, Maou? Why do you lose all your reasoning skills the moment Chiho Sasaki gets involved? Like, dude, did you have any better ideas for this?"

"You shut up!"

"My liege, calm yourself. You are getting grains of rice everywhere."

"No, you shut up, too! Arrrgh, I hate you guys!"

Maou was lashing out at pretty much everything at the moment.

After the Spear vanished, the rest of the zirga's events were cancelled for the first time in Northern Island history. The image of Adramelech, the disappearance of his Spear, and the rise of the new one—it was no time for partying. So Chief Herder Dhin Dhem Wurs exercised her authority to commission an immediate investigation, enlisting every clan in the land to aid the effort. Wurs fully knew where the vision came from and where the Spear went, of course—but Chiho's frozen arrow, and the pillar of ice that resulted, wasn't in anybody's game plan.

The original operation called for Chiho to borrow Laila and her Yesod fragment's power to break all zirga records in the archery exhibition. Then, once she knocked 'em dead in the Bowman's Offering, Libicocco would use his Malebranche-born necromancy and illusion magic to summon a vision of Adramelech. This burst of demonic force would serve as a smoke screen for Suzuno to use her angel's feather pen to transport the Spear through a Gate without the Northern Island's sorcerers noticing the rush of holy force that resulted. It was a miracle, but a human-engineered one.

But then, a miracle really did happen, one not in the script. The thorns of ice that supported Chiho's third shot were, beyond a doubt, the kind of ice magic Adramelech was best at, and the spear of ice that resulted still stood strong, showing zero sign of melting at all. Wurs had already reported to the Holy Magic Administrative Institute through Rumack that her preliminary investigation revealed no sign of demonic force in the edifice, but nobody had any idea why it stayed so perfectly frozen.

"I suppose," Ashiya said, "some kind of anomaly in holy force, like what Laila and our landlord talked about, reacted in some unforeseeable way with Sasaki's Yesod force and the demonic power left behind by Adramelech around Phiyenci. That is all I can surmise."

When Chiho had Laila's backing in the fight on Tokyo Tower, the arrows she shot dispelled the demonic force gathered around

Maou and his friends. And given the ice-tree towers that Adramelech drove into the ground across the Northern Island, serving as a sort of antenna network for demonic force, perhaps Chiho's power reacted somehow with what part of Adramelech's force was left in the groundwater. But the nature of that "somehow" was a mystery, as was everything about the ice tower for the time being.

"Honestly, though, I'm happy just leaving the Northern Island to clean up this mess for us. Plus, having that ice tower helps Rumack and Emeralda a bunch, right?"

Word of the miracle of the zirga had already spread worldwide, and with much greater speed and accuracy than anything about the Eastern Island conflict or Emilia's and Alciel's return. Thus, Rumack and Emeralda, playing dumb about the whole thing, had made contact with Chief Herder Dhin Dhem Wurs to stage a tandem investigation of the incident, the pretext being that the analysis of Sankt Ignoreido's groundwater conducted by Albert at the Institute could help with figuring out the mystery ice coming up from underneath Phiyenci.

The idea that anyone had made off with the original Spear was sheer conjecture at this point. Instead, a litany of wild, wholly nonscientific rumors spread around the island—the Spear shot into the heavens to pursue its master, or returned to the demon realm, or Adramelech popped back in from the afterlife to pick up his forgotten relic, or he saw that the people of the Northern Island had accepted the Spear and used Chiho Sasaki Wurs to replace it with another one.

But regardless of the results or subsequent reactions, the recovery of the Spear of Adramelechinus, the trickiest part of the relic search, ended in great success.

After the Bowman's Offering, Maou and Emi were brought to Chiho at the arena. They greeted her with silence, wholly unsure what to say at first. She had left her bow and arrow with Nord, so her hands were in the slits in her *hakama* pants as she idly fluttered them around.

"Come on," Rika finally said to break the ice, "say something!" She pushed Maou a step forward to make the point clearer.

Chiho, cheeks reddened, looked up at Maou, like a child who expected to be punished shortly.

"Um, Maou, I…"

"Yeah, um…"

Maou, for his part, had trouble dealing with those eyes. He had to work hard not to avert his gaze but somehow managed to succeed. If he avoided her eyes now, he thought, he might not ever be able to look straight at her again.

"Chiho Sasaki…"

"Yes?!"

Chiho, called very unexpectedly by her full name, arched her back upward.

"You did great. That was amazing."

"…Maou."

"I'm sure Adramelech is happy, too."

He looked at the spear of ice. It truly was a symbol of the Great Demon General, the one who supported his great, lofty ambition with the power of demonic ice.

Chiho nodded at the observation, then took a deep breath, looking straight at Maou.

"Your Demonic Highness…"

It was the first time she called him that.

"I, the Great Demon General Chiho Sasaki, have completed my mission!"

"…Well done."

And that was the limit.

"Haaahhhhhhh!"

She let out a deep sigh, then crumpled to the ground.

"Ohh, I was sooo nervous. I was so, so nervous!"

"Y-you okay?!"

Maou brought a hand down to support her. It brought the two of them close together. Their eyes met at point-blank range. It sent Maou into panic for a moment, but Chiho simply gave him a shy, red-tinged smile.

"…Hee-hee! But I think I'm better now."

"Wha… Oh, uh…yeah."

"Sorry I did all this dangerous stuff without telling you."

"N-no, um, it wasn't dangerous at all. It was a real sight to see. Like, amazing. And Chi, your bow, uh…"

He couldn't get the words out well, but Chiho still smiled on.

"I've received help from a lot of people. I really don't have much strength on my own."

"No, of course you do. Laila herself told me you've got a strong foundation."

"Well, I'm just glad you got to see me. It made the effort worth it."

"Y-yeah…"

"If you want to praise her, just *do* it."

The overjoyed Chiho and awkward Maou were interrupted by an exasperated Emi behind them.

"E-Emi!"

"Yusa…"

"I swear, Chiho, you do nothing but surprise us. This time, though, I thought I was gonna have a heart attack… Next time, I hope you'll talk it over with us first."

"All right. I promise I won't do this behind your back anymore."

She gave her a happy nod, then had Maou help her return to her feet.

"Akiko's already taken over my shifts, and thanks to this zirga, I think I have a clearer view of what's ahead, Maou."

A new resolve was in her voice.

"I don't mind if we wind up taking the long way around. Now I know, no matter how much time it takes, we're both aiming for the same place. So…I'm ready to follow you as far as it takes."

"Y-yeah…" That weak reply was about the best Maou could muster.

"Man… Today has been terrible on my heart. In more ways than one…"

"What, you're still going on about that?"

For once, it wasn't Urushihara yelling at a whining Maou, but Rika.

"Gnhh... S-Suzuki?!"

Ashiya reacted to her before Maou could.

"Hey there, guys." Rika was dressed for the outdoors, as if she had recently finished her shift at work. A large paper bag was in her hands. The throne room was far above the ground, and it was doubtful that Rika had made it up here by herself. She had probably used her feather pen to build a Gate that led right here.

Maou gave her a half-dejected smile. "Damn, you can make Gates whenever you want to now, huh?"

"It's just like taking the plane or bullet train," Rika indifferently replied. "The first time, you're all freaking out, worrying if you screwed up your ticket or whatever, but once you're used to it, it's like, *What was I so scared of?*"

Neither Maou, nor Ashiya, nor Urushihara had been on either of those transports, so the analogy didn't mean much to them, but they understood well enough that Rika was now fully used to cross-planetary travel.

"Oh, also, this is late, but..."

"Hmm?"

Rika took her shoes off to go on the tatami-mat floor, then pulled three gift-wrapped boxes out from the bag. She placed them in front of all three demons, the box facing Ashiya notably larger and wrapped fancier than the others.

"The hell's this?"

"Well, that's not a very nice way to put it, Maou. It's your Valentine's Day chocolate. It's past the fourteenth now, but we're still kind of in the general range, so..."

Maou glanced at the Japanese calendar atop the nearby plastic shelving. It was two days past Valentine's, but considering Kusuda provided her chocolate gift way back on the seventh, this was certainly permissible.

"Why's Ashiya's so much bigger?" Urushihara asked, though

it was unclear whether he was deliberately trying to make things awkward.

"Well, why do you think? The chocolate for Maou and Urushihara is just for politeness's sake. My real gift is for Ashiya."

"?!"

Ashiya suspected this would happen, but the spoken statement still shook him.

"Y-you, Suzuki...?"

"Oh, don't worry about getting me something for next month, either. I know you're gonna be busy, so...whenever is fine."

"Um, I'm not sure if it's..."

Ashiya had already refused Rika's advances once. As far as he was concerned, he couldn't have made that clearer to her. It was why he could barely bring himself to see Rika for the past month; they barely even interacted at all.

"You're not? So what is it?"

"That...um..."

"Because you're not being too specific." Rika smiled, knowing how thrown Ashiya was. "You know, I just realized that, come to think of it, you never did dump me, so..."

"Huh? Uhm..."

"In the end, Alciel, you're exactly like someone else I know. Never giving a clear answer."

"..."

That someone now had his back turned to her, grimacing.

"I mean, if you really don't like it, say so. But until then, I'm about as resolute on this as Chiho is, so... Oh, hey, where is Chiho? Down on the ground?"

"Huh? Um, yeah."

"Oh. I better say hi to her, then."

With that, she whipped out her feather pen, as casually as if she was about to write a note to herself, and drove it into the ground, hopping inside the Gate that resulted. Presumably, she used it to head for ground level in an instant. Maou shrugged at how quick and easy she made it seem, but turning back toward the table, he was faced with the full brunt of Urushihara's exasperated gaze upon him.

"Dudes..."

"What?"

"Both of you guys, getting manipulated by women like that... Doesn't that make you question your lives at all? As, like, demons?"

Having Urushihara accuse them of that seemed like a death knell. But for a change, Maou and Ashiya had no words to counter him with.

"Well, guess I'll clean up the dishes."

"Oh, me too..."

"Ughh..."

It was right when Maou and Ashiya stood up, attempting to flee Urushihara's admonishment at all costs, that Farfarello came through the throne-room door, with Libicocco and Ciriatto behind him.

"My liege, Lord Lucifer, and the Great Demon General of the East, pardon us for interrupting you."

"Mm? What's up?"

All three were naturally in their full, demonic Malebranche forms, but in all their clawed mandibles, they seemed to be carrying some manner of boxes.

"Your Demonic Highness... My lords..."

The three chieftains gave one box each to Maou, Ashiya, and Urushihara. All three looked at them, only to find pink heart stickers on each one. Question marks popped over all their heads at once.

"My liege," Libicocco dared to begin, "we understand there is a custom in Japan where one gifts those they respect with food as a symbol of their devotion."

Urushihara was the first to furrow his eyebrows. "...Huh?"

"We of the Malebranche," Ciriatto continued, "seek your forgiveness for so troubling not only you, but also your Great Demon Generals, and your regent, Camio."

"...Mm?" Ashiya tilted his head to the side, unsure what Ciriatto meant.

"This is a symbol of our appreciation, and of our renewed loyalty. We only hope you will accept it."

"...No way." For the first time in a while, Maou wasn't sure how to react. "Can I open this?"

The Malebranche nodded at him. He carefully pulled the box open—and inside, accompanied by the sweet aroma of cacao, was a heart-shaped piece of chocolate, a little crudely molded but no doubt crafted with honest love.

"Huh?"

"Th-this...?"

Urushihara and Ashiya, watching from the sides, stared blankly at the chocolate, unsure what was happening before their eyes.

"Uh, Farfarello?"

"Yes, my liege!"

Maou forced his face into an uneasy smile. "Was this...handmade?"

"It was, my liege. I understand that crafting your gift by hand is a sign of one's sincerity."

"...Phew... That, uh, wow. Thanks."

Maou looked at the people surrounding him, unsure how to express the churning emotions in the pit of his stomach. Then, he looked at the box of "polite" chocolate Rika left for him a moment ago. For a moment, he thought about these gruesome Malebranche fighters, working their massive claws and gnarled hands to work melted chocolate into a heart shape, and what could have possibly been the cause behind this spectacle.

"Devil King! Are you here?"

Then, a familiar voice heralded the entrance of a fairly large group of people into the throne room.

"Ugh..."

"N-no..."

It was a small horde of demons, led by Suzuno. There were Blue-horns, there were Iron Scorpions, there were Malebranche, there were smaller goblins and Pájaro Danino—all told, fifty or so demons who had escaped the postwar hunting on the Central Continent. They were in a neat line, nervous looks on their faces, and every one of them carried tiny boxes that didn't look at all correctly proportioned to their sizes.

"Y-you...?"

Realizing the three chieftains came here first, Suzuno glared at them, eyebrows down.

"I told you we would all give them together!"

"Hah!" Libicocco shrugged, not looking particularly guilty. "We are nimbler than you rabble, so we finished ahead of you. What is so wrong about delivering our wares first?"

"My apologies," Farfarello said, looking much more remorseful. "He insisted."

"B-Bell," muttered Ashiya as he beheld this monstrous lineup, "what is this...?"

"What does it look like?" Suzuno matter-of-factly stated. "It is their Valentine's gifts. We wanted to surprise you, but those three just had to come first..."

"Um, this goes well beyond the level of 'surprise,' I would say..."

So all those boxes contained handmade chocolate? Suzuno, surmising the doubt written all over Maou's face, gave him a brisk nod.

"Yes. All of them. We worked hard."

"You 'worked hard'?! What the hell're you making them do?!"

"What is the matter? Are you saying you will not accept the gifts prepared by your beloved staff, each piece molded with love, sincerity, and thankfulness?"

"I-I'm not saying that... I just, like, I really appreciate it, but..."

"Then good. All right, everyone, line up. The Devil King and his Generals are eager to accept your offerings."

"Wha—"

"N-no, uh..."

"Wait a..."

Under Suzuno's order, the demons swarmed Maou with their gifts. Suzuno smiled at his subsequent screaming.

"Ah," she shamelessly added, "what a joy it is to see such honest love for my leader!"

"Wh-what's going on? What is this?"

"I—I do not know! I do not know, but..."

"Holy crap, dude, if we let this spread around, we're gonna have the whole army in here..."

The boxes of handmade chocolate began to pile up. Each one seemed pretty full—and heavy, as Maou found out when he picked one up. By the time the demons filed out, the tatami-mat space looked a bit like a living room with all the stuff packed in boxes for the movers; some of them had even spilled out onto the throne room's floor.

The three demons, unable to believe what just happened, simply stared at the pile for a while.

"Do not worry," Suzuno said. "We used three kinds of chocolate—dark, milk, and tea-flavored. You will never be bored, I guarantee it!"

"I'm gonna get so bored of chocolate before I get... Hmm?"

Before he could finish sassing Suzuno, Urushihara spotted a small box atop the chocolate mountain, wrapped in light-green paper with a golden bow around it.

"And that, um... It contains matcha and *wasanbon* candies. And...well, perhaps it is not as infused with affection as the gifts from your faithful horde, but take it anyway."

"...Uh?"

"I left you entirely out of the loop this time. Call this...an apology."

Suzuno didn't look quite as gung ho about this as she did when she sent all those demons in here.

"...Well, thanks. Hmm... *Wasanbon* is, like, high-grade Japanese sugar candy, right?" Maou carefully scoped out the package, then the Spear on the side of the room. "But yeah, thanks for handling the Spear. Pulling that off really helps me a lot. I'll have to repay you sometime. Aren't I supposed to gift you something next month in response to this?"

Ashiya blanched a bit at the term "repay," but Suzuno blinked a couple of times in surprise, then gave Maou a happy smile.

"I only did what any Great Demon General would do, but if you insist, I will be glad to accept any medals of honor you provide me—"

"Ahhhhhhh! Suzuno!!"

The shout echoed across the throne room like lightning, startling the two of them.

"You said we would all do this together!"

"What could we do, Chiho? All those demons would have crushed you."

"Daddy! Chocolate! Chocolate!!"

Chiho, Emi, and Alas Ramus were here, and they, too, had some boxes with them. Running up to the three demons, Chiho gave each of them a box, much like Rika from before, each one done up in cute wrapping. In terms of size, it was actually Urushihara who got the largest one, followed by Ashiya, then Maou.

"I got Urushihara a few different brands of snack chips, and Ashiya, I got you a set of rice seasonings."

The salty selections came as an apparent relief to them both, not that it'd be any better for their health than chocolate. For Maou, however, she had a small box filled with the symbol of her sweet affection.

"And for you, Maou, I have some homemade chocolate, crafted with love!"

"Oh, um, thanks. You made your own chocolate, too, Chi?"

He asked the question even though the answer was obvious from the exquisite wrapping job.

"Yes, I actually made it with all the demons."

""""Huh?"""""

The bombshell of a confession took all three of them aback.

"Yeah, some of the demons asked what she was doing when she brought all the supplies over from Japan. So she told them, and you can see the results now."

"For real...?"

Would a passing idea from a high school teenager create an entirely new custom in the demon realm? And considering this chocolate came from Earth, what kinds of things would they concoct with the supplies available in Ente Isla? And for that matter, why did demons, who didn't have to eat food in the first place, respond so eagerly to the idea of giving out chocolate on Valentine's Day?

"Are they starting to change, too?"

"What are you muttering about? Here."

"......Huh?"

Maou honestly had no idea what was in the box Emi just presented to him. Emi apparently expected as much.

"It's not from me, stupid. Alas Ramus made this."

"!!" Maou immediately snatched the box away from Emi. "A-Alas Ramus made this?!"

"Yeh! I helped!!"

"That's right," Chiho explained. "She poured the chocolate into the heart mold all by herself!"

Maou broke into a wide smile. "W-wow... Wooow! You made Daddy so happy! So you can do hard stuff like that now? Thank you so much, Alas Ramus! I'll get something for you later, okay?"

"Huh? Okeh."

Alas Ramus wasn't fully up on the Valentine's tradition yet, but having her hair done up in an Emi-style side ponytail and getting patted on the head was all the reward she needed for now.

Just then, Acieth strolled inside, conspicuously helping herself to the contents of the box in her hands.

"Oh, is it all calm now? Maou, this is the box of me. You must pay me back the double on White Day!"

And Maou, still smiling and patting Alas Ramus's head, yelled, "Get out!!"

"But are you sure this was the best of ideas, Chiho?"

"I think it's about the best way we could've done it. That didn't put any stress on him, did it?"

"Maybe stress on his teeth and blood sugar, but not on his spirit, no."

Suzuno, Chiho, and Emi were at the base of Devil's Castle, having lunch as they watched the demons scarf down the extra chocolate lying around. It turned out that each demon had a raging sweet tooth, apparently, making them wonder if the conventional wisdom of them not eating food was really accurate after all.

"For now," Chiho said once more as she surveyed the view, "this is good."

As Emeralda, Acieth, Erone, and the demons warred bitterly over the chocolate, Rika was enjoying some *senbei* crackers (a gift from Japan) with Rumack, and a distance away, Laila and Nord were doing their own chocolate exchange, just like the loving couple they were. Gabriel was watching all this from his perch atop a hammock—or he would have been, if he wasn't currently napping.

Emi, seeing all this, turned her head down a bit.

"For now, huh?"

"Yusa?"

"...No, it's nothing."

For now, this was good. This was natural. A natural sort of scene, one that would've been impossible to imagine a short time ago.

"For now, it's good."

It was later in the evening, the mountain of chocolate from the all-star parade of demons now stacked up neatly on the *kotatsu* table like a brick wall. It wasn't going anywhere soon—too much to eat, too much to take back to Sasazuka—so presumably, Ashiya or someone tried to organize them a bit in the meantime. Rika's, Suzuno's, and Chiho's boxes, with their uniquely fancy packaging, were separated from the rest of the pile, but not even they were touched today.

"..."

Now, atop the wall of chocolate from the demons, a simple, plain-looking box was placed, decorated with one of Chiho's heart stickers and the kind of cheap paper that came in sets of ten sheets in the bargain bin.

"It's not like I want him to be happy or anything."

Only the mountain of chocolate could hear the whispering.

"But I just want to be polite, is all. For now."

The spoken excuse, directed toward nobody in particular, disappeared behind the edifice of the throne—and the presence of the hand that placed that final box on the stack soon vanished into the night.

EPILOGUE

"Uggghhhh, I'm exhausted!"

Flinging her large Boston bag to the floor, Chiho let out all her tension and threw herself onto her bed.

Traveling between worlds for five days in a row had left her feeling run-down. Her mother was unfortunately at home for all those days, with no plans for extended outings, so she needed to schedule things so as not to arouse her suspicion. It made navigating the zirga a major hassle. Through it all, though, she successfully gave Maou his chocolate and helped secure Adramelech's spear for the Devil King's Army. Even better, she received heaps of praise from the fellow fighters she looked up to—people who treated her with nothing but kindness, but were in another world in terms of mental makeup.

"Hee-hee… Hee-hee-hee-hee-hee!"

Chiho, her face buried in a pillow, recalled how Maou had embraced her when she had collapsed after finishing the Bowman's Offering.

"Hee-hee-hee-hee-hee-hee…"

For the first time, he had called her by her first name. She was "Sasaki" for the first little while at MgRonald, then always "Chi" after that. Then, out of nowhere, he had called her "Chiho"—"Chiho Sasaki," to be exact, but same difference.

"Hee-hee-hee-hee-hee-hee-hee-hee-hee-hee-hee-hee!"

Excitement, embarrassment, and pride filled her as she rolled around in bed for a bit. Then, coming back to her senses, she got up.

"Right. Better unpack my stuff."

Chiho opened up the Boston bag. She never overnighted in Ente

Isla, but it was still a trip to an unfamiliar land for her, so she had brought along a coat, some changes of clothes, and a few other things she thought would be necessary.

"I never really used any of this except for my digital camera..."

She giggled at the towel and clothing inside, still neatly folded. Suzuno and Nord, well versed in Japanese life, had provided her with most of the things she needed, and Wurs and Albert handled everything else.

"Ah well. The camera sure came in handy. I took a ton of photos."

Chiho had never traveled outside Japan before. In the Central Continent, she made sure not to go farther than around a quarter mile from Devil's Castle, to avoid causing too much trouble for the people and demons there. For her, getting to see the culture, customs, climate, language, races, animals, and more all over Phiyenci was an incredibly fresh experience.

"What should I do with them, though? Can I get away with printing out a few pics from Phiyenci?"

By this point, she was intimately familiar with demons and angels, even in Japan. While the castle on Isla Centurum and the many different demons she saw were a surprise, it didn't really feel like another world to her. Only when she ventured into Phiyenci did that feeling hit home—the realization that this was a wholly different realm, filled with millions of people living out their lives.

Her unpacking completed, Chiho went through the photos on her camera.

"It should be fine as long as I avoid the animals you don't see on Earth, huh?"

The people she met could all pass for regular human beings. The elephant-sized goat she instinctively shot a pic of was out of the question, but as long as she wasn't showing these photos off to everyone she knew, she figured it'd be all right.

"Hee-hee! That old lady was so surprised."

Chiho smiled as she looked at the photo she had Laila take of her with Dhin Dhem Wurs. They first met in the speaker's office in Phiyenci's National Congress building, overlooked by the Spear of

Adramelechinus. To her, Chiho was a "visitor from another planet," which she naturally had trouble believing at first—after all, Chiho looked like anybody else on Ente Isla. Being surrounded by holy force allowed her to send off Idea Links at will without the aid of 5-Holy Energy β or her cell phone, which meant she could speak with Ente Islans like a native.

To win her over, Chiho whipped out her camera. In a land like Ente Isla, which lacked even daguerreotype-style photography, carrying a device that captured a perfect image of your surroundings in an instant was more than convincing enough for Wurs. She scrutinized the camera and its LCD screen carefully, and in the end, she had to admit it: Chiho wasn't from around there.

✳

"Well, well! Live as long as I have, and you certainly do see a thing or two. Imagine, a girl from another world competing in the zirga!"

Dhin Dhem Wurs let out a deep sigh as she returned the camera to Chiho, then sized up the four people accompanying her in the Northern Island.

"Laila... Ranga... Stumpy Scythe... Hazel. I would like to speak with this girl in private. Can you leave us alone for a bit?"

"Huh?"

"But..."

"Chief Wurs, that..."

Laila, Rumack, and Suzuno were surprised, while Albert merely stood there silently.

"I'll be fine, guys."

"Yeah, we can't be frank with each other with you guys all watching her. She's no fighter, right? You've convinced me she's from that other world, but I can certainly picture you browbeating her into coming here."

"Lidem!"

Laila objected to the sentiment, but without Wurs's cooperation, they were headed nowhere. Suzuno resigned herself to it and dragged Laila out with Albert. In another moment, Chiho was alone in front of a desk, the leader of one of Ente Isla's five continents facing her, the crackling of a fire in the fireplace the only sound. It was a little nerve-racking.

"Well, I'd tell you to relax, but that's probably tough for you right now. Your name was Chiho, you said?"

"Yes."

"How much of what they're telling me about you is the truth?"

"Huh?"

"Because no offense meant, of course, but you really don't seem like the sort of person who could lead Satan and the Hero Emilia by the nose, no matter what Laila and Stumpy Scythe tell me. I'd be more ready to believe it if they called you a spoiled rich kid who knows nothing about the world."

Leading them around by the nose? How had Suzuno described Chiho to Wurs anyway?

"Hazel and Ranga, on the other hand; I can trust in their word. They wouldn't be singing the praises of somebody unless they really meant it. So I'm just not sure."

Wurs stood up. In her old age, she was now shorter than even Chiho, but in Chiho's eyes, she was like a mighty mountain shifting.

"I suppose what I'm asking is this: What are you to Emilia and all the rest?"

"I…"

Chiho felt like she was being interviewed for a part-time job. She didn't know what Wurs was driving at with this question, but she wasn't the type to try to lie or bluff her way out of situations like this. So she told the truth.

"I'm their friend."

"Huh? Their friend?"

"Right. Their friend. There's no other way to describe it."

Wurs blinked, as if this was a mighty shock to her. Chiho, sensing suspicion, panicked a bit.

"I'm well aware of what was going on in Ente Isla until two years ago. I guess putting it this way might offend you, Chief Wurs, but if you ask me why I got involved with things in this world, all I can say is it's because I was friends with Emilia and the Devil King."

"Friends...with Emilia...and the Devil King. You sure you know what the word *friend* means, girl?"

"If it means eating together, going out together, working and cooking and chatting about whatever, that's the kind of thing I've always been doing with them."

"Well, well, well..."

Wurs adjusted her monocle, having trouble taking this in.

"But I guess I'm always causing trouble for Emilia and Satan, too. They have to protect me all the time, and I didn't have the power to repay them ever. So I really want to make the most of this opportunity Suz...um, Crestia Bell and Laila gave me!"

"...Hold on just one moment. This stuff you're telling me is all too new and unfamiliar to an old woman like me. I'm having trouble comprehending it."

Wurs tossed a few more questions Chiho's way. She truthfully answered all of them. The queries had a probing aspect at first, as if testing Chiho out, but midway, they switched to how Emi, Suzuno, and Maou were doing over in Japan, the main subject of Wurs's curiosity. Chiho started calling them "Yusa" and "Maou" again, and toward the end, they were chatting about how Laila's inability to keep her place tidy was still an issue on Earth.

"Well, I take back what I said earlier about you being a spoiled rich girl. You've been through a lot, haven't ya? More than an entire band of knights could handle, I bet."

"I never overcame any of it by myself. I had Yusa and Maou and Suzuno helping me out the whole time."

"You can be as modest as you want about it, but that isn't gonna win you the zirga over the attention sponges you'll be competing against. Stumpy Scythe and Laila are treating the archery exhibition as the main event here, and I'm gonna be the one nominating you, so I want you to push yourself as hard as you do for the demon you're head over heels for."

"That... That's enough of that! Wait, do you mean...?!"

Being picked on for her love of Maou in the midst of the conversation distracted Chiho from it at first, but Wurs had apparently just agreed to get her into the competition.

"I can personally trust someone a lot more if they're in it to help out their lover or their best friend, instead of wanting to save all humanity or whatever. So why not? I'd be happy to recommend you for the exhibition."

"Th-thank you…"

Only Kaori and Chiho's mother would be so direct as to call Maou her "lover." Wurs seemed to be rapidly taking a shine to her. But then, she frowned, growing more serious.

"But let me ask you one more thing. I'm not sure Laila and Stumpy Scythe have really thought this through, but I'm sure Hazel and Ranga have and just haven't voiced it yet. Considering that, I want you to hear me out before you decide what to do. If you decide you want out, be honest with me about it. I'll simply tell 'em I turned you down or something, so don't get all weirdly obstinate about it, all right?"

"O-okay."

"Right. So I've heard you're going up to the moon to slay a god or whatever, and that if you do that, all the holy force in the world might disappear. Without holy force, none of us in Ente Isla will be able to cast magic. You get me so far?"

"…Yes."

"So you're going to borrow Laila's force to obtain the Spear with your archery skills. Your skills with a bow and arrow are going to be watched by a huge crowd at the zirga."

"Right."

"And the better those skills are, the more people are likely to lose their lives from other people's bows and arrows in the not-too-distant future. Are you all right with that?"

Chiho's expression was unchanged, something Wurs interpreted to mean she didn't understand what she was driving at.

"What I'm saying is that if we lose magic as a useful long-range weapon, it's gonna be replaced with the kind of archery skills you're about to show off, no doubt about it. This zirga might change the whole direction of Ente Islan warfare. Do you—"

"That's not related," Chiho interjected.

"It's not?"

"No, it's not." She squared up against the quizzical chief herder. "Me using a bow at the zirga and archery becoming a part of warfare in the far future are two totally different things. Besides, Chief Wurs, you already know everything, so whether I do this or not, you're going to promote archery more than ever for the sake of the Wurs clan's and the Northern Island's future, aren't you?"

"..."

"General Rumack and the people from the Eastern Island are the same way. They're actively joining this campaign, taking on all these burdens that people elsewhere don't comprehend, so they can take action before their rivals. I'm not arrogant enough to think I have enough power to change the world singlehandedly. Even if I wound up being the source for the next generation of battle tactics or whatever, it's up to the people involved to figure out how to use their powers, not me."

She smiled.

"Besides, in this zirga, I need to step up and help out Maou, Yusa, and Alas Ramus. Now's no time to hesitate and worry about whether I change the world or not. You said it yourself, Chief Wurs. That you trust people who want to support their loved ones more than people who want to save the world."

She sat up in her chair, determined.

"That's why I'm joining the zirga."

"...Well, well."

Wurs sat silent for a few moments, then broke into a breezy smile.

"Perhaps I've been relying on my own fragment too much. My ability to judge character's going on me."

Then, for the first time, she removed her monocle before Chiho's eyes, pointing out the purple fragment on it.

"The fragment on this monocle uses colors to show me whether someone is telling the truth or not. It doesn't tell me if someone's telling a falsehood which they believe is true, which has certainly given me trouble on more than one occasion, let me tell you. But if someone's hiding their fear and talking big with nothing to back it up, I can tell that right out. Perhaps, though, relying on such a useful tool made me fail to notice the courageous light you've been showing me from the beginning."

Wurs kept smiling as she returned to her desk and took out a sheet of paper.

"A spoiled little rich girl? Why, just listen to the junk coming out of my mouth. Stumpy Scythe has certainly played her trump card here. I'd say you've got more hero potential inside you than Emilia ever did."

She tossed the monocle in her pocket, staring straight at Chiho with both eyes.

"It's a pity you aren't my real granddaughter, Chiho Sasaki Wurs."

"Thank you very much, Grandma Lidem."

Chiho bowed her head deeply to this great leader, a woman who loomed larger than the Devil King's Army as she kept an entire continent together.

✵

She had managed to make a grand statement earlier, but the thought of her actions impacting the future of Ente Isla unnerved Chiho. Perhaps, she thought, Dhin Dhem Wurs was picking up on that. But still, it was that exchange that convinced Wurs to put her in the zirga, after all. She hoped they could have an even franker conversation next time; she wanted to hear more about what "working for those you love" meant to her, or the idea of a single person changing the world, given her broad view of history and being a wide-eyed ruler for so many years. "How strange."

Compared to angels and demons, whose lives go on for centuries or millennia, Wurs hadn't even made it a hundred years—but in Chiho's eyes, it seemed like she knew more about the world than any of them. Was that because Chiho herself was unlikely to make it to a hundred? Because the way they felt time was different?

"…"

Did that mean she couldn't walk together, her and Maou, along the same timeline? Even if they were destined to be united, Chiho would grow old sooner or later, while Maou would remain as young as ever. Would they share the same feelings, as living, breathing people, when that happened? No. Maybe it was impossible from the start.

Coming to this conclusion, Chiho felt her blood run cold. Just as a year's worth of time meant different things to a person and an animal, time from Chiho's perspective didn't work like time from Maou's. The thought was a constant presence in Laila's and Nord's minds, and they still hadn't come to terms with it. As Wurs hinted at, time flowed for Laila at an incomparably slower pace than it did for normal people. For her, it was downright languid.

But what about Maou? There was that answer he kept delaying. There was a future no one could see. And she was doomed to depart this world before the one she loved.

She didn't want that.

"Ahhh."

Chiho collapsed back into bed, spotting the moon out the window as she looked upward.

"I guess this is how it feels to want eternal youth."

She could already feel something deep, and dark, gouging a hole in a corner of her mind, something that went beyond the base concept of "right" and "wrong." But as it did:

"?!"

Suddenly, there was a loud *thud* of something hitting the window. Chiho, surprised, leaped out of bed. Something soft, spherical, but heavy had bounced off the glass, making a terrific noise before falling toward the ground below. And at the same time:

"Just now…something…"

The holy force within her picked up on something stirring.

Something nearby her. But before she could investigate, she had to see if the window was broken, and what that object was.

"Chiho!" her mother shouted from downstairs. "What was that noise?"

"I don't know! Some kind of ball bounced off the window... Lemme see what it is!"

Carefully, she opened the window that had been struck. It hadn't shattered, luckily, but whatever hit it had left an obvious smudge on the glass.

"Wow, what is this... Huh?"

Then, she noticed something sticking to the window frame. It astonished her.

"A feather?"

It was a black bird's feather.

"Oh, weird. Maybe a crow or something flew into the window by accident."

There wasn't enough light to fly by outside, but Chiho looked out the window anyway, squinting at the ground below. There, in the compact front yard, she saw a black lump of some sort, the size of a basketball. She didn't recognize it at first, but as the "night-blinded crow" theory solidified in her mind, she heard a sound...or, really, a voice.

"Nnngh......*cheep...*"

This was familiar to her. That low, hoarse voice, unbefitting the reverberation behind it. A bird with black feathers.

"—?!"

Chiho gasped, extending her lungs to their limits, then tore down the stairs, not even pausing to shut the window.

"Chiho? What's up?"

Ignoring the calls of her mother emerging from the living room, Chiho flew out the door and into the yard. There, squirming in the middle of the lawn:

"C-Camio?!"

It wasn't a black chicken—just a demon who looked kind of like one.

"Who…goes there…*cheep…cheep…*"

Camio, the Devil's Regent, the Pájaro Danino demon who helped raise a young Satan and was one of the first members of his force, was here for the first time since that trip to Choshi. But why was he in chicken form, and how did he get bashed against the window?

"Hey, hang in there! What happened to you?! Let's get you up to my room… Huh?!"

Chiho tried to pick up the curled-up ball of feathers at her feet, but the moment she did, her face tensed up at the feeling of a warm, thick liquid in her hands. She brought one of them up to a dim streetlight nearby. It was covered in blood. He was badly hurt.

"You—you need treatment… Camio, please, stay awake for me!"

"Rr…ngh… I know not who you are, but I thank *yeep…*"

The voice was weak, ready to evaporate away at any moment. Did he not remember her? Was he blinded by the darkness around him? Or did his injuries make him delirious? Chiho was starting to panic. Plus, as she now realized, a grown chicken was a bit larger than she thought—could she get him into her room without her mom noticing?

The bigger question, though, was how to treat him. Based on experience, she knew that demonic force was the best way to heal a wounded demon, but Maou, Ashiya, and Urushihara were all at Ente Isla's Devil's Castle, unable to immediately return. Was this something she could tackle with the family first aid kit? She was pretty sure she had heard something recently about demons formerly being humans, but she was starting to wonder if he was really a bird-man, or just a chicken all along. Wild, disorganized thoughts ran through her mind.

"N-now what? I hope Mom's back in the living room…"

"Hnn…gh…*chirrrrr…*"

"Well, whatever! If worse comes to worst, I'll have her call a nearby vet…!"

No time left to hesitate. Even the peeping was starting to draw out. Steeling her resolve, Chiho decided to bring him inside—but waiting at the front door for her was someone completely unexpected.

"Sorry. I had to have your mom take a nap for me. Get some hot water going and bring me as many towels as you can—ones you don't mind getting dirty."

"A-Amane…?!"

Standing there was a sleepy-eyed Amane Ohguro, her hair let down and a bit of it stuck to her cheek, wearing wrinkled socks and gray sweats under a body-length black coat. Clearly, she had been enjoying a lazy night in until mere moments earlier.

"H-How?! When did you get here? How'd you get inside?!"

"I detected something weird with the network Gabe set up to keep the house safe, so I went through your open window half a minute ago."

She took Camio from Chiho's hands as she explained.

"Wash your hands, okay? This is blood from someone bearing demonic force; it might affect your body in bad ways. You should probably have one of those energy shots, just in case."

"Um, okay."

Without another word, Amane trundled Camio upstairs. Chiho stared blankly at her for a moment but quickly snapped out of it, ran to the bathroom, and got the red blood off her hands.

"…She's sleeping."

Her mother was on the living-room sofa, sleeping in front of the blaring TV like her father tended to do after work. Chiho brought her ear close to her mother's face, anxious for a moment, but soon confirmed she was resting soundly. So off she went into the bathroom again, fetching some towels, and then to the kitchen to put a kettle on the stove. And as she was nervously waiting for the water to boil:

"Agh?!"

From upstairs, she heard the ominously loud sound of something falling to the floor. It made her jump into the air. Not even a toppled chest of drawers would produce that much of a shuddering impact. Forgetting about the kettle, she jogged upstairs.

"A-Amane…huh?"

At the door to her room, she froze, transfixed by the scene greeting her. Amane had used her hand to stop the tip of…something coming in from the open window. It was a three-pronged spear. Blood was pouring from her hand as she sneered at whatever was on the other side of it.

"Don't worry. He's already fled."

"Gnhh...*chirrrr*..."

Camio was hanging from her other hand, meaning both of her arms were covered in blood like a scene from a horror film.

"Uh, all right... Is your hand okay?"

"If you could get some bandages later..."

The job looked far too big for bandages to handle, but Amane's attention was already focused on the weapon, blood dripping from it.

"Well, this ain't good. If they come for us this way, I'll never make it in time, no matter what. I think they were targeting this chicken, Chiho, and not you, but we're gonna have to reconsider our security measures around here."

Amane tried pulling the trident inside but gave up once it became clear it was longer than the diagonal length of the room.

"Hmm. Pretty old-fashioned weapon to break out. Probably something from the heavens. Look familiar to you?"

"Yes," Chiho said, solemnly nodding. A giant, three-pronged spear, with images of flames ensconced on it. It belonged to Camael, the Sephirah guardian angel, who used it in his attack on Sasahata North High School.

"But I thought Maou and Acieth broke this spear in Ente Isla."

"You already know the guy's just a normal dude like the rest of us. They go on about these 'sacred relics' or whatever, but if they have the original maker or his plans, plus some materials and instructions and tools, they can fix it or make a new one any time... Hey, what's that sound?"

"Oh, noooo, I left the kettle on the stove!"

Chiho spun around at the high-pitched whistle and bounded back down the stairs.

"That's what panics her...?"

Amane chuckled at the sight of a teen casually examining a massive weapon coming through her window, then freaking out at the sound of a kettle. Then, she looked at the two things in her hands and scowled.

"Something tells me there's some stuff goin' down in the demon realm."

Amane already knew that this black chicken was a major authority figure in demondom. If someone like that showed up in Japan looking like this, it was natural to assume an urgent emergency.

"Ugh, I hate this! It's driving me nuts! This has nothing to do with me! Go somewhere else! Stay away from here!"

In one hand, a bloodied chicken-demon. In the other, a gigantic weapon of murder. And Camio, tasked with finding the Astral Gem and completing the Noah Gear search, was the only one around to listen to the Sephirah descendant's whining.

"...My liege... I am sorry...*peep*..."

THE AUTHOR, THE AFTERWORD, AND YOU!

I once heard that the person we all should thank the most on Valentine's Day is the guy who invented the concept of giving out chocolate for politeness's sake.

It can be hard to drum up the courage to give chocolate to the one you truly love, but if you're handing out little treats to the people you deal with on a daily basis, most people are like *Fair enough* to that or use it as an excuse to go all out. The end result is more people purchasing chocolate, and it means that a good fifth of all the chocolate sold in Japan each year is consumed on February 14.

You don't see this custom quite as much as you used to in Japanese workplaces, as part of an effort to get rid of useless formalities and encourage nonhostile work environments. In the future, then, Valentine's Day is going back to its original function—women relating their feelings to the one they truly love, or people giving out sweet treats for fun.

Looking back on the history of Valentine's, I have to say they dropped the ball right at the end with White Day, a tradition that was invented and propagated by Japan. The origins of Valentine's Day itself can be traced back years and years, perhaps all the way back to the Roman Empire; White Day, meanwhile, was declared to be March 14 by Japan's National Confectionery Industry Association in 1980. Nobody's quite sure who first sold sweets as a way to "answer" Valentine's gifts, but White Day was entirely an invention by the candy industry to get men to "repay" women for their thoughts.

In Japan, it's traditionally considered rude to accept a gift without offering something in return, maybe half or a third of the value, as compensation of a sort. That explains how White Day got its start, but somewhere along the line, it turned into this "Pay her back three times over for Valentine's!" thing, and people started giving accessories and other regular presents instead of chocolate. The Japan National Confectionery Industry Association was, of course, trying to get men to buy candy to "answer" women's Valentine's overtures, but I've never read anything that indicated candy sales going through the roof on March 14 or anything. I'm not sure it really fulfilled what the co-op was trying to do with it.

Some people like to warp this around, saying Valentine's Day is all just a conspiracy by the sweets industry—but with White Day, that really *is* the case. A tradition is something started by people reacting to the times, the weather, their homeland, or the local natural features, eventually taking root and evolving over time before acquiring its current form. Those same things are still gradually changing our traditions today, perhaps turning them into completely different things in the future—or maybe even causing them to die out.

The Devil Is a Part-Timer! Volume 16 is all about how even the smallest passing thoughts or actions have the potential to affect how we live and which customs we observe. You don't need to use fancy terms like "the butterfly effect" to see how you, being alive, have a small yet noticeable effect, direct or indirect, on the world around you. It's not easy to change customs once they take hold, but the world is changing, little by little, right this instant, whether you want it to or not.

Hopefully, you enjoyed this story of people struggling in this whirlpool of changes, trying to find a path for themselves. See you in the next volume!